SPECIAL EDUCATOR'S
COMPLETE GUIDE TO
109 DIAGNOSTIC TESTS

ROGER PIERANGELO, Ph.D. ♦ GEORGE GIULIANI, Psy.D.

THE CENTER FOR APPLIED
RESEARCH IN EDUCATION
West Nyack, New York 10994

Library of Congress Cataloging-in-Publication Data

Pierangelo, Roger.
    Special educator's complete guide to 109 diagnostic tests :
  How to select & interpret tests, use results in IEP's, and remediate
  specific difficulties / by Roger Pierangelo, George Giuliani.
        p.   cm.
      Includes bibliographical references (p.   ).
      ISBN 0-87628-893-X
      1. Handicapped children—Psychological testing.   2. Handicapped
  children—Ability testing.   3. Handicapped children—Remediation.
  4. Examinations—Interpretation.   5. Educational tests and
  measurements.   I. Giuliani, George A.   II. Title.
      LC4019.P53   1998
      371.9'04—dc21   97-46821
                                                              CIP

Acquisition Editor: *Susan Kolwicz*
Production Editor: *Mariann Hutlak*
Formatting: *DM Cradle Associates*
Interior design: *Dee Coroneos*

Printed in the United States of America

10   9   8   7   6   5   4   3

ISBN 0-87628-893-X

**THE CENTER FOR APPLIED RESEARCH
IN EDUCATION**

West Nyack, NY 10994

On the World Wide Web at http://www.phdirect.com

DEDICATIONS

This book is dedicated to my wife, Jackie, and children, Jacqueline and Scott, who gave me the purpose to expand my horizons, the support to undertake this project, and the understanding while I was writing this book.

I also dedicate this book to my parents, who gave me a truly loving foundation from which to grow, my sister Carol, who has been more special to me than she realizes, and my brother-in-law George, whose invaluable guidance, support, and direction greatly contributed to my professional opportunities and experiences and who was always there when I needed him.

Roger Pierangelo

This book is dedicated to my wife, Anita, and son, Collin, who gives me all the joy and happiness an individual can possibly feel. Anita has always been a most supportive and caring wife. I thank her for her constant encouragement and understanding, especially while writing this book.

George Giuliani

ACKNOWLEDGMENTS

- All the students, parents, and teachers of the Herricks Public School District that I have had the pleasure of meeting, knowing, and helping in my 24 years in the district.

- Again, to Ollie Simmons, an extraordinary individual and personal friend, who always helps me start the day with a smile.

- Helen Firestone, one of the most instrumental individuals in my career, who always believed in me.

- In memory of Bill Smyth, a truly "extraordinary ordinary" man and one of the best guidance counselors and individuals I have ever known.

- To Susan Kolwicz, my editor, who makes my life of writing textbooks very easy through her organization, efficiency, manner, and good humor.

Roger Pierangelo

- My mother, Carol Giuliani, a truly caring and wonderful woman, who has always given me the support and love to help me strive to be the very best that I can be.

- My father, Dr. George A. Giuliani, the most intelligent, moral, compassionate, and caring individual I have ever known.

- My brother and sister, Roger and Claudia, for always being there for me when I needed them most.

- My in-laws, Manfred and Ursula Jenkeleit, two of the kindest and most sincere people I have ever met.

- Dr. Kenneth Schneider and the entire faculty at Rutgers, who always showed the greatest faith and belief in my abilities.

- St Joseph's College, a college that understands the meaning of education and follows its motto—*Esse Non Videri, to be and not to seem.*

- Dr. Paul Hawryluk, Chairperson of the Psychology Department at St. Joseph's College, who believed in me and had the faith in my ability to teach at the college level.

- My grandfather and my grandparents (in memory), who always let me know that I could excel in whatever I set out to do.

- Dr. Roger Pierangelo, who had faith in me and guided me in my years as an intern and school psychologist.

- Susan Kolwicz, my editor, who gave me the chance to write this book, I will be forever appreciative of the opportunity.

George Giuliani

Authors' Professional Acknowledgments

In the course of writing this book we have encountered many professionally outstanding sources. It has been our experience that these resources have and continue to contribute enormous information, support, guidance, and education to parents, students, and professionals in the area of special education. While we have experienced many worthwhile sources and sites, we would like to take this opportunity to acknowledge the following: National Information Center for Children and Youth with Disabilities (NICHCY).

ABOUT THE AUTHORS

Dr. Roger Pierangelo has over 25 years of experience as a regular classroom teacher, school psychologist in the Herricks Public School system in New Hyde Park, NY, administrator of special education programs, full professor in the graduate special education department at Long Island University, private practitioner in psychology, member of Committees on Special Education, evaluator for the New York State Education Department, director of a private clinic, and consultant to numerous private and public schools, PTA and SEPTA groups.

Dr. Pierangelo earned his B.S. from St. John's University, M.S. from Queens College, Professional Diploma from Queens College, and Ph.D. from Yeshiva University. Currently he is working as a psychologist both in the schools and in private practice, teaching at the college and serving as director of a private clinic.

Dr. Pierangelo is a member of the American Psychological Association, New York State Psychological Association, Nassau County Psychological Association, New York State Union of Teachers, and Phi Delta Kappa.

Dr. Pierangelo is the author of *Survival Kit for the Special Education Teacher* and *The Special Education Teacher's Book of Lists*, and coauthor of the *Parent's Special Education Survival Kit* and *The Complete Guide to Transition Services*, all published by Simon and Schuster, and *301 Ways To Be A Loving Parent*, published by Shapolsky Publishers of New York.

Dr. George A. Giuliani is a full-time Assistant Professor at St. Joseph's College in the Psychology department. Dr. Giuliani earned his B.A. from the College of the Holy Cross, M.S. from St. John's University, J.D. from City University of New York Law School, and Psy.D. (Doctor of Psychology) from Rutgers University—The Graduate School of Applied and Professional Psychology.

Besides college teaching, Dr. Giuliani is involved in Early Intervention for children with special needs and is a consultant for school districts and early childhood agencies. Dr. Giuliani has provided numerous workshops for parents and teachers on a variety of psychological and educational topics.

Dr. Giuliani is a member of the New York Association of School Psychologists and the National Association of School Psychologists.

ABOUT THIS GUIDE

Special Educator's Complete Guide to 109 Diagnostic Tests has been developed to provide any individual involved in the special education process with a comprehensive overview of the most frequently used tests for diagnosing suspected disabilities—including intelligence, perception, and language to achievement, psycho/social behavior, and social maturity—from the early childhood years to adolescence.

Filled with practical tools, information, and suggestions, the *Guide* thoroughly covers the various stages of evaluation, interpretation, diagnosis, prescription, and remediation for those unfamiliar with this process. In addition, it offers up-to-date guidance on gathering information, the parents' role during the assessment process, understanding a subject's behavior during testing, writing and developing IEPs, and implementing remediation techniques in the classroom.

Furthermore, the *Guide* contains the following test information designed to assist readers in selecting and understanding the wide range of tests available to them today:

- Thorough explanations of the most commonly used diagnostic tests
- In-depth coverage of the areas measured by each test
- Easy-to-understand interpretation of test patterns for commonly used measures
- Diagnostic categories frequently exhibited by test patterns
- Strengths and weaknesses of each test
- How results/scores are evaluated for each test

HELPFUL AND UNIQUE FEATURES

Most current books on test information do not deal with the practical, day-to-day needs of the special education teacher as a diagnostician. They either explain the tests or cite statistical information, yet rarely include information on what scores mean or how to utilize their results.

The most commonly used measures found in the Guide offer teachers everything necessary to go from interpretation to remediation in one book. All 14 sections of the *Guide* have been designed to make readers more secure and aware about the often overwhelming process of special education testing and interpretation.

Following are several additional features:

- Developmental, step-by-step approach takes readers through a variety of topics and procedures necessary for a realistic, complete awareness of children with disabilities.
- Easy-to-read format contains a wealth of information and proven suggestions taken from the authors' extensive experiences.

- Material is presented in such a way as to help readers utilize its content to provide students with the most appropriate education available in the least restrictive environment.

- An overview of the issues associated with assessing students who are culturally or linguistically diverse is presented.

- Charts and tables help clarify often confusing topics.

- Useful information can be applied immediately to the various experiences that teachers encounter in the classroom.

- Thorough appendices contain tests organized by category (intelligence, perception, achievement, etc.) and also alphabetically, a list of test publishers with their addresses, phone and fax numbers, a complete glossary of testing terms, and references to readings on assessment.

In Closing

From our experiences, we know that educational diagnosticians and teachers need assistance in understanding the etiology (cause), nature, and meaning of the vast amount of diagnostic material available to them. With the proper tests and the proper interpretation, many problems exhibited by students with special needs can be more rapidly and appropriately addressed. As with any event, early diagnosis and intervention can mean all the difference in an individual's life.

Roger Pierangelo & George Giuliani

CONTENTS

≡ **Section 3** ≡
THE WECHSLER SCALES OF INTELLIGENCE / 31

≡ **Section 4** ≡
OTHER INTELLECTUAL ASSESSMENT MEASURES / 49

═══ Section 5 ═══

ACHIEVEMENT ASSESSMENT MEASURES / 67

═ Section 6 ═
PERCEPTUAL MEASURES / 131

〰 **Section 7** 〰

AN OVERVIEW OF LANGUAGE, PSYCHOLOGICAL & SOCIAL, AND ADAPTIVE MEASURES / 163

≡PSYCHOLOGICAL AND SOCIAL ASSESSMENT / 181

≡ **Section 8** ≡

AN OVERVIEW OF EARLY CHILDHOOD, HEARING IMPAIRED, OCCUPATIONAL & PHYSICAL THERAPY, AND BILINGUAL TESTS / 203

═══ Section 9 ═══

IDENTIFICATION OF POSSIBLE HIGH-RISK CHILDREN / 257

═══ Section 10 ═══

UNDERSTANDING A STUDENT'S BEHAVIOR DURING TESTING / 265

═ Section 11 ═

THE PARENTS' ROLE IN THE ASSESSMENT PROCESS / 269

═ Section 12 ═

WRITING AND DEVELOPING AN INDIVIDUALIZED EDUCATION PLAN / 275

═ Section 13 ═

CLASSROOM REMEDIATION TECHNIQUES / 287

═ Section 14 ═

APPENDICES / 299

Section 1

INTRODUCTION TO ASSESSMENT

The special educator in today's schools plays a very critical role in the overall education of students with all types of disabilities. For instance, the special educator can be assigned as a teacher in a self-contained classroom, categorical or noncategorical resource room, or an inclusive classroom. Often, teachers are important members of the Child Study Team (CST) or Pupil Personnel Team (PPT), the Committee on Special Education, or of multi-disciplinary teams educating secondary students.

Whatever the role, special educators encounter a variety of situations that require practical decisions and relevant suggestions on students' educational futures. No matter what role one assumes in this field, it is always necessary to understand fully, symptomatology, causality, evaluation, diagnosis, prescription, and remediation, and to communicate clearly vital information to professionals, parents, and students.

One of the most important roles that a special educator assumes is that of diagnostician. This role is crucial since it helps determine the extent and direction of a child's personal journey through the special education experience. The importance of this position should never be underestimated. Consequently, the skills one must possess in order to offer a child the most global, accurate, and practical evaluation should be fully understood. The development of these skills should include a good working knowledge of the following parts of the *assessment process* to determine the presence of a suspected disability:

- **Collection**—the process of tracing and gathering information from the many sources of background information on a child, such as school records, observation, parent intakes, and teacher reports

- **Analysis**—the analysis of patterns in the child's educational, social, developmental, environmental, medical, and emotional history

- **Evaluation**—the evaluation of a child's academic, intellectual, psychological, emotional, perceptional, language, cognitive, and medical development in order to determine areas of strength and weakness

- **Determination**—the determination of the presence of a suspected disability and the knowledge of the criteria that constitute each category

- **Recommendation**—the recommendations concerning educational placement and program that need to be made to the school, teachers, and parents

1

PREVENTIVE MEASURES PRIOR TO EVALUATION

Prior to beginning a full assessment on a child, it is important to make sure that the school has made every effort to ameliorate learning and/or behavioral problems through other means. The assessment process is a very significant and important piece in addressing such problems, but should never be the first step. Determine if the school has tried other avenues, such as the following, before initiating assessment:

- **PPT (Pupil Personnel Team) discussions**—This procedure should be used so that several staff members are able to view the symptoms and provide a variety of preventive suggestions prior to evaluation.

- **Team meeting with teachers**—Sometimes a group meeting with all the child's teachers can preclude the need for further involvement. One or several teachers may be using techniques that could benefit others also working with the child. By sharing information or observations, it is possible to identify patterns of behavior reflective of some particular condition or disability. Once these patterns are identified, the student may be handled in a variety of ways without the need for more serious intervention.

- **Parent interviews**—Meeting the parent(s) is always recommended for a child having some difficulty in school. This initial meeting can be informal with the purpose of clarifying certain issues and gathering pertinent information that may help their child as well as the teacher in the classroom. If testing or serious intervention is required, then a more formal and in-depth parent meeting will take place.

- **Classroom management techniques**—There are times when the real issue may not be the child, but the style of the classroom teacher. If that is the case, then help for the teacher can come in the form of classroom management techniques. These practical suggestions may be offered by an administrator, psychologist, or any realistic and diplomatic team member who feels comfortable with this type of situation. There are many classroom techniques and modifications that should be tried before taking more serious steps. (Many modifications and suggestions are discussed later.)

- **Help classes**—Some children may just require a temporary support system to get them through a difficult academic period. Some schools provide extra nonspecial education services, such as help classes that may be held during lunch or after school. These classes can clarify academic confusion that could lead to more serious problems if not addressed.

- **Resource Room assistance**—This option can only be tried when the school district offers such services for nonspecial education students and prior to any CSE (Committee on Special Education) review. Some schools provide resource room for students who are having academic problems that are not severe enough to warrant classification. If this option is available, then the school may want to try to see if this type of support helps.

- **Reading services**—These services can be recommended when reading is the specific area of concern. Eventually, the need for a complete and comprehensive reading diagnostic battery may be called for by the team when students show slow or no improvement in this area. Below are some symptoms that may necessitate this type of help:

  — inability to develop a sight word vocabulary by second grade
  — consistent inability to remember what is read

— constant loss of place while reading
— inadequate development of word-attack skills

- **Remedial reading or math services**—These types of services do not require a review by the CSE. Remedial reading or math classes are not special education services and can be instituted as a means of alleviating a child's academic problems.

- **Recommendation for in-school counseling**—Sometimes children may experience a *situational or adjustment disorder* (a temporary emotional pattern which may occur at any time in a person's life without a prior history of problems) resulting from separation, divorce, health issues, newness to school district, and so forth. When this pattern occurs, it may temporarily interfere with the child's ability to concentrate, remember, and attend to tasks. Consequently, a drop in academic performance can occur. If such a pattern occurs, the school psychologist may want to institute in-school counseling with the parent's involvement and permission.

  This recommendation should only be instituted to address issues that can be resolved in a relatively short period of time. More serious issues may have to be referred to outside agencies or professionals for longer treatment. When a psychologist makes a recommendation for longer treatment, he/she must provide a minimum of three names from which the parents may choose.

- **Daily/Weekly progress reports**—Sometimes children who have fallen behind academically "hide" from the real issues by avoiding reality. Daily progress reports for a week or two at first and then weekly reports may provide the child with the kinds of immediate gratification necessary to get back on track. They offer a child a greater sense of hope and control in getting back to a more normal academic pattern.

- **Hearing test**—This evaluation should be one of the first recommended by the team if one has not been administered within the last six months to one year. Be aware of inconsistencies in test patterns from year to year that might indicate a chronic pattern. Below are some symptoms that might indicate an updated audiological examination:

  — child turns head when listening
  — child asks you to repeat frequently
  — child consistently misinterprets what he/she hears
  — child does not respond to auditory stimuli
  — child slurs speech, speaks in a monotone voice, or articulates poorly

- **Vision test**—As with the hearing exam, results of the vision screening should also be considered first by the PPT. Again, if a vision screening has not been done within six months to a year, then request this immediately. Possible symptoms that may necessitate such an evaluation are listed below:

  — child turns head when looking at board or objects
  — child squints excessively
  — child rubs eyes frequently
  — child holds books and materials close to the face or at unusual angles
  — child suffers frequent headaches
  — child avoids close work of any type
  — child covers an eye when reading
  — child consistently loses place when reading

- **Disciplinary action**—This recommendation is usually made when the child in question needs a structured boundary set involving inappropriate behavior. If a child demonstrates a pattern of inappropriate behavior, disciplinary action is usually used in conjunction with other recommendations since such patterned behavior may be symptomatic of a more serious problem.

- **Medical exam**—Evaluators should try to rule out any possibility of a medical condition causing or contributing to the existing problems. If the PPT feels that there is any possibility of such a condition and the need for a complete medical work-up is evident, then a recommendation for a medical examination should be made. The team should review available records and if they are inadequate in light of the presenting problems and symptoms, the team should make the necessary outside recommendations to the parents (neurological examination, ophthalmological examination, etc.).

- **Change of program**—This recommendation usually occurs when a student has been placed in a course that is not suited to his/her ability or needs. If a student is failing in an advanced class, then the student's program should be changed to include more modified classes.

- **Consolidation of program**—There are times when reducing a student's courseload is necessary. If a child is "drowning in school," then that child's available energy level may be extremely limited. In such cases you may find that he or she is failing many courses. Temporarily consolidating or condensing the program allows for the possibility of salvaging some courses since the student's available energy will not have to be spread so thin.

- **In-school counseling**—This may be another option considered by the school prior to a full assessment. This option is explained in greater detail later in this book.

- **PINS Petition**—A PINS Petition stands for "Person in Need of Supervision" and is a family court referral. This referral can be made by either the school or the parent and is usually made when a child under the age of 16 is out of control in terms of attendance or behavior, or exhibits some socially inappropriate or destructive pattern.

- **Referral to Child Protective Services**—A referral to Child Protective Services (CPS) is mandated for all educators if there is a suspicion of abuse or neglect. The school official or staff does not have a choice as to referral if such a suspicion is present. Referrals to this service may result from physical, sexual, or emotional abuse, or educational, environmental, or medical neglect.

While all of these suggestions need not be tried before an evaluation is attempted, parents may be more willing to sign a release for evaluation if they see that other methods have been used and proven unsuccessful.

By law, the process of assessment must involve much more than just giving the student a standardized test in the area of his or her suspected disability. As previously indicated, valuable information about the student's skills and needs can come from many sources, including parents, teachers, and specialists, and by using a variety of assessment approaches:

— classroom observations
— interviews
— informal testing
— dynamic assessment
— ecological assessment

In this way, a comprehensive picture of the student can be obtained and used to guide eligibility decisions and educational programming.

The range of factors that might arouse the teacher or special education evaluator's concerns includes the following:

— difficulty following directions
— difficulty completing assignments on time
— problems progressing in reading and spelling
— difficulties interacting with peers
— delays in developing mobility and daily living skills
— declining grades
— slowness in processing information
— poor writing skills
— historical problems in mathematics

Many children, different as they may be, may require at some point in their education the special education services in their school system. If it is determined that a child requires an evaluation, and if other efforts to ameliorate difficulties have been exhausted, then that child should undergo an evaluation conducted by specially trained educational personnel such as the following:

— school psychologist
— special education evaluator
— speech/language pathologist
— regular education teachers
— social workers
— school nurse teacher
— medical personnel (when appropriate)
— reading teacher
— occupational therapist
— physical therapist

DEFINING ASSESSMENT

Assessment is a complex process that involves many ways of collecting information about a student. Testing, one part of the assessment process, is the administration of specifically designed measures to assess a child's academic or perceptual strengths and weaknesses as well as his or her emotional dynamics. Roth-Smith (1991) suggests that this information-gathering process involves the following:

♦ observing the student's interactions with parents, teachers, and peers

♦ interviewing the student and significant others in his or her life

♦ examining school records and past evaluation results

♦ evaluating developmental and medical histories

♦ using information from checklists completed by parents, teachers, or the student

♦ evaluating curriculum requirements and options

♦ evaluating the student's type and rate of learning during trial teaching periods

♦ using task analysis to identify which task components already have been mastered and in what order unmastered skills need to be taught

♦ collecting ratings on teacher attitude towards students with disabilities, peer acceptance, and classroom climate

Clearly, gathering information about the student using such a variety of techniques and information sources should shed considerable light upon the student's strengths and needs, the nature of the student's disability and its effect upon educational performance, and realistic and appropriate instructional goals and objectives to set for the student. More detail about many of these methods of collecting information about a student will be presented throughout this book.

PURPOSE OF ASSESSMENT

Following a referral to the CSE with written parental or guardian permission, an individual evaluation is conducted. This means that formal tests, observations, and assessments take place. The results help to determine if special education is needed. They also help to determine whether factors unrelated to disabilities are affecting a child's school performance. Evaluation results provide information that is useful for determining or modifying a child's program, if necesary.

Assessment in educational settings serves five primary purposes:

• **Screening and identification of suspected disabilities**—to screen children and identify those who may be experiencing delays or learning problems

• **Evaluation**—to evaluate a student's strengths, weaknesses, and overall progress

• **Eligibility and diagnosis**—to determine whether a child has a suspected disability and is eligible for special education services, and to diagnose the specific nature of the student's problems or disability

• **IEP development and placement**—to provide detailed information so that an IEP (Individualized Education Plan) may be developed and appropriate decisions may be made about the child's educational placement

• **Instructional planning**—develop and plan instruction appropriate to the child's special social, academic, physical and management needs

COMPONENTS OF A THOROUGH ASSESSMENT

An evaluation should be conducted on an individual basis for any child suspected of having a disability. It should be a comprehensive assessment of the child's abilities, and should include the following:

♦ An individual psychological evaluation (when determined necessary by the multidisciplinary team), including general intelligence, instructional needs, learning strengths and weaknesses, and social–emotional dynamics

♦ A thorough social history

♦ A thorough academic history including interviews or reports from past and present teachers

- A physical examination, including specific assessments that relate to vision, hearing, and health

- A classroom observation of the student in his or her current educational setting

- An appropriate educational evaluation specifically pinpointing the areas of deficit or suspected disability, including but not limited to educational achievement, academic needs, learning strengths and weaknesses, and vocational assessments

- A bilingual assessment for students with limited English proficiency

HOW STUDENTS ARE IDENTIFIED FOR ASSESSMENT

There are several ways in which a student may be identified for testing or assessment:

1. The *school* may suspect the presence of a learning or behavior problem, and will ask the student's parents for permission to evaluate the student individually. For example, when a student scores too far below his or her peers on some type of screening measure, this alerts the school to the possibility of a potential problem.

2. The *student's classroom teacher* may identify that certain symptoms exist within the classroom that seem to indicate the presence of some problem. For example, the student's work is below expectations for his or her grade or age, or the student's behavior is so disruptive that he or she is unable to learn.

3. The *student's parents* may also call or write to the school or to the director of special education, and request that their child be evaluated. They may feel that the child is not progressing as he or she should, or they may notice particular problems in how the child learns. When parents note a problem and request an evaluation, what is referred to as a Parent Request for a CSE Review, the school must follow through on the assessment process. This is the parents' right under due process. If the school disagrees, it may ask the parent to rescind the request for review in writing. However, if the parent refuses, the process must continue and the decision for classification must be made at the CSE level.

ASSESSMENT AND FEDERAL LAW

The Individuals with Disabilities Education Act (IDEA), Public Law 101-476, lists 13 separate categories of disabilities under which children may be eligible for special education and related services:

- **autism**—a developmental disability significantly affecting verbal and nonverbal communication and social interaction, generally evident before 3 years of age

- **deafness**—a hearing impairment that is so severe that the child is impaired in processing linguistic information, with or without amplification

- **deaf-blindness**—simultaneous hearing and visual impairments

- **hearing impairment**—an impairment in hearing, whether permanent or fluctuating

- **mental retardation**—significantly subaverage general intellectual functioning existing concurrently with deficits in adaptive behavior

- **multiple disabilities**—the manifestation of two or more disabilities (such as mental retardation and blindness), which requires special accommodation for maximal learning

- **orthopedic impairment**—physical disabilities, including congenital impairments, impairments caused by disease, and impairments from other causes, such as an accident

- **other health impairment**—having limited strength, vitality, or alertness due to chronic or acute health problems

- **serious emotional disturbance**—a disability where a child of typical intelligence has difficulty, over time and to a marked degree, building satisfactory interpersonal relationships; inappropriate behavioral or emotional response under normal circumstances; pervasive mood of unhappiness; the tendency to develop physical symptoms or fears

- **specific learning disability**—a disorder in one or more of the basic psychological processes involved in understanding or in using language, spoken or written, which may manifest itself in an imperfect ability to listen, think, speak, read, write, spell, or do mathematical calculations

- **speech or language impairment**—a communication disorder such as stuttering, impaired articulation, a language impairment, or a voice impairment

- **traumatic brain injury**—an acquired injury to the brain caused by an external physical force, resulting in total or partial functional disability or psychosocial impairment, or both

- **visual impairment**—a visual difficulty (including blindness) that, even with correction, adversely affects a child's educational performance

To determine if a child is eligible for classification under one of these areas of exceptionality, an individualized evaluation or assessment of the child must be conducted. The IDEA specifies a number of requirements regarding evaluations of children suspected of having a disability. These requirements are briefly summarized as follows:

♦ Before a child is evaluated for the first time, the school district must notify his or her parents in writing. Parents must give written permission for the school system to conduct this first evaluation (known as a preplacement evaluation).

♦ Evaluations must be conducted by a multidisciplinary team (e.g., speech and language pathologist, occupational or physical therapist, medical specialists, school psychologist) and must include at least one teacher or specialist who is knowledgeable about the area of the child's suspected disability.

♦ The assessment must thoroughly investigate all areas related to the child's suspected disability.

♦ No single procedure may be used as the sole criterion for determining a child's eligibility for special services or for determining his or her appropriate educational placement. Rather, the evaluation process must utilize a variety of valid assessment instruments and observational data.

♦ All testing must be administered on an individual basis.

♦ Tests and other evaluation materials must be provided in the child's primary language or mode of communication, unless it is clearly not feasible to do so.

♦ All tests and other evaluation materials must be validated for the specific purpose for which they are used. This means that a test may not be used to assess a student in a particular area (e.g., intelligence) unless the test has been designed and validated through research as measuring that specific area.

♦ Assessments must be conducted in a nondiscriminatory way. This means that the tests and evaluation materials and procedures that are used may not be racially or culturally discriminatory (biased) against the child.

♦ The evaluation team must ensure that any test used is administered appropriately by a person trained to do so, that the test is being used for the purposes for which it was designed, and that the child's disability does not interfere with his or her ability to take any test measuring specific abilities (e.g., visual impairment affects the child's ability to read and correctly answer the questions on an achievement test).

Appropriately, comprehensively, and accurately assessing a child with a suspected disability clearly presents a significant challenge to the assessment team.

PARENTAL CONSENT AND THE ASSESSMENT PROCESS

In order to protect the due process rights of parents and their children, the school must obtain written permission before any school evaluation for a suspected disability is undertaken. Requesting consent for an evaluation should not be misinterpreted as a decision that a child has a disability. Rather, it is a means of assuring that parents have full knowledge of school actions *and* involvement in the decision-making process. It is essential that parents fully understand the reasons for an individual evaluation so that they feel comfortable with the decisions that they must eventually make.

If parents have questions about the purpose or type of evaluation proposed, or if they do not want their child evaluated, they may request an informal conference. This conference may be held with the CSE, other professionals familiar with the proposed evaluation, the person who referred the pupil, and/or an advisor of their choice. Such a conference may ease parents' concerns about the proposed evaluation and could also result in an agreement between the person who made the referral and the parents to withdraw the referral. If such an agreement cannot be reached, the school is required to initiate an impartial hearing during which a hearing officer can determine whether to waive parental consent and proceed to an evaluation.

Section 2

METHODS OF GATHERING INFORMATION

The most appropriate and acceptable approach in determining a student's eleigibility for special education placement is to develop the decision from a variety of procedures. The child must be assessed in all areas related to the suspected disability:

♦ health

♦ vision

♦ hearing

♦ social and emotional status

♦ general intelligence

♦ academic performance

♦ communicative status

♦ motor abilities

Because of the convenient and plentiful nature of standardized tests, it is perhaps tempting to administer a battery (group) of tests to a student and make an eligibility or placement determination based upon the results. However, tests alone will not give a comprehensive picture of how a child performs or what he or she knows or does not know.

There are, recently, a number of other approaches being used to collect information about students as well. These include:

♦ curriculum-based assessment

♦ ecological assessment

♦ task analysis

♦ dynamic assessment

♦ assessment of learning style

These approaches can yield important information about students, especially when assessing students who are from culturally or linguistically diverse backgrounds, and, there-

11

fore, are critical methods in the overall approach to assessment. Students possessing medical or mental health problems may also have assessment information from sources outside of the school. Such information would need to be considered along with assessment information from the school's evaluation team in making appropriate diagnoses, placement decisions, and instructional plans.

Only through collecting data through a variety of approaches (observations, interviews, tests, curriculum-based assessment, and so on) and from a variety of sources (parents, teachers, specialists, peers, and student) can an adequate picture be obtained of the child's strengths and weaknesses. Synthesized, this information can be used to determine the specific nature of the child's special needs, whether the child needs special services and, if so, to design an appropriate program.

THE SCREENING AND REFERRAL PROCESS

Referral Forms

Usually the first time a psychologist, special education teacher, or PPT (Pupil Personnel Team) becomes aware of a problem is when a classroom teacher fills out a referral form on a specific child. The major purpose of such a form is to alert other school professionals that a student is exhibiting difficulties in the classroom that may require further attention. These referral forms usually appear in one of two formats, as an *open-ended referral form* or as a *structured referral form*. An open-ended referral form may look like the following:

OPEN-ENDED REFERRAL FORM

Name: Matthew Jones   **Date of Referral:** November 9, 1997

Grade: 4

Teacher: Mrs. Brown

Why are you referring this child?

Matthew is experiencing severe academic difficulties in the classroom. He procrastinates, is easily distracted, refuses to hand in work, has a short attention span, and has difficulty with social skills. The other children tolerate him, but are losing patience. I have contacted his mother, and she has mentioned that these problems have been around for some time.

I have estimated Matthew's academic ability to be at least average, but his academic performance is well below grade level in all areas. He further exhibits low frustration tolerance, an unwillingness to attempt new concepts, self-criticism, and intolerance for those around him.

I am very concerned about Matthew's deterioration this year and would like some advice on how to handle the situation.

Has parent been notified of this referral?

yes _____   no _____

Administrator's signature _____ date _____

This type of referral form allows the teacher to fill in what he/she considers the most important issues about the child. However, the information given to the team may not be the type of information necessary for an overall indication of severity, history, and nature of the symptoms presented.

A structured referral form, on the other hand, may look like the following:

Name: _____

Grade: _____

Teacher: _____

Please answer the following questions using behavioral terms:

_____

_____

What symptoms is the child exhibiting that are of concern at this time?

_____

_____

What have you tried that has worked?

_____

_____

What have you tried that does not seem to work towards alleviating these symptoms?

_____

_____

What are the child's present academic levels of functioning?

_____

_____

What is the child's social behavior like?

_____

_____

Have the parents been contacted ? yes _____ no _____ If no, why not?

Further comments?

_____

_____

As you can see, in the structured referral form, the teacher is guided through a series of questions that define the specific areas determined as important by the PPT. Room is also given at the end for any further comments that the teacher feels are necessary to the understanding of the child.

Regardless of the version of form used, the special education teacher should begin to look for signals in the symptoms being presented and should ask him/herself the following questions at the time of the referral:

What are the comments from past teachers?

Never assume that the child has always had difficulties. Obtaining comments from past teachers may give a different picture and may also help pinpoint the changes that have led to the referral. A child who has had positive teacher feedback for several years and all of a sudden begins to deteriorate may have experienced something upsetting over the summer, experienced changes in the home, or may be experiencing difficulty adjusting to the personality or teaching style of his or her present teacher.

What is going on at home?

Home issues affect every child and some more than others. Many symptoms in school may be the result of tension or problems emanating from the home. If an evaluator misdiagnoses a student's home-related as school–related problems, the source of the problem will be overlooked and symptoms rather than problems will be treated. A brief conversation with the classroom teacher can possibly determine any *situational disturbances* (brief, but intense sources of tension, e.g., a parent's loss of a job, death of a relative, parental separation, etc.) that may be causing the child to have difficulty focusing or performing in school.

What are the achievement test scores and what patterns do they reflect?

Group achievement tests can be good indicators of certain types of problems. While individual achievement tests should only be used when evaluating a child with a disability, group tests may offer certain types of evidence. For example, a pattern of inconsistent strengths and weaknesses in the same skill area over time may be more reflective of emotional interference, while consistent weaknesses over time may be more reflective of a learning deficit.

What does the child's developmental history look like?

A child's developmental history can be like a fingerprint in determining possible causes or influences that may be contributing to the child's present problem. A thorough intake that covers all areas of a child's history is a crucial factor in the proper diagnosis of a problem. A look at developmental milestones, traumatic experiences, hospitalizations, prior test scores, and other factors offer a closer look at the total child.

When was the last time both vision and hearing were checked?

These two factors should be ruled out immediately as having any influence on the presenting problem. If the child has not been evaluated in either area within at least one year, or if symptoms indicate possible visual or auditory involvement (e.g., squinting, eye fatigue, failure to hear directions, etc.) then a retest in that area is indicated. A referral form should be considered as a list of signals that need to be investigated. It is important that the teacher writing the referral distinguish between symptoms and problems with the understanding

that the purpose of an evaluation, if required, is to define problems manifested through the child's pattern of symptoms.

Rating Scales

There may be times when an evaluator needs to refine the information received on a referral form into something more objective. This can be accomplished through the use of a personal interview with the child's teacher or employment of a *rating scale*. Rating scales are useful for qualifying behaviors or characteristics. Having a teacher answer yes or no to a question such as "Is the child easily distracted?" reveals very little. Having that same teacher rate the child's activity level across a 5-point scale allows for a better measure of the problem.

Classroom teachers have the best long-term observational opportunities with a child and provide excellent visions of children's status if given the right tools such as rating scales, and if the items of the scale are mutually understood by the teacher and the evaluator. Since the terms presented may be open to interpretation—for example, "impulsivity" may be defined by various people very differently—an evaluator should sit with the teacher involved in the evaluation and discuss the behaviors to be observed, before the teacher completes the rating scale. This will operationalize the scale and provide a more consistent interpretative tool. It is also sometimes helpful for the evaluator to sit with the classroom teacher so they can fill out the scale together. This will allow the evaluator to ask pertinent questions as they proceed along the scale and it will allow the teacher to clarify his or her insights about the child. Evaluators need to make sure that teachers know that the purpose of the rating scale is to help identify the source of a child's problem, not to indicate inferior ability, lack of potential, or an unwillingness to learn. If teachers fully understand the nature of symptoms, such misinterpretations can be avoided.

The rating scale is an excellent tool in the overall analysis of a child's potential problems and can begin to narrow down a child's specific areas of concern. It is important that the rating scale employed is of an effective length: If it is too short it will not provide an adequate picture of the child, and if it is too long it will burden the classroom teacher. It is also important that the rating scale be relevant to the child's needs. There are many types of rating scales that focus on different academic, behavioral, social, self-help, developmental, and perceptual areas.

The following is just an example of how a rating scale can be used to qualify a series of observations by the classroom teacher and shed some light on the severity of a student's symptoms.

Sample A

Student Rating Scale

	Always	Most of the time	Sometimes	Seldom	Never
Academic Behavior					
♦ Has trouble comprehending what he/she reads	—	—	—	—	—
♦ Uses adequate word attack skills	—	—	—	—	—

Student Rating Scale (*Continued*)

	Always	Most of the time	Sometimes	Seldom	Never
Academic Behavior					
◆ Loses his/her place while reading	—	—	—	—	—
◆ Slows down when reading aloud	—	—	—	—	—
◆ Exhibits good sight word vocabulary	—	—	—	—	—
◆ Shows adequate math computational skills	—	—	—	—	—
◆ Understands word problems	—	—	—	—	—
◆ Applies mathematical skills in solving problems	—	—	—	—	—
◆ Exhibits appropriate handwriting for age	—	—	—	—	—
◆ Exhibits adequate spelling skills for age	—	—	—	—	—
Classroom Behavior					
◆ Exhibits impulsivity	—	—	—	—	—
◆ Exhibits distractibility	—	—	—	—	—
◆ Gets along with peers	—	—	—	—	—
◆ Follows rules of a game	—	—	—	—	—
◆ Willing to reason	—	—	—	—	—
◆ Conforms to boundaries and rules in the classroom	—	—	—	—	—
◆ Attends to task	—	—	—	—	—
◆ Completes homework	—	—	—	—	—
◆ Completes classwork in allotted time	—	—	—	—	—
◆ Listens carefully	—	—	—	—	—
◆ Becomes easily frustrated	—	—	—	—	—
◆ Cooperates with others	—	—	—	—	—
Language Behavior					
◆ Exhibits adequate vocabulary	—	—	—	—	—
◆ Exhibits limited verbal fluency	—	—	—	—	—
◆ Exhibits faulty articulation	—	—	—	—	—

Sample B

Student Rating Scale

Please rate the following behaviors according to the following scale:

Rating

1—The behavior does not apply to this child and is never observed
2—The behavior is rarely exhibited
3—The behavior occurs some of the time
4—The behavior occurs most of the time
5—The behavior always occurs

____Anxious	____Tires easily
____Disruptive	____Defies authority
____Fights frequently	____Fears criticism
____Unhappy	____Critical to others
____Withdrawn	____Controlling
____Moody	____Painfully shy
____Distractible	____Slow starter
____Impulsive	____Inconsistent
____Does not complete work	____Hyperactive
____Short attention span	____Hypoactive
____Daydreams	____Fearful of new situations
____Argumentative	____Procrastinates
____Disorganized	____Rarely takes chances
____Easily Confused	____Overreactive
____Poor speller	____Problems with writing
____Poor reader	____Problems with math
____Limited reading comprehension	____Poor vocabulary usage
____Faulty articulation	____Poor expressive language ability
____Poor grammar	____Inadequate word attack skills
____Problems judging time	____Poor balance and coordination
____Poor fine-motor skills	____Poor gross-motor skills
____Slow in completing tasks	____Difficulty tracing and drawing
____Poor logical reasoning and thinking	____Difficulty with abstract concepts
____Poor number concepts	____Problems with auditory memory tasks

Observation Scales

Observing children in different settings is a necessary part of the screening and referral process and offers further perspective on a child. A child who has been referred should be observed in a variety of settings, including the classroom, playground, gym, and lunchroom regarding basic behaviors—attention, focus, aggressiveness, compliance, flexibility, rigidity, oppositional behavior, shyness, controlling behavior, distractibility, impulsivity, social interaction, and so on.

WHAT EVALUATORS SHOULD LOOK FOR WHEN OBSERVING

While observing a child, evaluators should seek answers to the following kinds of questions:

Is there a difference between the child's behaviors in a structured setting, i.e., the classroom, and the child's behaviors in an unstructured setting, i.e., the playground?

This factor may shed light on the child's need for a more structured environment in which to learn. Children who do not have well-developed internal control systems need a highly structured environment to maintain focus and appropriate behavior. Some children cannot shift between structured and unstructured and back again. They may not possess the internal monitor that regulates conformity and logical attendance to rules. These children may be more successful in a structured play setting set up by teachers during the lunch hour.

Does the child seem to respond to external boundaries?

This factor is important to the teacher since it is a monitor of potential learning style. If a child who lacks internal controls does conform to external boundaries, e.g., time out or teacher proximity during worktime, then this factor needs to be taken into consideration when prescribing classroom management techniques for the child. When the child conforms to such boundaries, then his or her behavior is a message of what works best.

What is the child's attention span during academic tasks?

Attention span at different ages is normally measured in minutes or hours. Evaluators should become aware of the normal attention span for children of all ages and then compare the attention span of the child being observed over several activities and days to see if a pattern of inattention is present. If the attention span is very short, relative to the norm for children of his or her age, then modifications of work load, i.e., shorter but more frequent assignments, may be appropriate.

Does the child require constant teacher supervision or assistance?

A child who requires constant teacher supervision or assistance is exhibiting a wide variety of possible symptomatic behavior that may be resulting from difficulties such as attention deficit disorder, processing problems, emotional difficulties involving need for attention, a need for control, high anxiety, stress, limited intellectual capacity, and hearing problems. All of these areas need to be assessed and a good evaluation should determine the root of such behavior. It is important to remember the indicative importance of the frequency, intensity, and duration of the child's symptoms.

Does the child interact appropriately with peers?

Observing a child at play can reveal a great deal about that child's self-esteem, tension levels, social maturity, physical development, and many other factors. Keeping in mind that social interaction is more common in children over the age of six or seven while parallel play is still common in younger children, observing play behavior gives us insight into a child's own internal boundaries and organization. A child who always needs to control may really be masking high levels of tension. The more controlling a child is, the more out-of-control he or she may be feeling. A child who can appropriately conform to group rules, delay his or her needs for the good of the team, conform to rules and various changes or inconsistencies in rules, may be a child who is very self-assured and has low anxiety levels. The opposite is most always typical of children at risk. It is important that evaluators be thoroughly familiar with and always consider developmental stages since certain behaviors, such as control, may be more typical at early ages.

Is the child a high or low status child?

Observing a child in different settings allows the opportunity to see the social status of the child and its impact on his or her behavior. Often, children with learning disabilities are viewed by their peers as having low status. Consequently, they don't receive the positive social cues that would reinforce positive self-esteem. Their lack of self-esteem increases the peer designation as low status, and so the destructive cycle continues. These children are also more apt to feel insignificant relative to their peers because they don't receive positive social cues. Having the school psychologist begin a counseling group of five or six low status children enables them to feel empowered with feelings of connection, and allows them to build positive and reinforcing relationships.

The type of checklist that allows the observer to fill in information on specific observable behaviors is referred to as an observation scale. The following is just one example:

Observation Report Form

Name of Student Observed: Observer:
Date of Observation: Place of observation:

Behaviors to Observe	Classroom	Playground	Lunchroom	Gym	Other
1. Impulsivity	—	—	—	—	—
2. Attention to Task	—	—	—	—	—
3. Attention Span	—	—	—	—	—
4. Conformity to rules	—	—	—	—	—
5. Social interaction with peers	—	—	—	—	—
6. Aggressiveness	—	—	—	—	—
7. Level of teacher assistance required	—	—	—	—	—
8. Frustration levels	—	—	—	—	—
9. Reaction to authority	—	—	—	—	—
10. Verbal interaction	—	—	—	—	—
11. Procrastinates	—	—	—	—	—
12. Organizational skills	—	—	—	—	—
13. Developmental motor skills	—	—	—	—	—

As seen by the above example, any of a number of behaviors in any number of settings can and should be observed. It can also serve to fulfill the Committee on Special Education's requirement for a classroom observation, which must be part of the packet when a review for classification is required. The spaces provided allow for comments and notes of observations that may shed some light on the child's overall pattern of behavior and severity of symptoms.

COMMON OBSERVATIONAL TECHNIQUES

Besides rating scales and observation checklists, there are several other common observational techniques used to gather information about a child's behavioral patterns. These include:

Anecdotal Records: The observer describes incidents or behaviors observed in a particular setting in concrete, narrative terms (as opposed to drawing inferences about feelings or motives). This type of record allows insight into cause and effect by detailing what occurred before a behavior took place, the behavior itself, and consequences or events that occurred after the behavior.

Event Recording: The observer is interested in recording specific behavioral events (such as how many times the student hits or gets out of his or her seat). A tally sheet listing the behaviors to be observed and counted is useful; when the observer sees the behavior of interest, he or she can simply make a tic mark on the sheet.

Duration Recording: This method usually requires a watch or clock, so that a precise measurement of how much time a student spends doing something of concern to the teacher or assessment team (e.g., talking to others, tapping, rocking) can be recorded.

Time-sampling Recording: With this technique, observers count the number of times a behavior occurs during a specific time interval. Rather than observe for long periods of time and tally all incidences of the behavior causing concern, the observer divides the observation period into equal time units and observes and tallies behavior only during short periods of time. Based upon the time sampling, predictions can then be made about the student's total behavior.

The observer needs to keep in mind that there are a number of errors that can occur during observations that will distort or invalidate the information collected. One source of error may come from the observer who must record accurately, systematically, and without bias. If his or her general impression of the student influences how he or she rates that student in regards to specific characteristics, the data will be misleading and inaccurate. This can be especially true if the student comes from a background that is different from the majority culture. In such cases, it is important that the observer have an understanding of, and a lack of bias regarding, the student's cultural or language group.

Often, multiple observers are used to increase the reliability of the observational information collected. All observers should be fully trained in how to collect information using the specific method chosen (e.g., time-sampling using a checklist) and how to remain unobtrusive while observing and recording, so as not to influence the student's behavior. It is also important to observe more than once, in a number of situations or locations, and at various times, and to integrate these data with information gathered through other assessment procedures. In short, decisions should not be made based upon a narrow range of observational samples.

CHILD STUDY TEAMS/PUPIL PERSONNEL TEAMS

Many schools are moving towards a more global approach to the identification of potential high-risk students through the development of the Pupil Personnel Team, Child Study Team, School-Based Support Team, and so on. The members of such teams work as a single unit in determining the possible etiology, contributing behavioral factors, educational status, prognosis, and recommendations for a student. Bringing together many disciplines and professional perspectives to help work on a case is the major objective of the team so that a single person is not required to determine and assimilate all of the factors impacting a particular child. The members of a team are responsible for gathering all the necessary information on a child in order to determine the most effective and practical direction for that child.

Membership or the Pupil Personnel Team (PPT)

A PPT is usually made up of the following individuals:

- Administrator
- Psychologist
- Nurse Teacher
- Classroom Teacher
- Social Worker
- Special Education Teacher
- Guidance Counselor
- Reading Teacher
- Speech and Language Teacher

The members of this team usually meet on a regular basis, once or twice a week depending upon the case load. This is a local school-based support team and should not be confused with the Committee on Special Education, which is a district based-team required to have a parent member. The Pupil Personnel Team does not, and is not, required to have a parent member.

Questions Considered by the Pupil Personnel Team

When a PPT first receives a referral from a teacher, its members must consider many issues. These may include the following:

Has this child ever been referred to the PPT before?

Prior referral may indicate a *historical disturbance*, or long-term problem, and therefore a more serious situation, especially if the same pattern was reported previously. *Situational disturbances*, problems that are linked to a specific change or event and that have not been preceded by similar disturbances, usually have a better prognosis.

Are there any prior psychological, educational, language, or other evaluations?

This information is very important insofar as it prevents the child's undergoing unnecessary testing. Such evaluations also offer the team another perspective on the problem.

Is anyone on the PPT familiar with other members of the child's family?

Family patterns of behavior may help define contributing factors to the child's problem. Familiarity with patterns of behavior within the family may afford the team perspective on the best approach to take with this family.

Are there any medical issues that might impact on this case?

Medical issues are crucial, and their existence should always be determined first. Difficulties with hearing and eyesight, being on medication, having severe allergies, etc., can be significant contributors to poor performance that may be mistakenly attributed to the child's being "unmotivated," "lazy," "stubborn," and so on.

What do the child's present and past report cards look like? What patterns are exhibited?

Some children have trouble starting off in a new situation and end up playing catch-up the entire year. Others do well the first marking period and slowly decline to a pattern of poor grades. Others exhibit the roller-coaster effect—consistently receiving inconsistent grades. Knowing the child's report card "style" may help determine the type of support, remediation, and program offered by the PPT.

What are the child's group achievement test score patterns?

Achievement test scores can offer a great deal of useful information about a child's scholastic patterns. If the team suspects a learning disability, then the areas affected should be consistently low from year to year. Many fluctuations of scores and wide ranges of results may indicate more emotional involvement than a learning disability. A child who is not functioning well in the classroom but consistently receives achievement scores within the ninetieth percentile may be performing poorly for reasons other than learning disabilities.

If the results of prior testing are not available, is there any group IQ test information that would offer some idea of intellectual ability?

While group IQ tests should never be used to determine a high-risk child's true intellectual potential, they may offer a general idea of ability. The problem with group tests for a child with learning and emotional problems is that the child may lack the energy or motivation to take such tests. Since the test would have been administered to a group, the child's behavior toward the test could have gone unnoticed.

Has anyone in an official capacity observed this child?

This piece of information is required if the team sees the possibility of referring the child to the CSE. In any case, observation should always be part of the information presented to the PPT. One PPT member—usually the psychologist, social worker, guidance counselor, or special education teacher—should observe the child in a variety of situations prior to the first PPT meeting. It is very important for the team to know how this child functions in structured and unstructured settings.

Does the PPT have samples of the child's classwork?

Samples of classwork over a period of time offer a clearer overview of the child's abilities and attitude toward classwork. This also gives several team members an opportunity to observe possible academic symptoms that may first appear in written work.

Have the child's parents been notified of the teacher's concerns?

It is the responsibility of the classroom teacher, not the PPT, to alert the child's parents that he or she is concerned about the child and would like the PPT to take a closer look. Parents do not have a legal right to refuse such requests since they are considered normal school procedures. The teacher should also notify the parents that someone from the team will be in touch with them to gather more information. At this point such a parent intake is frequently requested of the parent to enhance the diagnosis of the problem or problems.

Options of the Pupil Personnel Team

Depending on delays, conflicts, procedures, the organizational ability of the team, and so on, several weeks might pass while the PPT has meetings and gathers information about the child under consideration—work samples, academic records, group achievement test scores, observations, medical records, teacher reports, parent intake—and decides on the appropriate direction to follow. There are several directions and recommendations that the PPT can institute:

Psychoeducational Evaluation: Such an evaluation is frequently recommended when a child's academic skill levels (reading, math, writing, and spelling) are unknown or inconsistent and when his or her learning process shows gaps (e.g., memory and expression). The evaluation will determine if a discrepancy between intellectual potential and academic achievement required for the classification of LD (learning disability) exists, and it will determine strengths and weaknesses in the child's academic and processing levels. Some symptoms that might suggest this recommendation are:

- Consistently low test scores on group achievement tests
- Indications of delayed processing when faced with academic skills
- Labored handwriting after grade 3
- Poor word recall
- Poor decoding (word attack) skills
- Discrepancy between achievement and ability
- Consistently low achievement despite remediation

Language Evaluation: This recommendation usually occurs when the child is experiencing significant delays in speech or language development, problems in articulation, or problems in receptive or expressive language. Some symptoms that might warrant such an evaluation would follow:

- Difficulty pronouncing words through grade 3
- Immature or delayed speech patterns
- Difficulty labeling thoughts or objects
- Difficulty putting thoughts into words

Psychological Evaluation: This recommendation is appropriate when the child's intellectual ability is unknown or when there is a question about his/her inability to learn. It is useful when the PPT suspects a potential learning, emotional, or intellectual problem.

The psychological evaluation can rule out *or* rule in emotionality as a primary cause of a child's problem. Ruling this factor out is necessary before the diagnosis of LD can be made. Some symptoms that might signal the need for such an evaluation follow:

- High levels of tension and anxiety exhibited in behavior
- Aggressive behavior
- Lack of motivation or indications of low energy levels
- Patterns of denial
- Oppositional behavior
- Despondency
- Inconsistent academic performance, ranging from very low to very high
- History of inappropriate judgment
- Lack of impulse control
- Extreme and consistent attention-seeking behavior
- Pattern of provocative behavior

Referral to CSE for a meeting to discuss the parent's resistance to evaluation: If a parent refuses to sign a release for testing and the school feels strongly that such a procedure is in the best interests of the child, then both parents should be urged to attend a meeting so that some agreement or compromise can be made. While it may be impossible for both parents to attend due to work schedules, family responsibilities, unwillingness to face the problem, or divorce, the school should make every attempt to have at least one parent present. Whatever the evaluation recommended by the Pupil Personnel Team, representatives of the PPT should come to the meeting with all the most recent available information on a child. Such recommendations may have tremendous implications and should never be taken lightly.

If the child's parents remain uncooperative, it may become necessary to involve the CSE (Child Study Team) to resolve any disputes.

REVIEWING SCHOOL RECORDS

Schools usually have a wealth of information about all of the students, distributed among a number of people and a number of records. Gathering and reviewing this information after a referral and prior to evaluation could reduce the need for testing the child, and could provide a very thorough picture of the child and his or her abilities and patterns. Investigating the following areas will contribute to the overall "picture" of the child:

Prior teacher reports: Comments written on report cards or in permanent record folders can provide a different perspective on the child under a different style of teaching. Successful years and positive comments may be a clue to the child's learning style and the conditions under which the child responds best.

Reports of prior parent-teacher interviews: Write-ups about conferences between previous teachers and parents can provide information important to understanding the child's patterns and history.

Cumulative school record: This particular file may contain standardized achievement test results, group IQ results, teacher comments dating back to kindergarten, records from previous schools, individual reading test results, and family information.

Group IQ test information: This information is usually found in the permanent record folder. Many schools administer this type of test (e.g., Otis Lennon, Henmon Nelson) in grades 3, 6, and 9. It is important to be aware that within the past year or so the term *School Abilities Index* has replaced the term "IQ" or Intelligence Quotient.

Standardized test scores: These scores should be analyzed for patterns of strengths and deficiencies. The older the child, the greater the number of scores that can be compared.

Report card grades: These materials can be reviewed for comments and for patterns of productivity and difficulty.

Attendance records: These records should be reviewed for patterns of lateness or absence. If such patterns exist, the reasons should be determined so as to rule out medical causes (hospital stays, illnesses), psychological causes (dysfunctional family patterns, school phobia, etc.) or social causes (peer rejection or isolation).

Number of schools attended: There are instances when a child could be enrolled in several schools over several years. The reasons for the many moves should be investigated as the many moves and/or their causes could contribute to a child's adjustment difficulties.

Prior teacher referrals: Investigate school records for prior referrals from teachers. There could have been a time when a teacher referred but no action was taken due to time of year, parent resistance, delay in evaluation procedures, or other reasons. These referrals may still be on file and may reveal information that can be useful.

Medical history in the school nurse's office: Investigate school medical records for indications of visual or hearing difficulties, prescribed medication that may have an effect on the child's behavior (i.e., antihistamines), and medical conditions in need of attention or that could be contributing to the child's present difficulties.

LOOKING AT THE STUDENT'S WORK

Often, an initial part of the assessment process includes examining a student's work, either by selecting work samples that can be analyzed to identify academic skills and deficits, or by conducting a portfolio assessment, where folders of the student's work are examined. When collecting work samples, the teacher should select work from the areas where the student is experiencing difficulty and should systematically examine it. The teacher might identify elements across the work—such as how the student was directed (e.g., orally or in writing), how long it took the student to complete the activity, the pattern of errors (e.g., reversals when writing), and the pattern of correct answers. Analyzing the student's work in this way can yield valuable insight into the nature of his or her difficulties and suggest possible solutions.

INTERVIEWS

Interviewing the student in question, his or her parents, teachers, and other adults or peers can provide a great deal of useful information about the student. Preparing for the interview may involve a careful review of the student's school records or work samples, for these may help the assessment team identify patterns or areas of specific concern that can help determine who should be interviewed and some of the questions to be asked.

TESTING

When gathering information on a child, the evaluator may use a variety of measures for assessment:

Standardized Tests: Unlike informal tests, standardized tests have detailed procedures for administration, timing, and scoring. There is a wide variety of tests available to assess different skill areas.

Criterion Referenced Tests: Some tests are known as *criterion-referenced tests*. This means that they are scored according to a standard, or criterion, that the teacher, school, or test publisher decides represents an acceptable level of mastery. An example of a criterion-referenced test might be a teacher-made spelling test where there are 20 words to be spelled and where the teacher has defined an "acceptable level of mastery" as 16 correct (or 80%).

Content-Referenced Tests: These tests are concerned with the mastery of specific, defined skills; the student's performance on the test indicates whether or not he or she has mastered those skills.

Norm-referenced Tests: Other tests are known as *norm-referenced tests*. Scores on these tests are interpreted not according to an absolute standard or criterion (i.e., 8 out of 10 correct) but, rather, according to how the student's performance compares with that of a particular group of individuals. In order for this comparison to be meaningful, a valid comparison group, called a norm group, must be defined. A norm group is a large number of children who are representative of all the children in that age group. Individual schools will then compare the scores of children being evaluated to the scores obtained by the norm group. This helps evaluators determine whether a child is performing at a level typical for, below, or above that expected for children of a given ethnicity, socioeconomic status, age, or grade.

Selecting an Appropriate Testing Instrument

Choosing which test is appropriate for a given student requires investigation on the part of the evaluator. It is extremely important that those responsible for test selection do not just use what is available to or "always used by" the school district or school. The child's test results will certainly influence eligibility decisions, instructional decisions, and placement decisions—all of which have enormous consequences for the child, his or her parents, as well as the classroom teacher. Therefore, selecting instruments with care is vital, as is the need to combine any information gathered through testing with information gathered by other means (e.g., interviews, observations, dynamic assessment).

Before choosing an assessment instrument, the evaluator should ask:

♦ Is the focus of the test directly relevant to the skill area(s) to be assessed?

♦ Will the student's results on the test address the educational questions being asked? (In other words, will the test provide the type of educational information that is needed?)

♦ Is the test *reliable* (consistency of results over time) and *valid* (does the test measure what the publisher claims)?

♦ Is the content/skill area being assessed by the test appropriate for the student, given his or her age and grade?

♦ If the test is norm-referenced, does the student resemble the norm group?

♦ Is the test intended to evaluate students, to diagnose the specific nature of a student's disability or academic difficulty, to inform instructional decisions, or to be used for research purposes?

♦ Is the test administered in a group or individually?

♦ Does the examiner need specialized training in order to administer the test, record student responses, score the test or interpret results?

♦ Will the student's suspected disability impact upon his or her taking of the test? (e.g., If a student has weak hand strength or dexterity, his or her performance on a timed test that requires holding a pencil or writing will be negatively affected by the disability.)

♦ How similar to actual classroom tasks are the tasks the child is asked to complete on the test?

NEW OUTLOOKS ON ASSESSMENT

Recent developments in assessment strategies have resulted in a variety of ways in which an evaluator can gather information. Some of these assessment techniques have been gaining recognition within the actual school setting. These include:

Ecological Assessment

Ecological assessment basically involves directly observing and assessing the child in the many environments in which he or she routinely operates. The purpose of conducting such an assessment is to probe how the different environments influence the student and his or her school performance. For instance:

♦ Where does the student manifest difficulties?

♦ Are there places where he or she appears to function appropriately?

♦ What is expected of the student academically and behaviorally in each type of environment?

♦ What differences exist in the environments where the student manifests the greatest and the least difficulty?

♦ What implications do these differences have for instructional planning?

Direct Assessment

Direct assessment of academic skills is one alternative that has recently gained in popularity. While there are a number of direct assessment models that exist, they are similar in that they all suggest that assessment needs to be directly tied to instructional curriculum. Curriculum-based assessment (CBA) is one type of direct evaluation. "Tests" of performance in this case come directly from the curriculum. For example, a child may be asked to read from his or her reading book for one minute. Information about the accuracy and the speed of reading can then be obtained and compared with other students in the class, building, or district. CBA is quick and offers specific information about how a student may differ from peers.

Dynamic Assessment

One of the chief characteristics of dynamic assessment is that it includes a dialogue or interaction between the examiner and the student. The interaction allows the examiner to draw conclusions about the student's thinking processes (e.g., why he or she answers a question in a particular way) and his or her response to a learning situation (i.e., whether, with prompting, feedback, or modeling, the student can produce a correct response, and what specific means of instruction produce and maintain positive change in the student's cognitive functioning).

Typically, dynamic assessment involves a test-train-retest approach. The examiner begins by testing the student's ability to perform a task or solve a problem without help. Then, a similar task or problem is given to the student, and the examiner models how the task or problem is solved or gives the student cues to assist his or her performance.

Task Analysis

Task analysis is very detailed; it involves breaking down a particular task into the basic sequential steps, component parts, or skills necessary to accomplish the task. The degree to which a task is broken down into steps depends upon the student in question; "it is only necessary to break the task down finely enough so that the student can succeed at each step" (Wallace, Larsen, & Elksnin, 1992, p. 14). Taking this approach to assessment offers several advantages to the teacher. For one, the process identifies what is necessary for accomplishing a particular task. It also tells the teacher whether or not the student can do the task, which part or skill causes the student to falter, and the order in which skills must be taught to help the student learn to perform the task.

Outcome-Based Assessment

Outcome-based assessment is another approach to gathering information about a student's performance. Outcome-based assessment involves considering, teaching, and evaluating the skills that are important in real-life situations and is based on the assumption that learning such skills will result in the student becoming an effective adult. Assessment, from this point of view, starts by identifying what outcomes are desired for the student (e.g., being able to use public transportation). In steps similar to what is used with task analysis, the team then determines what competencies are necessary for the outcomes to take place, and identifies which subskills the student has mastered and which he or she still needs to learn. The instruction that is needed can then be pinpointed and undertaken.

Learning Styles Assessment

Learning styles theory suggests that students may learn and problem solve in different ways, and that some ways are more natural than others. When they are taught or asked to perform in ways that deviate from their natural style, they are thought to learn or perform less well. A learning styles assessment attempts to determine those elements that impact on a child's learning.

Some of the common elements involved in a learning styles assessment include:

♦ The way in which material is typically presented (visually, auditorily, tactilely) in the classroom

♦ The environmental conditions of the classroom (hot, cold, noisy, light, dark)

♦ The child's personality characteristics

♦ The expectations for success that are held by the child and others

♦ The response the child receives while engaging in the learning process (e.g., praise or criticism)

♦ The type of thinking the child generally utilizes in solving problems (e.g., trial and error, analyzing)

Identifying the factors that positively impact the child's learning may be very valuable in developing effective intervention strategies.

Section 3

THE WECHSLER SCALES OF INTELLIGENCE

The Wechsler Scales are one of the most widely used individual evaluation measures of intelligence utilized in today's schools. Most cases involving a suspected disability require some form of intellectual evaluation. While the Wechsler Scales are usually administered by psychologists, there is a great deal of useful information that can be obtained from this test. Since it is inevitable that special education teachers will more than likely come in contact with this test, it is critical that they understand the nature of the scores and the implications of the results. Strengths and weaknesses of a child's learning style, indications of greater potential, organizational skills, processing abilities, reasoning abilities, and adjustment to timed tasks are examples of useful information that can be obtained from this test. Consequently, this entire chapter will focus solely on an in-depth analysis of the three Wechsler Scales of Intelligence:

— Wechsler Preschool and Primary Scale of Intelligence (WPPSI-R)
— Wechsler Intelligence Scale for Children—III (WISC-III)
— Wechsler Adult Intelligence Scale—Revised (WAIS-R)

THE WECHSLER SCALES OF INTELLIGENCE

GENERAL TEST INFORMATION

Author:	David Wechsler
Publisher:	The Psychological Corporation
Address of Publisher:	555 Academic Court
	San Antonio, Texas 78204-2498
Phone Number of Publisher:	800-211-8378
Fax of Publisher:	800-232-1223
TDD of the Publisher:	800-723-1318

Purpose of Test: Some of the most commonly used tests in the measurement of intelligence, and the most widely used individual intelligence tests in education, are the Wechsler Scales. These are three separate tests that measure a variety of intellectual areas and compute a Verbal, Performance, and Full Scale IQ.

Description of Test: Test comprises two areas of assessment: Verbal and Performance. The verbal areas are considered *auditory/vocal* tasks (auditory input and vocal output) while the performance areas are *visual/vocal and visual/motor* tasks (visual input and vocal or motoric output). The three tests include:

— Wechsler Preschool and Primary Scale of Intelligence (WPPSI-R)
— Wechsler Intelligence Scale for Children—III (WISC-III)
— Wechsler Adult Intelligence Scale—III (WAIS-III)

Type of Test:	Standardized, norm referenced
Administration Time:	60–75 minutes
Type of Administration:	Individual
Who Administers This Test:	Psychologist
Age/Grade Levels:	The three tests are designed for children and adults ages 4½ to adult. The age ranges for the three Wechsler tests are:

⊛ The Wechsler Preschool and Primary Scale of Intelligence (WPPSI-R)—ages 4½ to 6½

⊛ Wechsler Intelligence Scale for Children—III (WISC-III)—ages 6½ to 16½

⊛ Wechsler Adult Intelligence Scale—III (WAIS-III)—ages 16 and over

Subtest Information: The three Wechsler Scales consist of a total of 19 possible subtests. Unless otherwise noted, all subtests are contained in each scale. The specific subtests for each Wechsler Scale are:

Verbal Tests (auditory/vocal tasks)

- *Information*—Measures general information acquired from experience and education, remote verbal memory, understanding, and associative thinking. The socioeconomic background and reading ability of the student may influence the subtest score.

- *Similarities*—Measures abstract and concrete reasoning, logical thought processes, associative thinking, and remote memory.

- *Arithmetic*—Measures mental alertness, concentration, attention, arithmetic reasoning, reaction to time pressure, and practical knowledge of computational facts. This is the only subtest directly related to the school curriculum, and is greatly affected by anxiety.
- *Vocabulary*—Measures a child's understanding of spoken words, learning ability, general range of ideas, verbal information acquired from experience and education, and kind and quality of expressive language. This subtest is relatively unaffected by emotional disturbance, but is highly susceptible to cultural background and level of education. It is also the best single measure of intelligence in the entire battery.
- *Comprehension*—Measures social judgment, common-sense reasoning based on past experience, and practical intelligence.
- *Digit Span*—Measures attention, concentration, immediate auditory memory, auditory attention, and behavior in a learning situation. This subtest correlates poorly with general intelligence.
- *Sentences*—Measures attention, concentration, immediate auditory memory, auditory attention, and behavior in a learning situation. (*This subtest is part of the WPPSI-R only.*)
- *Letter-Number Sequencing*—Measures working memory. A series of orally presented letters and numbers are presented in a mixed-up order; examiner must reorder and repeat the list in a predetermined order. (*This subtest is part of the WAIS-III only.*)

Performance Subtests (visual and vocal/visual motor tasks)

- *Picture Completion*—Measures visual alertness to surroundings, remote visual memory, attention to detail, and ability to isolate essential from nonessential detail.
- *Picture Arrangement*—Measures visual perception, logical sequencing of events, attention to detail, and ability to see cause-effect relationships. (*This subtest is part of the WISC-III and WAIS-III only.*)
- *Block Design*—Measures ability to perceive, analyze, synthesize, and reproduce abstract forms, visual motor coordination, spatial relationships, general ability to plan and organize.
- *Object Assembly*—Measures immediate perception of a total configuration, part-whole relationships, and visual motor spatial coordination. (*This subtest is part of the WISC-III and WAIS-III only.*)
- *Coding*—Measures ability to associate meaning with symbol, visual motor dexterity (pencil manipulation), flexibility, and speed in learning tasks. (*This subtest is part of the WISC-III only.*)
- *Digit Symbol*—Measures ability to associate meaning with symbol, visual motor dexterity (pencil manipulation), flexibility and speed in learning tasks. (*This subtest is part of the WAIS-III only.*)
- *Symbol Search*—Measures visual discrimination. (*This subtest is part of the WISC-III and WAIS-III only.*)
- *Mazes*—Measures ability to formulate and execute a visual-motor plan, pencil control and visual-motor coordination, speed and accuracy, and planning capability. (*This subtest is part of the WPPSI-R and WISC-III only.*)
- *Animal House*—Measures ability to associate meaning with symbol, visual motor dexterity, flexibility, and speed in learning tasks. (*This subtest is part of the WPPSI-R only.*)
- *Geometric Design*—Measures a child's pencil control and visual-motor coordination, speed and accuracy, and planning capability. (*This subtest is part of the WPPSI-R only.*)
- *Matrix Reasoning*—Measures perceptual organization. This is a traditional type of nonverbal task where the examinee looks at a picture of geometric shapes and either names or points to the correct answer from five response options. (*This subtest is part of the WAIS-III only.*)

SCORING INFORMATION

All three scales result in three IQ measures: Verbal IQ, Performance IQ, and Full Scale IQ. The resulting IQ scores fall into several classification ranges:

IQ Range	Classification	Percent Included
130 and over	Very Superior	2.2
120-129	Superior	6.7
110-119	High Average	16.1
90-109	Average	50.0
80-89	Low Average	16.1
70-79	Borderline	6.7
69 and below	Intellectually Deficient	2.2

When scoring the Wechsler Scales, there are several interpretive areas that need to be analyzed besides the resulting IQ scores. One of the first areas to analyze is whether or not the student's results reflect his or her greatest potential. Since academic expectations are often based on intellectual ability, it is crucial to determine if the resulting scores are indicative of the child's true ability. This is also useful in determining realistic expectations of a child at a given age level. Consequently, the first step to analyze involves the possibility of greater potential.

Indications of Greater Potential on the Wechsler Scales

Let's take a look at some of the factors that need to be analyzed when determining intelligence and see the types of information that an analysis of the Wechsler Scales can offer.

Once a child has finished taking an IQ test and received a score, it is crucial to determine whether or not that score is truly reflective of his/her potential ability or is an underestimate of that ability. Frequently, expectations, educational plans, placement, and so on are determined for a child as a result of his/her testing and what it reveals about intellectual potential. At this point the special educator may want to secure a copy of the *protocol* (the booklet or sheet on which the answers to a test are written) from the psychologist to facilitate calculations and diagnosis. There should be no problem with this request since special educators are allowed to see this information as part of the diagnostic team and as long as the psychologist is reassured that the purpose is to get a better understanding of learning style, approach to tasks, modality strengths and weaknesses, etc., and that the copy will be returned to his/her files. However, if there is some resistance, you may have to accomplish this in the psychologist's office. Either way, don't hesitate to complete this area of diagnosis since it is a crucial piece of the overall assessment.

The protocol reveals many things about the test and its cover contains a great deal of useful information. The first thing we want to look at is the pattern of *scaled scores* (scores converted from raw scores for purposes of interpretation and a common standard) that appear next to the *raw scores* (the number of correct responses on a given test) on the front of the protocol. The scale scores can range from a low of 1 to a high of 19 with 10 considered the midpoint. However several scaled scores may constitute a specific range (i.e., scaled scores of 8, 9, 10, and 11 are considered average) as can be seen by the chart below.

To get a better idea of the value of a scaled score simply multiply it by 10 and that will give you a "rough" idea of the correlated IQ value. It is from these scaled scores that our investigation of greater potential begins.

Relationship Among IQ Ranges, Scaled Scores and Percentiles		
RANGE	SCALED SCORE	PERCENTILE
Very Superior	19	99.9
Very Superior	18	99.6
Very Superior	17	99
Very Superior	16	98
Superior	15	95
Superior	14	91
Above Average	13	84
Above Average	12	75
Average	11	63
Average	10	50
Average	9	37
Average	8	25
Low Average	7	16
Low Average	6	9
Borderline	5	5
Borderline	4	2
Mentally Deficient	3	1
Mentally Deficient	2	0.4
Mentally Deficient	1	0.1

Note: The above chart is used only for a general relationship between IQs, scaled scores, and percentiles and is not statistically exact. The conversion tables used by the psychologist in deriving the actual IQ from test results are different and located within the manual.

The IQ results from the Wechsler Scales may not always indicate an individual's true intellectual potential. While the Wechsler Scales are valid tests, the resulting scores can be influenced by many factors—tension, poor self-esteem, language difficulties—and may not be valid, therefore necessitating further analysis. In order to determine if the resulting scores are valid, four indicators of an individual's true ability are applied to the results of the test. Any one indicator by itself should bring into question the true validity of the results and initiate an analysis of the factors which may contribute to such variability.

I. Check for INTERTEST SCATTER

Intertest scatter is scatter or variability between subtests that may indicate an unevenness of performance. To ascertain verbal intertest scatter and performance intertest scatter, first find the range of verbal scores from low to high and do the same for performance scores. If the range on either the verbal or performance scale is greater than 3 points, then the possibility of intertest scatter should be explored with the psychologist.

EXAMPLE: Information-8
Similarities-15
Arithmetic-6
Vocabulary-13
Comprehension-10
Digit Span-5

In the above illustration of verbal scaled scores, for example, the range of scores is from 5 (Digit Span) to 15 (Similarities). While different levels of scatter may be due to a variety of reasons, including chance, the pattern should be noted and discussed with the psychologist who would determine, by criteria, if the variability of intertest scatter is significant.

Such scatter can also be the result of emotional factors, processing problems, or neurological factors. However, intertest scatter is only one signal of a potential invalid IQ result but, if it exists, it should be noted.

2. Check for INTRATEST SCATTER

Intratest scatter is variability in performance within a subtest. It can only be ascertained by scrutiny of responses of the subject on the test protocol. Since IQ tests are made with questions increasing in difficulty, one would expect a subject to answer easier ones and miss on the more difficult questions. However, the opposite exists, where a subject will continuously miss easier questions and be able to correctly respond to harder ones. When this occurs in several subtests, intratest scatter may exist, indicating greater potential than the test scores indicate. The more frequently a respondent's subtests reflect intratest scatter, the greater the respondent's potential.

3. Check for Verbal/Performance Scatter

The normal range difference of scores between the two test levels—verbal and performance—should be under 15 points so as to indicate a more consistent pattern of performance. A 15 or more point difference between Verbal IQ and Performance IQ is considered by many to be an indicator of scatter and an uneven performance that could be the result of, for example, emotional problems, language difficulties, or processing problems.

4. Check for Vocabulary/Similarities Scatter

If a respondent's Vocabulary and/or Similarities scaled scores are more than 3 points higher than the respondent's *Verbal Mean Scaled Score* (the average of all the verbal scaled scores given) then another type of scatter may exist. *Vocabulary and/or Similarities* have the greatest correlation with intelligence on the Wechsler Scales. If an individual is able to score significantly higher on these subtests than on the others, then the possibility exists that greater potential is present regardless of the scores on other subtests.

HOW TO DETERMINE RELATIVE PROCESS STRENGTHS AND WEAKNESSES ON THE WECHSLER SCALES

Each subtest of the Wechsler Scales measures a different process. Therefore, we can determine a great deal about a child's strengths and weaknesses and consequent learning style by looking closely at that child's subtest results relative to his/her performance overall. Taking a closer look involves determining the **Mean Verbal Scaled Score** (average of all the scaled scores for the verbal subtests) and the **Mean Performance Scaled Score** (average of all the scaled scores for the performance subtests). You then subtract each verbal scaled score from the Verbal Mean Scaled Score and each of the performance scaled scores from the Performance Mean Scaled Score. Any subtest that is greater than 3 points from the mean may be considered a significant strength and any subtest that is greater than 3 points below the mean is considered a significant weakness for a particular individual. Let us take a look at an example:

VERBAL		PERFORMANCE	
Information	7	Picture Completion	12
Similarities	15	Picture Arrangement	5
Arithmetic	4	Block Design	10
Vocabulary	14	Object Assembly	4
Comprehension	6	Coding	11
Digit Span	5	Symbol Search	10
		Mazes	3

Verbal Mean Scaled Score:

$51 \div 6 = 8.5$ rounded to 9

Performance Mean Scaled Score:

$55 \div 7 = 7.8$ rounded to 8

Verbal IQ = 95   **Performance IQ = 90**   **Full Scale IQ = 92**

In the above example, the Verbal Mean Scaled Score is 9. If we find the difference between that mean and each verbal subtest we get the following:

Subtest	Mean Scaled Score	Scaled Score	Deviation from the Mean
Information	9	7	−2
Similarities	9	15	+6
Arithmetic	9	4	−5
Vocabulary	9	14	+5
Comprehension	9	6	−3
Digit Span	9	5	−4

When we look at these results of the verbal subtests we notice that two subtests (Similarities and Vocabulary) are significant strengths, and two subtests (Arithmetic and Digit Span) are significant weaknesses. Therefore, we find that the processes of abstract reasoning (Similarities) and word knowledge (Vocabulary) are strengths, and the processes of arithmetic reasoning (Arithmetic) and auditory sequential memory (Digit Span) are weaknesses.

Now if we do the same for the Performance subtests (Mean Scaled Score of 8) we get the following results:

Subtest	Mean Scaled Score	Scaled Score	Deviation from the Mean
Picture Completion	8	12	+4
Picture Arrangement	8	5	−3
Block Design	8	10	+2
Object Assembly	8	4	−4
Coding	8	11	+3
Symbol Search	8	10	+2
Mazes	8	3	−5

In this example we have one significant process strength (Picture Completion) and two significant process weaknesses (Object Assembly and Mazes). Therefore, we find that the processes of visual alertness and memory (Picture Completion) are significant strengths, while the processes of whole relationships and visual motor spatial coordination (Object Assembly), and visual motor dexterity (Mazes) are significant weaknesses. Such patterns are important since certain trends may be indicative of specific disorders.

DIAGNOSTIC PATTERNS ON THE WECHSLER SCALES

The patterns of scaled scores can sometimes reflect a certain type of pattern more reflective of certain learning styles. While one test should never be used by itself to diagnose a child's problems, common patterns throughout a test battery might offer insight about a child. Some of the more common diagnostic patterns may include the following:

Diagnostic Pattern 1—Slow Learner

Definition: The definition for slow learner requires the following:

♦ intellectual ability consistently falls within the low average (80–89) range over repeated measures

♦ scaled score pattern reveals the absence of any scatter or greater potential

The diagnosis of a slow learner is sometimes mistaken for that of a learning disabled (LD) child who may also score in the 80s on an intellectual measure. However, at least two factors differentiate these populations:

1) A slow learner may not be able to meet grade-level expectations regardless of the type of support he/she receives, while an LD child can be expected to attain grade-level performance with assistance.

2) While both populations may obtain IQ scores within the 80 range, the LD child's pattern will usually indicate greater potential through factors such as scatter.

The diagnostic pattern for the Slow Learner on the Wechsler might be reflected as follows:

VERBAL		PERFORMANCE	
Information	6	Picture Completion	7
Similarities	7	Picture Arrangement	7
Arithmetic	6	Block Design	7
Vocabulary	6	Object Assembly	7
Comprehension	6	Coding	7
Digit Span	7	Symbol Search	8
		Mazes	7

Verbal Mean Scaled Score:

$38 \div 6 = 6.3$ rounded to 6

Performance Mean Scaled Score:

$50 \div 7 = 7.1$ rounded to 7

Verbal IQ = 87   Performance IQ = 81   Full Scale IQ = 83

Note: All Verbal, Performance, and Full Scale IQs are derived from conversion tables presented in the Wechsler manual and not from any chart presented in this chapter.

1) There is an absence of intertest scatter: The range within either test level—verbal or performance—not greater than 3 points.

2) If one were to look at the protocol, there would likely be no indication of intratest scatter.

3) The Verbal IQ and the Performance IQ are only 6 points apart, indicating the absence of Verbal/Performance Scatter.

4) The Vocabulary subtest scaled score and/or the Similarities subtest scaled scores are not greater than 3 points from the Verbal Mean Scaled Score of 6.

5) The respondent would also have to have a history of IQ scores within this 80–89 range. A child scoring in the 80s with the above factors present would not be a slow learner if a separate individual IQ test taken a year or so earlier showed significantly greater potential or was within the average or higher range.

The importance of correctly diagnosing a child within this category lies in reducing the child's frustration with unrealistic expectations and workload. The teacher needs to be very aware of such a pattern so that goals and work requirements closely meet the ability levels of the child.

Diagnostic Pattern 2—Educable Mentally Disabled

Definition: The definition for educable mentally disabled requires the following:

⬥ a Verbal, Performance, and Full Scale IQ score within the mentally deficient range

⬥ no indications of greater potential

⬥ a low score on a measure of Adaptive Behavior. Adaptive Behavior Scales are tests that measure an individuals's social competence and ability to cope with the demands of the environment. (For examples of these tests, see section on Social Maturity and Behavior Scales later in this book.)

⬥ A history of academic performance commensurate with low intellectual ability

The diagnosis of a mental disability is the result of several factors as indicated. The absence of any one of these factors may prevent such a diagnosis. The IQ score is only one variable and no child should be diagnosed solely on this factor. However, certain patterns might exist on the Wechsler IQ Test that might contribute to the diagnosis of mental disability.

The diagnostic pattern for an Educable Mentally Disabled Child on the Wechsler Scales might be reflected as follows:

VERBAL		PERFORMANCE	
Information	4	Picture Completion	5
Similarities	4	Picture Arrangement	4
Arithmetic	4	Block Design	5
Vocabulary	4	Object Assembly	4
Comprehension	5	Coding	5
Digit Span	4	Symbol Search	4
		Mazes	4

Verbal Mean Scaled Score:

$25 \div 6 = 4.2$ rounded to 4

Performance Mean Scaled Score:

$31 \div 7 = 4.4$ rounded to 4

Verbal IQ = 67   Performance IQ = 68   Full Scale IQ = 65

1) There is an absence of intertest scatter: The range within either test level—verbal or performance—is not greater than 3 points.

2) If one were to look at the protocol, there would likely be no indication of intratest scatter.

3) The Verbal IQ and the Performance IQ are only 1 point apart, indicating the absence of Verbal/Performance Scatter.

4) The Vocabulary subtest scaled score and/or the Similarities subtest scaled scores are not greater than 3 points from the Verbal Mean Scaled Score of 5.

5) There are low scores on measures of adaptive functioning as described in the previous diagnostic pattern. (For examples of these tests, see section on Social Maturity and Behavior Scales later in this book.)

6) The correctly diagnosed respondent would also have a history of IQ test measures within the same range and no indications of greater potential.

Diagnostic Pattern 3—Trainable Mentally Disabled

Definition: The definition for trainable mentally disabled requires the following:

♦ IQ scores well within the low levels of the mentally deficient range

♦ a low score on a measure of Adaptive Behavior. While intelligence tests are sometimes administered for purposes of classification, a better measure for a student in this category is a Social Maturity Scale like the Vineland or Syracuse. (For other examples of these tests, see section on Social Maturity and Behavior Scales later in this book.)

The diagnostic pattern for the Trainable Mentally Disabled child on the Wechsler Scales might be reflected as follows:

VERBAL		PERFORMANCE	
Information	1	Picture Completion	3
Similarities	2	Picture Arrangement	2
Arithmetic	2	Block Design	1
Vocabulary	3	Object Assembly	1
Comprehension	1	Coding	1
Digit Span	2	Symbol Search	1
		Mazes	2

Verbal Mean Scaled Score:

$11 \div 6 = 1.8$ rounded to 2

Performance Mean Scaled Score:

$11 \div 7 = 1.5$ rounded to 2

Verbal IQ = 54   Performance IQ = 49   Full Scale IQ = 48

1) There is an absence of intertest scatter: The range within either test level—verbal or performance—not greater than 3 points.

2) If one were to look at the protocol there would likely be no indication of intratest scatter.

3) The Verbal IQ and the Performance IQ are only 5 points apart, indicating the absence of Verbal/Performance Scatter.

4) The Vocabulary subtest scaled score and/or the Similarities subtest scaled scores are not greater than the Verbal Mean Scaled Score. The Mean Verbal Scaled Score is 2 and neither subtest is more than 3 points from the mean.

5) There are low scores on measures of adaptive functioning. Adaptive Behavior Scales are tests that measure an individuals's social competence and ability to cope with the demands of the environment. (For examples of these tests, see section on Social Maturity and Behavior Scales later in this book.)

6) The correctly diagnosed respondent would also have a history of IQ test measures within the same range and no indications of significantly greater potential.

Diagnostic Pattern 4—Emotionally Disabled

Definition: The definition for emotionally disabled requires the following:

♦ a present dynamic state so tense and draining that the child's emotions greatly affect his/her ability to function commensurate with his/her potential

♦ an unstable emotional pattern of behavior that has been evident for a long period of time

While other measures are used to provide evidence for this diagnosis, certain patterns on the intelligence test may signal the presence of this area of dysfunction.

The diagnostic pattern for the emotionally disabled child on the Wechsler Scales might be reflected as follows:

VERBAL		PERFORMANCE	
Information	7	Picture Completion	11
Similarities	15	Picture Arrangement	4
Arithmetic	4	Block Design	10
Vocabulary	14	Object Assembly	4
Comprehension	5	Coding	13
Digit Span	6	Symbol Search	5
		Mazes	9

Verbal Mean Scaled Score:

$51 \div 6 = 8.5$ rounded to 9

Performance Mean Scaled Score:

$56 \div 7 = 8$

Verbal IQ = 94   Performance IQ = 91   Full Scale IQ = 92

1) There is a presence of extreme intertest scatter within each test level—verbal and performance—greater than 3 points.

2) If one were to look at the protocol, there would likely be many indications of intratest scatter and great variability of performance.

3) The Verbal IQ and the Performance IQ may or may not always be discrepant (more than a 15-point difference). In this particular case they are not. However, in many cases they are because the child's energy level is sporadic and sustained concentration is difficult. Therefore, after several subtests, he/she may give up. In addition, performance tests are sometimes more motivating for these students than the verbal tests, which are more school-related in their content, and that may account for some scatter in the results.

4) The Vocabulary subtest scaled score and/or the Similarities subtest scaled scores are more than 3 points from the Verbal Mean Scaled Score. (The Mean Verbal Scaled Score is 9, the Similarities score is 15, and the Vocabulary is 14.) The assumption here is that no matter how low an IQ, if these two scores are significantly higher than the rest, then greater potential is present because it is not possible to guess your way to a high score.

Diagnostic Pattern 5—Learning Disabled With Visual Motor Deficits

Definition: The definition for learning disabled with visual motor deficits requires exhibited and documented difficulties in the areas of:

♦ eye–hand coordination

♦ spatial relationships

♦ visual motor dexterity

♦ ability to see cause-and-effect relationships

♦ pencil control

The diagnostic pattern for Learning Disabled with Visual Motor Deficits on the Wechsler Scales might be reflected as follows:

VERBAL		PERFORMANCE	
Information	10	Picture Completion	13
Similarities	11	Picture Arrangement	5
Arithmetic	13	Block Design	6
Vocabulary	11	Object Assembly	6
Comprehension	10	Coding	7
Digit Span	11	Symbol Search	6
		Mazes	6

Verbal Mean Scaled Score:

$66 \div 6 = 11$

Performance Mean Scaled Score:

$49 \div 7 = 7$

Verbal IQ = 106   Performance IQ = 83   Full Scale IQ = 95

1) There is an absence of verbal intertest scatter which might indicate that this area should be considered the more valid indicator of the child's true ability (assuming there is no indication of intratest scatter on verbal tests). However, performance intertest scatter is present with the range of performance scores being greater than 3 points.

2) If one were to look at the protocol, there might not be an indication of intratest scatter on the performance areas since consistently low performance on this section would be expected from children with visual motor difficulties. However, the higher score noted on Picture Completion is common with these students, since it is the only performance test that does not require visual motor skills.

3) In this pattern, the Verbal IQ and the Performance IQ would be significantly different. However, there is no guarantee that verbal subtests might not be low as well. When a child's confidence and self-esteem are low, his/her willingness to venture a guess or expand upon an answer may suffer.

4) The Vocabulary subtest scaled score and/or the Similarities subtest scaled scores are not greater than the Verbal Mean Scaled Score. The Mean Verbal Scaled Score is 11,

and neither subtest is more than 3 points from the mean. However, the real discrepancy here is the difference between the Verbal tests which are Auditory Vocal (auditory channel input and vocal output) and the Performance tests which are Visual and Vocal/Visual Motor (visual input and vocal output, and visual input and motoric output).

Diagnostic Pattern 6—Language Impaired

Definition: The definition for language impaired requires difficulties in:

♦ receptive or expressive language abilities

♦ labeling

♦ naming

♦ retrieving

♦ remembering

♦ expressing ideas and concepts

The diagnostic pattern for the Language Impaired child on the Wechsler Scales might be reflected as follows:

VERBAL		PERFORMANCE	
Information	7	Picture Completion	11
Similarities	6	Picture Arrangement	12
Arithmetic	6	Block Design	13
Vocabulary	7	Object Assembly	13
Comprehension	6	Coding	14
Digit Span	7	Symbol Search	13
		Mazes	12

Verbal Mean Scaled Score:

39 ÷ 6 = 6.5 rounded to 7

Performance Mean Scaled Score:

88 ÷ 7 = 12.5 rounded to 13

Verbal IQ = 80   Performance IQ = 117   Full Scale IQ = 97

1) There is an absence of performance intertest scatter which might indicate that this area should be considered the more valid indicator of the child's true ability (assuming there is no indication of intratest scatter on performance tests). There is also an absence of verbal intertest scatter as well. A low consistent nonvariable pattern of performance might also occur when a specific area is so impaired.

2) If one were to look at the protocol, there might not be an indication of intratest scatter on the verbal areas since consistently low performance on this section would be expected from children with language difficulties.

3) The Verbal IQ and the Performance IQ are 37 points apart, indicating the presence of Verbal/Performance Scatter.

4) The Vocabulary subtest scaled score and/or the Similarities subtest scaled scores are not greater than the Verbal Mean Scaled Score. The Mean Verbal Scaled Score is 7, and neither subtest is more than 3 points from the mean. However, the real discrepancy here is the difference between the Verbal tests which are Auditory Vocal (auditory channel input and vocal output), and the Performance tests which are Visual and Vocal/Visual Motor (visual input and vocal output and visual input and motoric output).

Diagnostic Pattern 7—Gifted

Definition: The definition for gifted requires outstanding abilities and capacity for high performance and includes the following:

❊ a demonstrated achievement and/or potential in general intellectual ability

❊ specific high levels of academic aptitude

❊ creative and productive thinking

The diagnostic pattern for the gifted child on the Wechsler Scales may be reflected in the following ways:

VERBAL		PERFORMANCE	
Information	17	Picture Completion	17
Similarities	18	Picture Arrangement	18
Arithmetic	16	Block Design	17
Vocabulary	16	Object Assembly	18
Comprehension	16	Coding	19
Digit Span	15	Symbol Search	17
		Mazes	18

Verbal Mean Scaled Score:

98 ÷ 6 = 16.3 rounded to 16

Performance Mean Scaled Score:

124 ÷ 7 = 17.7 rounded to 18

Verbal IQ = 138   Performance IQ = 142   Full Scale IQ = 142

1) There is an absence of intertest scatter; the range within each level—verbal and performance—is not greater than 3 points.

2) If one were to look at the protocol there would likely be no indication of intratest scatter.

3) The Verbal IQ and the Performance IQ are only 4 points apart indicating the absence of Verbal/Performance Scatter.

4) The Vocabulary subtest scaled score and the Similarities subtest scaled scores are not more than 3 points greater than the Verbal Mean Scaled Score. The Mean Verbal Scaled Score is 16 and neither subtest is more than 3 points from the mean.

5) The presence of a hearing impairment as a contributing factor to the low verbal scores has been ruled out.

How to Determine Modality or Channel Strengths and Weaknesses on the Wechsler Scales

A *modality* or *channel* is the avenue through which information comes to us. As discussed later in the chapter on Perceptual Assessments, there are six modalities or channels:

♦ visual modality—information received through the eye

♦ auditory modality—information received through the ear

♦ kinesthetic modality—information obtained through a variety of body movements and muscle feelings

♦ tactile modality—information obtained through the sense of touch via the fingers and skin surfaces

♦ gustatory modality—information obtained through the sense of taste

♦ olfactory modality—information obtained through the sense of smell

The Verbal subtests of the Wechsler Scales are considered Auditory Vocal tasks, and the Performance subtests are considered Visual and Vocal/Visual Motor tasks.

One of the major purposes of an evaluation is to determine learning style, the various factors that contribute to an individual child's ability to learn. One of the factors involved in learning style is modality. It is important to determine if either or both modalities are strengths or weaknesses and therefore contribute to the child's ability to learn or inability to process information. One way to determine this on the Wechsler Scales is by comparing the difference between the Verbal and Performance areas IQs. If the difference in these scores is greater than 15 points, then the difference may serve as evidence of a stronger and weaker modality. It would be very important for teachers to know a child's different modality strengths and weaknesses so that they can adjust their manner of conveying information to the student.

Other Forms of Analysis Using the Wechsler Scales

There are some other forms of analysis that are possible using the Wechsler Scales. For instance, on the WISC-III there are four separate sub scales derived from the scores. These scores are calculated from the averages of certain combined subtests:

• **Verbal Comprehension** (VCI)—Information, Similarities, Vocabulary, and Comprehension.

• **Perceptual Organization** (POI)—Picture Completion, Picture Arrangement, Block Design, and Object Assembly

• **Freedom from Distractibility** (FDI)—Arithmetic and Digit Span

• **Processing Speed** (PSI)—Coding and Symbol Search

Other forms of analysis specific to all three Wechsler Scales—WPPSI-R, WISC-III, and WAIS-R—are derived from a combination of several subtests. Finding a pattern of strengths or weaknesses among these subtests can enhance diagnosis and help support the evidence for a specific learning style. Following are brief descriptions of an individual's strengths derived from scores on the verbal and performance subtests:

- **Abstract and Conceptual Thought**—This ability (often referred to as fluid intelligence) is present in individuals who are able to master and solve new and unique situations. The three subtests measuring this area are Similarities, Comprehension, and Block Design.

- **Memory**—This ability is present in individuals who have the capacity to retrieve and mentally represent information, images, and ideas. The four subtests involved in this area are Coding, Digit Span, Arithmetic, and Visual Memory.

- **Receptive and Expressive Language**—This ability is present in individuals who understand information, presented aurally or visually, and can express language understanding orally or in writing. The three subtests that most directly assess this area are Similarities, Vocabulary, and Comprehension.

- **Visual-Perceptual Organization**—This ability is present in individuals who are able to organize visual information in meaningful ways. The three subtests that assess this area are Picture Arrangement, Mazes, and Object Assembly.

- **Social Judgment and Common Sense**—This ability is present in individuals who have the sensitivity to social and environmental experiences. The two subtests that assess this area are Comprehension and Picture Arrangement.

- **Sequential Reasoning**—This ability is present in individuals who have the capacity to understand the time order of events and can logically move from one step to the next. The four subtests that assess this area are Arithmetic, Mazes, Digit Span, and Comprehension.

- **Psychomotor Speed and Coordination**—This ability is present in individuals who have the capacity to coordinate motor activity with facility and speed. The subtests that assess this area are Picture Arrangement, Block Design, Object Assembly, Mazes, Symbol Search, and Coding.

These scores are found on the front of the WISC-III protocol and should be reviewed to determine possible factors influencing learning style. Even though these subscales are not found in the WPPSI-R or WAIS-R manuals, research has found their use in interpreting these two tests encouraging.

STRENGTHS OF THE WECHSLER SCALES

- There is strong evidence of the test's reliability and validity.

- There is a thorough interpretation in the manual of information regarding interpretation of scaled score differences.

- Scores on the test correlate highly with academic achievement.

- The test provides valuable information as one of the measures in the diagnosis of learning disabilities.

- The test is well organized and easy to use.

- The test provides strong objective and projective potential.

WEAKNESSES OF THE WECHSLER SCALES

♦ Some of the test's questions may be culturally biased.

♦ The test does not allow for the distinction of full scale IQs below 40, making it less useful than other tests in distinguishing among levels of retardation.

♦ The test cannot be used alone in the diagnosis of learning disabilities.

Section 4

OTHER INTELLECTUAL ASSESSMENT MEASURES

The individual evaluation of a child should cover several areas, including the following:

◆ intellectual levels

◆ academic skills

◆ perceptual skills

◆ language skills

◆ background history

◆ academic history

◆ present levels of classroom functioning

◆ behavior

All of these factors play an important role in diagnosing the child's real problems and in determining the child's best learning style.

HOW TO ANALYZE A STUDENT'S INTELLECTUAL PROFILE EFFECTIVELY

The first area to explore may be the child's intellectual ability and potential. While this test is usually completed by a psychologist, it is very important that the special educator learn how to interpret the results of intellectual measures so that he or she can substantiate a diagnosis, help determine learning style, assist in making recommendations, and arrive at accurate levels of intellectual expectation.

Intelligence tests are most helpful (and probably most appropriate) when they are used to determine specific skills, abilities, and knowledge that the child either has or does not have, and when such information is combined with other evaluation data and then directly applied to school programming. There are a number of skills that an intelligence test attempts to measure:

◆ social judgment

◆ level of thinking

- language skills

- perceptual organization

- processing speed

- spatial abilities

- common sense

- long- and short-term memory

- abstract thinking

- motor speed

- word knowledge

The above skills are very dependent on experience, training, and intact verbal abilities of the child being tested. Responses to items concerning perceptual organization, processing speed, and spatial abilities are less dependent on experience and verbal skill.

Intelligence tests can also yield valuable information about a student's ability to process information. In order to learn, every person must take in, make sense of, store, and retrieve information from memory in an efficient and accurate way. Each of us can process certain kinds of information more easily than other kinds. In school, children need certain skills to function effectively, such as listening attentively so that other movements, sounds, or sights do not distract them. They must be able to understand the words spoken to them. This often requires children to hold multiple pieces of information in memory (e.g., page number, questions to answer) in order to act upon them. For example, they must be able to find the words they need to express themselves and, ultimately, commit these words to paper. This involves another whole series of processing skills—holding a writing implement, coordinating visual and motor actions, holding information in memory until it can be transferred to paper, transforming sounds into written symbols, and understanding syntax, punctuation, and capitalization rules. They also must be able to interpret the nonverbal messages of others, such as a frown, a smile, or a shake of the head. Moreover, they must do all of these things quickly and accurately and often in a setting with many distractions.

A thorough interpretation of an intelligence test can yield information about how effectively a child processes and retrieves information. Most individually administered intelligence tests can determine, at least to some degree, a child's ability to attend, process information quickly, distinguish relevant from less relevant details, put events in sequence, and retrieve words from memory.

Kamphaus (1993) summarizes a number of research findings related to the use of intelligence tests:

1) Intelligence test scores are more stable for school-aged children than for preschoolers and more stable among individuals with disabilities than among those without disabilities.

2) Intelligence test scores can change from childhood to adulthood.

3) It is likely that environmental factors, socioeconomic status, values, family structure, and genetic factors all play a role in determining intelligence test scores.

4) Factors such as low birth weight, malnutrition, anoxia (lack of oxygen), and fetal alcohol exposure have a negative impact on intelligence test scores.

5) Intelligence and academic achievement appear to be highly related.

Once the test is scored and the information is obtained, the psychologist can make several determinations and report back to parents and teachers the following information:

1) The child's present overall levels of intellectual ability

2) The child's present verbal intellectual ability

3) The child's nonlanguage intellectual ability

4) Indications of greater intellectual potential

5) Possible patterns involving learning style, such as verbal comprehension and concentration

6) Possible influence of tension and anxiety on testing results

7) Intellectual ability to deal with present grade-level academic demands

8) The influence of intellectual ability as a contributing factor to a child's past and present school difficulties (i.e., limited intellectual ability found in retardation)

STANFORD-BINET INTELLIGENCE SCALE
Fourth Edition (SB:FE)

GENERAL TEST INFORMATION

Authors:	R.L. Thorndike, E.P. Hagen, and J.M. Sattler
Publisher:	The Riverside Publishing Company
Address of Publisher:	8420 Spring Lake Drive Itasca, Illinois 60143-2079
Phone Number of Publisher:	800-323-9540
Fax of Publisher:	630-467-7192

Purpose of Test: The Stanford-Binet Intelligence Scale is an intellectual measure utilized by psychologists. The test attempts to serve the following purposes:

— To help differentiate between children who have a mental disability and those who have a specific learning disability

— To help teachers and psychologists understand why a particular child is having trouble learning in school

— To help in the identification of gifted children

— To help in the study of the development of cognitive skills of individuals from ages 2 to adult

Description of Test: This test is an individual intelligence test and is a measure of global or general intelligence; it offers results in terms of a mental age and IQ. This test is generally used with younger children and with intellectually limited youngsters.

Type of Test:	Standardized
Administration Time:	45–90 minutes
Type of Administration:	Individual
Who Administers This Test:	Psychologist
Age/Grade Levels:	Ages 2 to adult

Subtest Information: The Stanford-Binet comprises 15 tests divided according to *four areas*:

1. **Verbal Reasoning**—This area consists of four subtests:

   • *Vocabulary*—The respondent is required to name pictures of common objects.

   • *Comprehension*—The respondent is required to point to body parts on a picture of a child.

   • *Absurdities*—The respondent is required to point to which of three pictures shows something "wrong" or "silly."

   • *Verbal Relations*—The respondent is read four words and is required to tell how three words are alike and which of the four is different.

2. **Quantitative Reasoning**—This area consists of three subtests:

   • *Quantitative*—The respondent is required to use dice to match, count, add, subtract, or form logical series of numbers.

   • *Number Series*—The respondent is required to find the next two numbers that would be consistent according to a certain rule.

   • *Equation Building*—The respondent is required to build mathematical statements from a list containing several numbers and operational symbols.

3. **Abstract/Visual Reasoning**—This area consists of four subtests:

- *Pattern Analysis*—This test requires the child to complete a three-hole formboard with a circle, square, and triangle and then with combinations of pieces that together fit into the holes.
- *Copying*—This test requires the child to arrange blocks or draw copies of designs.
- *Matrices*—This test requires the child to choose from four or five options the symbol or picture that completes a pattern.
- *Paper Folding and Cutting*—This test requires the child to choose which of five drawings would look like a paper design if it were unfolded.

4. **Short-Term Memory**—This area consists of four subtests:

- *Bead Memory*—The respondent is required to identify beads or patterns of beads from memory.
- *Memory for Sentences*—The respondent is required to correctly repeat a sentence spoken by the examiner.
- *Memory for Digits*—The respondent is required to repeat a series of digits spoken by the examiner.
- *Memory for Objects*—The respondent is required to identify the correct order of pictures presented in a series.

Scoring Information: Once the examiner has obtained raw scores on single tests, those scores are converted to Standard Age Scores (SAS) using tables at the back of the manual. These Standard Age Scores have a mean of 50 and a standard deviation of 8. Standard Age Scores are then obtained on each of the four areas described above and summed up. This result is then converted to Area Standard Age Scores (Area SASs) using a different set of tables. Once these four scores are derived, the examiner sums up the scores and converts the results to a Composite SAS. This Composite SAS has a mean of 100 and a standard deviation of 16.

Overall Composite scores can then be classified as follows:

IQ Range	Classification
132 and above	Very Superior
121–131	Superior
111–120	High Average
89–110	Average
79–88	Low Average
68–78	Slow Learner
67 and Below	Mentally Retarded

The cover of the test booklet also contains a rating scale that can be used by the examiner to summarize clinical observations of the child. This scale then may provide those concerned with further insight into the child's learning style.

STRENGTHS OF THE SB:FE

- A rating scale is included on the cover of the test booklet.
- The Examiner's Manual includes many informative case studies.

STANFORD-BINET INTELLIGENCE SCALE (SB:FE)

(continued)

- ◆ The test employs "adaptive-testing" format (whereby tests are administered only to children at certain entry levels) which prevents excessive frustration or boredom for the very dull or very bright child.

WEAKNESSES OF THE SB:FE

- ◆ This is not a particularly valuable test for children in the $2^1/_2$- to 4-year age range, especially if there are developmental delays.
- ◆ Some of the subtests have a ceiling that is much too low for older and some very bright individuals (Spruill, 1987).
- ◆ Several subtests contain two types of items that seem quite dissimilar, i.e., easy items requiring pointing, harder items involving enhanced language responses.
- ◆ "Time limits" are suggested, but the examiner may have to rely on clinical judgment regarding enforcement of the limits.
- ◆ To keep testing time to 60–90 minutes, the test developers suggest several abbreviated batteries thereby reducing test reliability.
- ◆ The norming samples for some tests at some age levels are inadequate.

- Some of the subtests have a ceiling that is much too low for older and some very bright individuals (Spruill, 1987).

- Several subtests contain two types of items that seem quite dissimilar, i.e., easy items requiring pointing, harder items involving enhanced language responses.

- "Time limits" are suggested, but the examiner may have to rely on clinical judgment regarding enforcement of the limits.

- To keep testing time to 60–90 minutes, the test developers suggest several abbreviated batteries thereby reducing test reliability.

- The norming samples for some tests at some age levels are inadequate.

KAUFMAN ASSESSMENT BATTERY FOR CHILDREN (K-ABC): MENTAL PROCESSING SCALES

GENERAL TEST INFORMATION

Authors: Alan S. Kaufman and Nadeen L. Kaufman

Publisher: American Guidance Service
Address of Publisher: Publishers Building
Circle Pines, Minnesota 55014-1796

Phone Number of Publisher: 800-328-2560

Fax of Publisher: 512-786-5603

Purpose of Test: The test measures intelligence and achievement; it defines intelligence as the ability of children to process information and solve problems. The test is used for psychological and clinical assessment of children, especially the learning disabled, mentally disabled, gifted, preschoolers, and members of minority groups, and for neuropsychological research.

Description of Test: This individually administered intelligence test was developed in 1983 in an attempt to minimize the influence of language and acquired facts and skills on the measurement of a child's intellectual ability.

Type of Test: Standardized

Administration Time: 35–85 minutes, depending upon age group

Type of Administration: Individual

Who Administers This Test: Psychologist

Age/Grade Levels: Ages $2^1/_2$ to $12^1/_2$.

Subtest Information: The intelligence test contains 10 subtests divided into *two areas*:

1. **Sequential Processing Scale**—This area consists of the following subtests:

   - *Hand Movements*—The child (ages $2^1/_2/$ to $12^1/_2$) is required to perform a series of hand movements presented by the examiner.

   - *Number Recall*—The child (ages $2^1/_2$ to $12^1/_2$) is required to repeat a series of digits in the same sequence as presented by the examiner.

   - *Word Order*—The child (ages 4 to $12^1/_2$) is required to touch a series of silhouettes of objects in the same order as presented verbally by the examiner.

2. **Simultaneous Processing Scale**—This area consists of the following subtests:

   - *Magic Windows*—This test requires the child (ages $2^1/_2$ to 5) to identify a picture that the examiner exposes slowly through a window so that only a small part is exposed at a time.

   - *Face Recognition*—This test requires the child (ages $2^1/_2$ to 5) to choose from a group photo the one or two faces that were exposed briefly.

   - *Gestalt Closure*—This test requires the child (ages $2^1/_2$ to $12^1/_2$) to name an object or scene from a partially constructed inkblot.

   - *Triangles*—This test requires the child (ages 4 to $12^1/_2$) to assemble several identical triangles into an abstract pattern.

   - *Matrix Analogies*—This test requires the child (ages 5 to $12^1/_2$) to choose a meaningful picture or abstract design that best completes a visual analogy.

KAUFMAN ASSESSMENT BATTERY FOR CHILDREN (K-ABC): MENTAL PROCESSING SCALES

(continued)

- *Spatial Memory*—This test requires the child (ages 5 to 12½) to recall the placement of a picture on a page that was briefly exposed.
- *Photo Series*—This test requires the child (ages 6 to 12½) to place photographs of an event in the proper order.

Scoring Information: As can be seen by the ages provided after the test information above, some are administered only to younger children, some only to older, and some to both.

This test uses the following standard score ranges for interpretation:

Standard Score	Classification
130 and above	Upper Extreme
120–129	Well Above Average
110–119	Above Average
90–109	Average
80–89	Below Average
70–79	Well Below Average
69 and below	Lower Extreme

Other forms of score reporting include percentiles, confidence levels (a statistically-derived range of scores within which the subject's true score can be expected to fall), stanines, and age equivalents. This test also provides a Nonverbal Global score for children who are hearing impaired, language impaired, or non-English speaking students.

STRENGTHS OF THE K-ABC

- This test has excellent norming sample.
- This test has excellent reliability and validity data.
- This test provides substantial data profiles of various groups of exceptional children.
- This test provides the examiner with clues regarding what strengths and weaknesses may be demonstrated by children with various types of special needs.
- This test provides profile differences related to sex, socioeconomic status, and ethnic group membership.
- This test provides suggestions for educational programming.
- This test can be used with children under the age of 2½.

WEAKNESSES OF THE K-ABC

- The use of the term mental processing for some subtests and the term achievement for others may be misleading.
- The K-ABC should not be used in the intellectual diagnosis of the mentally disabled in the preschool years because low scores at this age are very difficult to obtain.
- The test's heavy reliance on short-term memory may affect children with attention and short-term recall difficulties.

KAUFMAN BRIEF INTELLIGENCE TEST (KBIT)

GENERAL TEST INFORMATION

Authors:	Alan S. Kaufman and Nadeen L. Kaufman
Publisher:	American Guidance Service
Address of Publisher:	4201 Woodland Road P.O. Box 99 Circle Pines, MN 55041-1796
Phone Number of Publisher:	800-328-2560
Fax of Publisher:	512-786-5603

Purpose of Test: This test is intended as a brief measure of verbal and nonverbal intelligence.

Description of Test: This test is an assessment device for developing and evaluating remedial programs for the mentally disabled. It may also be used for normal children aged birth to 10 years.

Type of Test:	Individual
Administration Time:	15–30 minutes
Type of Administation:	Individual
Who Administers This Test:	Psychologist
Age/Grade Levels:	Ages 4 to 90

Subtest Information: The test consists of two subtests:

1. Vocabulary—This subtest measures verbal knowledge through pictures.

2. Matrices—This subtest measures the ability to perceive relationships and complete analogies through pictures or abtract designs.

Scoring Information—This test provides:

- Percentiles
- Standard scores
- IQ Composite

STRENGTHS OF THE KBIT

- Instructions are given for motor items and the scoring sheet is clear and easy to complete.
- This test is a good quick screening measure of intelligence.
- This test is a psychometrically sound measure of verbal, nonverbal, and composite intelligence.

WEAKNESSES OF THE KBIT

- The manual lacks clarity and organization.
- Caution should be exercised in interpreting standard scores for older subjects—ages 20 to 90—because of the small number of subjects used in the norming sample.
- Further validation studies are needed.

COLUMBIA MENTAL MATURITY SCALE (CMMS)

GENERAL TEST INFORMATION

Authors:	Bessie B. Burgemeister, Lucille Hollander Blurn, and Irving Lorge
Publisher:	The Psychological Corporation
Address of Publisher:	555 Academic Court San Antonio, TX 78204-2498.
Phone Number of Publisher:	800-211-8378
Fax of Publisher:	800-232-1223
TDD of the Publisher:	800-723-1318

Purpose of Test: The test is intended to measure the intelligence of children with disabilities by using a pictorial type of classification.

Description of Test: The CMMS is an individual type scale that requires perceptual discrimination involving color, shape, size, use, number, kind, missing parts, and symbolic material. Items are printed on 95 six-inch by 19-inch cards that are arranged in a series of eight overlapping levels. The subject responds by selecting the picture in each series that is different from, or unrelated to, the others.

Type of Test:	Standardized
Administration Time:	15–30 minutes
Type of Administration:	Individual
Who Administers This Test:	Psychologist
Age/Grade Levels:	Ages 3$\frac{1}{2}$–10 years

Subtest Information: There are no formal subtests on this scale; rather, it is a 92-item test of general reasoning abilities.

Scoring Information: The test mean is 100, and the standard deviation is 16. The measured IQ range is from 50–150. An age equivalent score can also be obtained(also referred to as a Maturity Index).

STRENGTHS OF THE CMMS

- Most children enjoy taking this test.
- The test can be administered in a relatively short period of time.
- A trained examiner can get quality judgments of the child and his/her method of attacking problems.

WEAKNESSES OF THE CMMS

- The test manuals need to be updated.
- The test has been standardized on a nondisabled population only.
- Little has been determined about the test's possible educational or clinical value.

McCARTHY SCALES OF CHILDREN'S ABILITIES (MSCA)

GENERAL TEST INFORMATION

Author:	Dorothea McCarthy
Publisher:	The Psychological Corporation
Address of Publisher:	555 Academic Court San Antonio, TX 78204-2498
Phone Number of Publisher:	800-211-8378
Fax of Publisher:	800-232-1223
TDD of the Publisher:	800-723-1318

Purpose of Test: To determine general intellectual level as well as strengths and weaknesses in important abilities.

Description of Test: The test consists of 18 separate tests that are grouped into six scales: Verbal, Perceptual-Performance, Quantitative, Composite (General Cognitive), Memory, and Motor.

Type of Test:	Standardized, Norm-referenced
Administration Time:	45–60 minutes
Type of Administration:	Individual
Who Administers This Test:	Psychologist, Special Education Teacher
Age/Grade Levels:	Ages 2 years–4 months to 8 years–7 months

Subtest Information: The test consists of 6 scales comprising a variety of 18 subtests. Some subtests fall into more than one scale. Listed below is each scale and the corresponding subtests measuring that skill:

1. **Verbal Scale**—This scale consists of five subtests:
   - *Pictorial Memory*—The child is required to recall names of objects pictured on cards
   - *Word Knowledge*—In Part 1, the child is required to point to pictures of common objects named by the examiner. In Part 2, the child is required to give oral definitions of words.
   - *Verbal Memory*—In Part 1, the child is required to repeat word series and sentences. In Part 2, the child is required to retell a story read by the examiner.
   - *Verbal Fluency*—The child is required to name as many articles as possible in a given category within 20 seconds.
   - *Opposite Analogies*—The child is required to complete sentences by providing opposites.

2. **Perceptual Performance Scale**—This scale consists of seven subtests:
   - *Block Building*—The child is required to copy block structures built by the examiner.
   - *Puzzle Solving*—The child is required to assemble picture puzzles of common animals or foods.
   - *Tapping Sequence*—The child is required to imitate sequences of notes on a xylophone, as demonstrated by the examiner.
   - *Right-Left Orientation*—The child is required to demonstrate knowledge of right and left.

MCCARTHY SCALES OF CHILDREN'S ABILITIES (MSCA)

(continued)

- *Draw-A-Design*—The child is required to draw geometrical designs as presented in a model.
- *Draw-A-Child*—The child is required to draw a picture of a child of the same sex.
- *Conceptual Grouping*—The child is required to classify blocks on the basis of size, color, and shape.

3. **Quantitative Scale**—This scale consists of three subtests:
   - *Number Questions*—The child is required to answer orally presented questions involving number information or basic arithmetical computation.
   - *Numerical Memory*—In Part 1, the child is required to repeat a series of digits exactly as presented by the examiner. In Part 2, the child is required to repeat a digit series in exact reverse order.
   - *Counting and Sorting*—The child is required to count blocks and sort them into equal groups.

4. **Motor Scale**—This scale consists of three subtests:
   - *Leg Coordination*—The child is required to perform motor tasks that involve lower extremities, such as walking backwards or standing on one foot.
   - *Arm Coordination*—In Part 1, the child is required to bounce a ball. In Part 2, the child is required to catch a beanbag, and in Part 3, the child is required to throw a beanbag at a target.
   - *Imitative Action*—The child is required to copy simple movements such as folding hands or looking through a tube.

5. **General Cognitive**—This scale consists of fifteen subtests. Please refer to the four prior scales for a complete explanation of these subtests.

   - Pictorial Memory
   - Word Knowledge
   - Verbal Memory
   - Verbal Fluency
   - Opposite Analogies
   - Block Building
   - Puzzle Solving
   - Tapping Sequence
   - Right-Left Orientation
   - Draw-A-Design
   - Draw-A-Child
   - Conceptual Grouping
   - Number Questions
   - Numerical Memory
   - Counting and Sorting

MCCARTHY SCALES OF CHILDREN'S ABILITIES (MSCA)
(continued)

6. Memory: This scale consists of four subtests. Please refer to the first four scales for a complete explanation of these subtests.

- Pictorial Memory
- Tapping Sequence
- Verbal Memory
- Numerical Memory

Scoring Information: The general cognitive raw score is converted into a standard score with a mean of 100 and a standard deviation of 16. This score is called the General Cognitive Index and is the equivalent of an IQ score.

STRENGTHS OF THE MSCA

- The test's Technical Manual contains elaborate information about the standardization process, norm tables, and guidelines for administration and interpretation.
- The test creates a framework within which the child being tested can function comfortably.
- The test is gamelike with nonthreatening material.
- Reliability and validity are good determinants of achievement for children in school.

WEAKNESSES OF THE MSCA

- The test excludes exceptional children from the standardization sample.
- The test lacks social comprehension and judgment tasks.
- This test may not be appropriate for older or gifted children because of a low ceiling level.
- The test may take a long time to administer and interpret. Furthermore, there is a lengthy scoring procedure which may problematic for new users.

SLOSSON INTELLIGENCE TEST—REVISED (SIT-R)

GENERAL TEST INFORMATION

Authors: Richard L. Slosson. Revised by Charles L. Nicholson and Terry L. Hibpschman

Publisher: Slosson Educational Publications

Address of Publisher: PO Box 280
East Aurora, NY 14052-0280

Phone Number Publisher: 888-SLOSSON

Fax of Publisher: 800-655-3840

Purpose of Test: The test is designed to provide a quick screening measure of verbal intelligence.

Description of Test: This IQ test measures six different categories with 187 oral questions. Tasks are arranged in order of difficulty. This is a question-and-answer test with no reading or writing required.

Type of Test: Norm-referenced

Administration Time: 15–30 minutes

Type of Administration: Individual

Who Administers This Test: Psychologist

Age/Grade Levels: Ages 4 to 65

Subtest Information: This test measures six cognitive areas:

1. *Vocabulary*—33 items measuring word knowledge
2. *General Information*—29 items measuring general knowledge, and long-term memory
3. *Similarities and Differences*—30 items measuring abstract reasoning
4. *Comprehension*—33 items measuring social judgment and common sense
5. *Quantitative*—34 items measuring arithmetic abilities
6. *Auditory Memory*—28 items measuring short-term and sequential memory

Scoring Information: The test provides:

- Standard scores
- Age equivalents
- Percentiles
- Stanines

STRENGTHS OF THE SIT-R

- The test has excellent reliability.
- The test can be administered and scored quickly.
- The test can provide useful information about probable level of mental ability.

WEAKNESSES OF THE SIT-R

- The test is of limited use for young children with language difficulties.
- The test does not contain any performance tasks.
- Visual spatial difficulties may be difficult to assess on this test.

COMPREHENSIVE TEST OF NONVERBAL INTELLIGENCE (CTONI)

GENERAL TEST INFORMATION

Authors:	Donald D. Hammill, Nils A. Pearson, and Lee Wiederholt
Publisher:	PRO-ED, Inc.
Address of Publisher:	8700 Shoal Creek Blvd. Austin, TX 78758-6897
Phone Number of Publisher:	512-451-3246 or 800-897-3202
Fax of Publisher:	800-FXPROED

Purpose of Test: The test is designed to measure the nonverbal intelligence of students who are bilingual, speak a language other than English, or are socially/economically disadvantaged, deaf, language disordered, motor impaired, or neurologically impaired.

Description of Test: The CTONI measures six different types of nonverbal reasoning ability. No oral responses, reading, writing or object manipulation are involved.

Type of Test:	Norm-referenced
Administration Time:	60 minutes
Type of Administration:	Individual
Who Administers This Test:	Psychologist
Age/Grade Levels:	Ages 6 to 18

Subtest Information: There are six subtests arranged according to three abilities. The three ability areas are:

1. *Analogical Reasoning*—The two subtests in this section are Pictorial Analogies and Geometric Analogies. This section identifies the ability to recognize a fourth object that bears the same relation to the third as the second does to the first.

2. *Categorical Classification*—The two subtests in this section are Pictorial Categories and Geometric Categories. Categorical Classification assesses the ability to understand the common attributes by which objects are grouped.

3. *Sequential Reasoning*—The two subtests in this section are Pictorial Sequences and Geometric Sequences. Sequential Reasoning assesses the ability to understand the successive relationship of objects.

Scoring Information: Besides providing standard scores, percentiles, and age equivalents, the test also has three Composite Scores:

♦ Nonverbal Intelligence Quotient (NIQ)—Represents a blend of three different cognitive abilities (Analogical Reasoning, Categorical Classifying, and Sequential Reasoning)

♦ Pictorial Nonverbal Intelligence Quotient (PNIQ)—Measures problem solving and reasoning through the use of pictures of familiar objects

♦ Geometric Nonverbal Intelligence Quotient (GNIQ)—Measures problem solving and reasoning through the use of unfamiliar designs

STRENGTHS OF THE CTONI

♦ This test is designed and documented to be unbiased with regard to gender, race, and disability.

COMPREHENSIVE TEST OF NONVERBAL INTELLIGENCE (CTONI)
(continued)

♦ The test directions can be administered orally or through simple pantomime.

♦ The test can be individually administered in less than 60 minutes

WEAKNESSES OF THE CTONI

♦ Given the newness of the test, further study is required to determine the limitations, if any, of its validity and reliability.

TEST OF NONVERBAL INTELLIGENCE—THIRD EDITION (TONI-3)

GENERAL TEST INFORMATION

Author:	Linda Brown, Rita J. Sherbenou, and Susan Johnsen
Publisher:	PRO-ED, Inc.
Address of Publisher:	8700 Shoal Creek Blvd. Austin, TX 78758-6897
Phone Number of Publisher:	512-451-3246 or 800-897-3202
Fax of Publisher:	800-FXPROED

Purpose of Test: The test is designed to measure the nonverbal intelligence of students who are bilingual, speak a language other than English, or are socially/economically disadvantaged, deaf, language disordered, motor impaired, or neurologically impaired.

Description of Test: The TONI-3, a major revision of the popular and well designed Test of Nonverbal Intelligence, is a 50-item measure of intelligence, aptitude, abtract reasoning, and problem solving that is completely free of the use of language. The test requires no reading, writing, speaking, or listening skills on the part of the student.

Type of Test:	Norm-referenced
Administration Time:	15–20 minutes
Type of Administration:	Individual
Who Administers This Test:	Psychologist
Age/Grade Levels:	Ages 5 to 85

Subtest Information: There are no subtests.

Scoring Information: The test provides the following:

- Percentile ranks
- Deviation Quotients with a mean of 100 and standard deviation of 15

STRENGTHS OF THE TONI-3:

- The test is quick to score.
- The test is easy to administer.
- Required responses are motor reduced; only a meaningful gesture is required for response.
- The test is particularly well suited for individuals with multiple disabilities.

WEAKNESSES OF THE TONI-3:

- Given the newness of the test, further study is required to determine the limitations, if any, of its validity and reliability.

OTIS-LENNON SCHOOL ABILITY TEST (OLSAT)

GENERAL TEST INFORMATION

Authors:	Arthur S. Otis and Roger T. Lennon
Publisher:	The Psychological Corporation
Address of Publisher:	555 Academic Court San Antonio, TX 78204-2498
Phone Number of Publisher:	800-211-8378
Fax of Publisher:	800-232-1223
TDD of the Publisher:	800-723-1318

Purpose of Test: The test intends to measure abstract thinking and reasoning ability.

Description of Test: The test consists of 7 different levels covering ages 5 through 18. Twenty-one different types of subtests are organized into 5 clusters and an equal number of verbal and non-verbal items are included at each level.

Type of Test:	Standardized
Administration Time:	Levels A–C (grades K to 2), 75 minutes over two sessions; Levels D–G (grades 3 to 12), 60 minutes
Type of Administration:	Group
Who Administers This Test:	Psychologist, special education teacher, classroom teacher
Age/Grade Level:	Grades K to 12

Subtest Information: The five clusters are:

1. *Verbal Comprehension*—includes following directions, antonyms, sentence completion, and sentence arrangement
2. *Verbal Reasoning*—includes logical selection, verbal analogies, verbal classification, and inference
3. *Pictorial Reasoning*—includes picture classification, picture analogies, and picture series
4. *Figural Reasoning*—includes figural classification, figural analogies, and figural series
5. *Quantitative Reasoning* (given in Levels E through G)—includes number series, numeric inference, and number matrix

Scoring Information: The Otis-Lennon is hand or machine scorable. The scores can be reported in the following manners:

♦ Percentile rank
♦ Stanine
♦ Scaled scores
♦ NCEs by age
♦ NCEs by grade

STRENGTHS OF THE OLSAT

♦ The test is standardized on a large representative sample of the school population within the United States.
♦ The test provides a variety of derived scores for separate age and grade groups.

WEAKNESSES OF THE OLSAT

♦ There may be concerns about the overall validity of the test.
♦ Examiners are cautioned about using the upper three levels with pupils who are poor readers or easily distractible.

Section 5

ACHIEVEMENT ASSESSMENT MEASURES

After the child's intellectual ability has been measured, his or her academic achievement skills may be reviewed to determine how well he or she is performing in core skill areas such as reading, spelling, mathematics, and writing. The information obtained from the academic battery of tests is important both for the planning and evaluation of instruction.

It is important to remember that individual achievement tests are preferred for assessment of school performance in special education. The reasons are:

- ◆ Individually administered achievement tests are designed to assess children at all ages and grade levels.

- ◆ Individually administered achievement tests can assess the most basic skills of spelling, math, reading, and writing.

- ◆ Individually administered achievement tests allow the examiner to observe a child's test-taking strategies.

- ◆ Individually administered achievement tests can focus on a specific area of concern.

- ◆ Individually administered achievement tests can be given in oral, written, or gestural format.

- ◆ Individually administered achievement tests allow the examiner to observe the child's behavior in a variety of situations.

This section focuses on what to expect from reading, spelling, writing, and mathematics tests that are available to educators today.

READING ASSESSMENT

INTERPRETING READING TESTS

Reading provides a fundamental way for individuals to exchange information. It is also a means by which much of the information presented in school is learned. As a result, reading is the academic area most associated with academic failure. Reading is a complex process which requires numerous skills for its mastery. Consequently, identifying the skills that lead to success in reading is important.

There are numerous reading tests available for assessing a student's ability to read. Choosing which test to use depends upon what area needs to be assessed. Different reading tests measure different reading subskills:

— Oral Reading

— Reading Comprehension

— Word Recognition

— Word Attack Skills

Oral Reading Assessment

A number of tests or parts of tests are designed to assess the accuracy and fluency of a student's ability to read aloud. According to Salvia and Ysseldyke (1995), different oral reading tests record different behaviors as errors or miscues in oral reading. Common errors seen on oral reading tests include, but are not limited to, the following:

- **Omissions of a word or groups of words**—The student will skip individual words or groups of words.

- **Insertion of a word or groups of words**—The student inserts one or more words into the sentence being read.

- **Substitution of one meaningful word for another**—The student replaces one or more words in the passage by one or more meaningful words.

- **Gross mispronunciation of a word**—The student's pronunciation of a word bears very little resemblance to the proper pronunciation.

- **Hesitation**—The student hesitates for 2 or more seconds before pronouncing a word.

- **Inversion or changing of word order**—The student changes the order of words appearing in a sentence.

- **Disregard of punctuation**—The student fails to observe punctuation, such as pausing for a comma, stopping for a period, or indicating by vocal inflection a question mark or exclamation point.

ANALYZING ORAL READING MISCUES

An oral reading error is often referred to as a miscue. By definition, a miscue is the difference between what a reader states is on a page and what is actually on the page.

According to Vacca, et al. (1986, p. 445), "Differences between what the reader says and what is printed on the page are not the result of random errors. Instead, these differences are cued by the thought and language of the reader, who is attempting to construct what the author is saying."

Analysis of miscues can be of two types. These are:

- **Quantitative miscues**—With this type of miscue, the evaluator counts the number of reading errors made by the student.

- **Qualitative miscues**—With this type of miscue, the focus is on the quality of the error rather than the number of different mistakes. It is not based on the problems related to word identification, but rather, on the differences between the miscues and the words on the pages. Consequently, some miscues are more significant than others (Vacca, et al., 1991).

A miscue is significant if it affects meaning (Johns, 1985). Miscues are generally significant when:

1. The meaning of the sentence or passage is significantly changed or altered, and the student does not correct the miscue.

2. A nonword is used in place of the word in the passage.

3. Only a partial word is substituted for the word or phrase in the passage.

4. A word is pronounced for the student.

Miscues are generally not significant when:

1. The meaning of the sentence or passage undergoes no change or only minimal change.

2. They are self-corrected by the student.

3. They are acceptable in the student's dialect.

4. They are later read correctly in the same passage.

Through miscue analysis, teachers can determine the extent to which the reader uses and coordinates graphic sound, syntactic and semantic information from the text. According to Goodman and Burke (1972), to analyze miscues you should ask at least four crucial questions:

1. **Does the miscue change meaning?** If it doesn't, then it's semantically acceptable within the context of the sentence or passage.

2. **Does the miscue sound like language?** If it does, then it's grammatically acceptable within the context. Miscues are grammatically acceptable if they sound like language and serve as the same parts of speech as the text words.

3. **Do the miscue and the text word look and sound alike?** Substitution and mispronunciation miscues should be analyzed to determine how similar they are in approximating the graphic and pronunciation features of the text words.

4. **Was an attempt made to self-correct the miscue?** Self-corrections are revealing because they demonstrate that the reader is attending to meaning and is aware that the initial miscuing did not make sense.

Reading Comprehension Assessment

Diagnostic reading tests often assess six kinds of reading comprehension skills. According to Salvia and Ysseldyke (1995), these are:

- **Literal comprehension**—The student reads the paragraph or story and is then asked questions based on it.

- **Inferential comprehension**—The student reads a paragraph or story and must interpret what has been read.

- **Listening comprehension**—The student is read a paragraph or story by the examiner and is then asked questions about what he or she has read.

- **Critical comprehension**—The student reads a paragraph or story and then analyzes, evaluates, or makes judgments on what he or she has read.

- **Affective comprehension**—The student reads a paragraph or story, and his or her emotional responses to the text are evaluated by the examiner.

- **Lexical comprehension**—The student reads a paragraph or story, and his or her knowledge of vocabulary words is assessed by the examiner.

When evaluating the reading behavior of a child on reading comprehension subtests, it is important for the evaluator to ask the following questions:

- Does the student guess at answers to the questions presented?
- Does the student show an unwillingness to read or attempts at reading?
- Does the student skip unknown words?
- Does the student disregard punctuation?
- Does the student exhibit inattention to the story line?
- Does the student drop the tone of his or her voice at the ends of sentences?
- Does the student display problems with sounding out word parts and blends?
- Does the student exhibit a negative attitude towards reading?
- Does the student express difficulty attacking unknown words?(Mann and Suiter, 1979)

Word Recognition Skills Assessment

The purpose of word recognition tests are to explore the student's ability with respect to sight vocabulary. According to Salvia and Yselldyke (1995, p. 464), "A student learns the correct pronunciation of letters and words through a variety of experiences. The more exposure a student has to specific words and the more familiar those words become, the more readily he or she recognizes those words and is able to pronounce them correctly.

Word recognition subtests form a major part of most diagnostic reading tests. Students who recognize many words are said to have good sight vocabularies or good word-recognition skills."

Word recognition errors may be primarily due to auditory channel problems. According to Mann and Suiter (1979) some of these are:

- **Auditory Acuity and/or Discrimination**—The student may mispronounce words, for example, read the word "chimney" as "chimley."

- **Auditory-Visual Associative Memory**—(a) The student may take wild guesses, with no relationship between the word seen and the word read. (b) When stuck on a word, the student may not be able to sound it out. (c) The student may use a synonym, for example, saying "mommy" for "mother." (d) The student may substitute words, such as "a" for "the."

- **Auditory Closure**—The student may be poor in blending sounds together to make words.

Word recognition errors may also be due to visual channel deficits (Mann and Suiter, 1979) such as:

- **Rate of Perception**—(a) The student may exhibit word-by-word reading or poor phrasing. (b) The student may look at the beginning of a word and then say some other word that starts in the same way, for example, "surprise" for "something."

- **Visual Ground or Ocular Motor**—The student may be unable to keep his or her place and may skip lines or parts of lines when reading.

- **Visual Memory and/or Misperception**—The student may add words that may or may not change the meaning, for example, adding the word "the" when it is not there.

- **Receptive and/or Expressive Language Problems**—(a) The student may repeat parts of words, phrases, and sometimes whole sentences in an attempt to get the meaning. (b) The student may read through punctuation, distorting the meaning of what he/she reads.

- **Visual Sequential Memory**—The student may reverse words or letters.

- **Visual Memory and/or Spatial**—The student may invert words or letters.

Word Attack Skills Assessment

When assessing the reading abilities of the student, evaluators will often examine the word attack/word analysis skills of the child. Word attack skills are those used to derive meaning and/or pronunciation of a word through context clues, structural analysis, or phonics. In order to assess the word attack skills of the student, the examiner will normally read a word to the student who must then identify the consonant, vowel, consonant cluster, or digraph that has the same sound as the beginning, middle, or ending letters of the word.

According to Salvia and Ysseldyke (1995, p. 463), "Students must be able to decode words before they can gain meaning from the printed page. Since word-analysis difficulties are among the principal reasons students have trouble reading, a variety of subtests of commonly used diagnostic reading tests specifically assess word-analysis skills."

SUMMARY OF READING ASSESSMENT

Although most reading tests do cover many of the above areas of assessment, each has its own unique style, method of scoring, and interpretative value. However, when looking at a student's reading behavior, regardless of the test administered, there are certain questions that one must address:

1. Does the student have excessive body movements while reading?

2. Does the student prefer to read alone or in a group?

3. How does the student react to being tested?

4. Does the student avoid reading?

5. When the student reads, what types of materials will he or she read?

6. Does the student read at home?

7. Does the student understand more after reading silently than after listening to someone read the material orally?

8. Does the student value reading?

9. Is the student's failure mechanical or is he or she deficient in comprehension?

GATES-MacGINITE SILENT READING TESTS—
Third Edition

GENERAL TEST INFORMATION

Authors: Walter MacGinite and Ruth MacGinite

Publisher: The Riverside Publishing Company

Address of Publisher: 8420 Spring Lake Drive
Itasca, IL 60143-2079

Phone Number of Publisher: 800-323-9540

Fax of Publisher: 630-467-7192

Purpose of Test: The test is designed to measure silent reading skills.

Description of Test: The test comprises a series of multiple-choice, pencil-and-paper subtests designed to measure silent reading skills.

Type of Test: Standardized

Administration Time: About 1 hour

Type of Administration: Individually or in a group setting

Who Administers This Test: Special education teacher, reading specialist, psychologist, or classroom teacher

Age/Grade Levels: Grades 1 to 12

Subtest Information: The test provides a comprehensive assessment of reading skills in two domains:

- *Vocabulary*—This subtest domain assesses reading vocabulary. The difficulty of the task varies with the grade level.

- *Comprehension*—This subtest domain assesses the ability to read and understand whole sentences and paragraphs.

Scoring Information: Scores are presented in the following manners:

- Percentile ranks
- Stanines
- Grade equivalents
- Scale scores

STRENGTHS OF THE GATES-MacGINITE

- The student and teacher test booklets are written in easy-to-understand language which facilitates the administration of the test for first-time users.
- The test covers a wide age range.
- The test has alternate forms which are very useful for test-retest purposes.
- The test is excellent for screening purposes because of the various areas measured.

WEAKNESSES OF THE GATES-MacGINITE

- The silent reading format makes analysis of certain error types difficult, including but not limited to:
  - omission
  - repetition

73

— mispronunciation

— decoding skills

— substitution

♦ The comprehension section includes questions about facts not present in the paragraphs themselves.

♦ The comprehension section does not require the student to draw conclusions from what is read which is an important factor in comprehension.

GRAY ORAL READING TEST—3 (GORT-3)

GENERAL TEST INFORMATION

Authors:	J. Lee Wiederholt and Brian R. Byrant
Publisher:	PRO-ED
Address of Publisher:	8700 Shoal Creek Blvd. Austin, TX 78757-6897
Phone Number of Publisher:	512-451-3246
Fax of Publisher:	800-397-7633

Purpose of Test: The GORT-3 has four purposes:

1. To help identify those students who are significantly below their peers in oral reading proficiency and who may profit from supplemental help

2. To aid in determining the particular kinds of reading strengths and weaknesses that individual students possess

3. To document students' progress in reading as a consequence of special intervention programs

4. To serve as a measurement device in investigations where researchers are studying the reading abilities of school-age students

Description of Test: The GORT-3 comprises two alternate equivalent forms, each of which contains thirteen developmentally sequenced passages with five comprehension questions. The GORT-3 provides a means of assessing the accuracy and rate of a student's oral reading skill. A system for analyzing the student's oral reading errors is built into the test format.

Type of Test:	Standardized, Norm-referenced
Administration Time:	The time required to administer each form of the GORT-3 will vary from 15 to 30 minutes. Although the test is best administered in one session, examiners may use two sessions if the reader becomes fatigued or uncooperative.
Type of Administration:	Individual
Who Administers This Test:	Special education teacher, reading specialist, psychologist, or classroom teacher
Age/Grade Levels:	Grade 1 to College

Subtest Information: There are no subtests on the GORT-3.

Scoring Information: On the GORT-3 a student's oral reading performance can be discussed in terms of raw scores, standard scores, grade equivalents, percentiles, and a composite quotient.

1. **Raw scores**—The raw scores on the GORT-3 are the total points counted as correct on each separate form of the test. No tables are needed to calculate raw scores. These scores have very little clinical value and are primarily used to generate percentiles or standard scores.

2. **Standard scores**—Raw scores can be converted to standard scores based on a distribution with a mean of 10 and a standard deviation of 3. The guidelines for interpreting standard scores are presented on the following page.

3. **Grade equivalents**—These scores allow the examiner to state that a student is reading at a particular grade level.

GRAY ORAL READING TEST—3 (GORT-3)

(continued)

Standard Score	Rating	Percentage
17–20	Very Superior	2.34
15–16	Superior	6.87
13–14	Above Average	16.12
8–12	Average	49.51
6–7	Below Average	16.12
4–5	Poor	6.87
1–3	Very Poor	2.34

4. **Percentiles**—Raw scores on the GORT-3 can be converted to percentiles using the tables provided in the test manual. Percentiles, also called percentile scores or ranks, represent a value on a scale of 1 to 99 that indicates the test population to which the student's skills are equal.

5. **Composite Quotient**—The Oral Reading Quotient (ORQ) has a mean score of 100 (50th percentile) and a standard deviation of 15.

There are at least five areas of additional assessment that might be of interest to an examiner when a student's GORT-3 oral reading behavior is below what would be expected. These include the following:

1. Silent reading
2. Reading rate
3. Reading miscues in actual classroom reading materials
4. The reading environment
5. Oral language and cognition

If a student performs poorly on the GORT-3, a silent reading test should be administered. If the student's silent reading comprehension is average for his or her age and ability, then additional standardized assessment of reading is probably not warranted since the skills involved in oral reading may impair his/her ability to concentrate and comprehend.

STRENGTHS OF THE GORT-3

♦ There are convenient charts in the examiner's booklet that make scoring easier than it is in prior editions.

♦ The authors provide guidance in interpreting scores, seeking further assessment, and/or planning interventions.

♦ Test administration instructions are clear.

♦ The test results have high validity and reliability.

WEAKNESSES OF THE GORT-3

♦ The necessity of keeping track of separate basal and ceiling criteria may confuse some examiners in determining when to discontinue the test.

♦ The test manual omits normative data stratified along race, ethnic, and socioeconomic lines.

♦ Some slow readers with high accuracy levels may be penalized on this test because time is a variable in scoring.

DURRELL ANALYSIS OF READING DIFFICULTY (DARD)

GENERAL TEST INFORMATION

Authors:	Donald 0. Durrell and Jane H. Catterson
Publisher:	The Psychological Corporation
Address of Publisher:	555 Academic Court San Antonio, TX 78204-2498
Phone Number of Publisher:	800-211-8378
Fax of Publisher:	800-232-1223
TDD of the Publisher:	800-723-1318

Purpose of Test: This test is designed to screen for reading problems.

Description of Test: This test has long served a population of experienced teachers whose primary purpose was to discover and describe weaknesses and faulty habits in children's reading. The kit includes an examiners manual, student record booklets, tachistoscope, and a subtest presentation booklet containing reading passages.

Type of Test:	Standarized
Administration Time:	30–90 minutes
Type of Administration:	Individual
Who Administers This Test:	Special education teacher, reading specialist, psychologist, and classroom teacher
Age/Grade levels:	Grades 1–6

Subtest Information: The Durrell Analysis consists of 19 subtests designed to assess a student's reading and listening performance. They are included in the following sections:

1. *Oral Reading*—The student reads orally and answers questions that require the recall of explicit information.

2. *Silent Reading*—The student reads silently and answers questions that require the recall of explicit information.

3. *Listening Comprehension*—The examiner is directed to read one or two paragraphs aloud to determine the student's ability to comprehend information presented orally.

4. *Word Recognition*—The examiner reads lists of words at increasing difficulty levels and the score is based on the total number of words that the child recognizes correctly.

5. *Word Analysis*—The examiner reads lists of words at increasing difficulty levels and the score is based on the total number of words that the child analyzes correctly.

6. *Listening Vocabulary*—The student is required to listen to a series of words and indicate the category to which it belongs.

7. *Sounds in Isolation*—The student's mastery of sound/symbol relationships, including letters, blends, digraphs, phonograms, and affixes is assessed.

8. *Spelling of Words*—The examiner reads lists of words at increasing difficulty levels and the student's score is based on the total number of words he or she spells correctly.

9. *Phonic Spelling of Words*—The examiner reads lists of words at increasing difficulty levels and the student's score is based on the total number of words he or she spells phonetically correctly.

DURRELL ANALYSIS OF READING DIFFICULTY (DARD)

(continued)

10. ***Visual Memory of Words***—The examiner reads visually presented lists of words at increasing difficulty levels, and the student's score is based on the total number of words the student can recall correctly when the word list is presented again.

11. ***Identifying Sounds in Words***—The examiner reads lists of words at increasing difficulty levels, and the student's score is based on the total number of identifying sounds in words that the student can correctly recall.

12. ***Prereading Phonics Abilities Inventory***—This is an optional subtest that includes syntax matching, naming letters in spoken words, naming phonemes in spoken words, naming lower case letters, and writing letters from dictation.

Scoring Information: Scores are reported in grade levels.

STRENGTHS OF THE DARD:

- The manual for the *Third Edition* is improved, providing clearer procedures for testing.

- A continuing strength of the test is its set of behavioral checklists, urging close observation of individual reader characteristics.

- The addition of several new subtests makes for a more complete battery for assessment. However, the major focus of the test continues to be on specific skills.

WEAKNESSES OF THE DARD

- The test only provides grade levels which may not be accurate, especially in cases of children who have been retained.

- There is still a need for establishing the test's validity.

- The standardization sample is not well described in the manual.

GATES-McKILLOP-HOROWITZ READING DIAGNOSTIC TEST

GENERAL TEST INFORMATION

Authors:	Arthur I. Gates and Anne S. McKillop and Elizabeth Horowitz
Publisher:	Teachers College Press
Address of Publisher:	1234 Amsterdam Ave. New York, NY 10027
Phone Number of Publisher:	212-678-3929
Fax of Publisher:	212-678-4149

Purpose of Test: The test is designed to assess overall reading ability.

Description of Test: This test is an 11-part verbal paper-pencil test. Not all parts need to be given to all students. Subtests are selected based on the student's reading levels and reading difficulties.

Type of Test:	Standardized
Administration Time:	40–60 minutes
Type of Administration:	Individual
Who Administers This Test:	Special education teacher, reading specialist, psychologist, and classroom teacher
Age/Grade Levels:	Grades 1–6

Subtest Information: The subtests are listed and described below:

Oral Reading—The student is required to read seven paragraphs orally. No comprehension is required.

Reading Sentences—The student is required to read four sentences with phonetically regular words.

Words-Flash Presentation—The student is required to identify words presented by a tachistoscope in 1/2-second intervals.

Words-Untimed—The student is required to read the same word list as presented in Words/Flash Presentation. However, the student is given the opportunity to use word-attack skills in an untimed setting.

Syllabication—The student is required to read a list of nonsense words.

Recognizing and Blending Common Word Parts—The student is required to read a list of nonsense words made up of common word parts.

Reading Words—The student is required to read 15 one-syllable nonsense words.

Letter Sounds—The student is required to give the sound of a printed letter.

Naming Capital Letters—The student is required to name uppercase letters.

Naming Lower Case Letters—The student is required to name lowercase letters.

Vowels—The student is required to determine which vowel is associated with a nonsense word presented by the examiner.

Auditory Blending—The student is required to blend sounds to form a whole word.

Auditory Discrimination—The student is required to listen to a pair of words and to determine whether the words are the same or different.

Spelling—The student is required to take an oral spelling test.

GATES-McKILLOP-HOROWITZ READING DIAGNOSTIC TEST
(continued)

Informal Writing—The student is required to write an original paragraph on a topic of his or her choice.

Scoring Information: The scores are presented in the following manner:

- Grade level
- Age level
- Rating scale

STRENGTHS OF THE GATES-McKILLOP-HOROWITZ:

- Tests many critical reading skills.
- A careful selection of subtests allows every student some successful reading experiences during the testing procedure.
- Students can maintain a high level of interest throughout the test because of its varied format and the informal tone of the procedures.

WEAKNESSES OF THE GATES-McKILLOP-HOROWITZ:

- Manner of reporting results does not include percentiles which provide a more accurate measure in assessing students with other norms.
- The test offers no measure of comprehension.

GILMORE ORAL READING TEST

GENERAL TEST INFORMATION

Authors:	John V. Gilmore and Eunice C. Gilmore
Publisher:	The Psychological Corporation
Address of Publisher:	555 Academic Court San Antonio, TX 78204-2498
Phone Number of Publisher:	800-211-8378
Fax of Publisher:	800-232-1223
TDD of the Publisher:	800-723-1318

Purpose of Test: This test is intended to provide a means of analyzing the oral reading performance of pupils.

Description of Test: This test measures three aspects of oral reading competency: pronunciation, comprehension, and reading rate. It is used for diagnosing the reading needs of students identified as having reading problems.

Type of Test:	Standardized
Administration Time:	15–20 minutes
Type of Administration:	Individual
Who Administers This Test:	Special education teacher, reading specialist, psychologist, and classroom teacher
Age/Grade Levels:	Grades 1 to 8

Subtest Information: The test is made up of 10 paragraphs in increasing order of difficulty that form a continuous story about episodes in a family group. There are five comprehension questions on each paragraph and a picture that portrays the characters in the story.

Scoring Information: The test manual provides separate scores for grade equivalency, percentile, and stanines. Individual scores are given for accuracy, comprehension, and rate of reading.

STRENGTHS OF THE GILMORE ORAL READING TEST

- The updated Gilmore is among the best standardized tests of accuracy in oral reading of meaningful material.
- The test directions are clear and concise.
- No special training is required to administer this test satisfactorily.

WEAKNESSES OF THE GILMORE ORAL READING TEST

- The test seeks to measure comprehension ability with an oral test. This may be a problem since certain oral reading skills may interfere in a child's ability to recall what he or she is reading.

SLOSSON ORAL READING TEST—REVISED (SORT-R)

GENERAL TEST INFORMATION

Authors:	Richard L. Slosson; Revised by Charles L. Nicholson
Publisher:	Slosson Educational Publication Inc.
Address of Publisher:	P.O. Box 280 East Aurora, NY 14052-0280
Phone Number of Publisher:	716-652-0930
Fax of Publisher:	800-655-3840

Purpose of Test: This test was designed to predict a quick estimate of word-recognition levels for children and adults.

Description of Test: The Slosson Oral Reading Test-Revised (SORT-R) contains 200 words arranged in ascending order of difficulty in groups of 20 words. These word groups approximate reading grade levels. For example, group 1 is at the first-grade level, and group 5 is at the fifth-grade level, etc. The last group, listed as grades 9–12, contains the most difficult words and words frequently encountered at the adult level.

Type of Test:	Standardized
Administration Time:	Untimed (approximately 3–5 minutes)
Type of Administration:	Individual
Who Administers This Test:	Special education teacher, reading specialist, psychologist, and classroom teacher
Age/Grade Levels:	Preschool to adult

Subtest Information: The test has no subtests.

Scoring Information: Scores on the SORT-R are determined from the tables in the Appendix of the manual. Grade-equivalent and age-equivalent scores can be calculated from manual tables. Also, there are tables to determine the standard score. The mean standard score is 100, and the standard deviation is 16 at all age/grade levels.

STRENGTHS OF THE SORT-R

- The test is easy to administer.
- The test is easy to score.
- The test can be administered quickly.

WEAKNESSES OF THE SORT-R

- The test has limited relevance to school-based instruction because of the nature of the questions presented.
- Given the newness of the revision, further research is necessary to assess the test's validity and reliabilty.

SPACHE DIAGNOSTIC READING SCALES (DRS)

GENERAL TEST INFORMATION

Author:	George D. Spache
Publisher:	CTB MacMillan/McGraw-Hill
Address of Publisher:	Del Monte Research Park Garden Road, Monterey, CA 93940
Phone Number of Publisher:	800-538-9547
Fax of Publisher:	800-282-0266

Purpose of Test: The test is designed to identify the strengths and weaknesses that affect a student's reading proficiencies at the grade levels in which reading is normally taught.

Description of Test: The Diagnostic Reading Scales consist of a battery of individually administered tests that are used to estimate the instructional, independent, and potential reading levels of a student.

Type of Test:	Standardized
Administration Time:	60 minutes
Type of Administration:	Individual
Who Administers This Test:	Special education teacher, reading specialist, psychologist, and classroom teacher
Age/Grade Levels:	Grades 1–7 and poor readers in grades 8–12

Subtest Information: The subtests are listed and described below:

1. *Word Recognition List*—This test contains graded word lists that are used to determine a student's reading ability.
2. *Oral Reading*—The student is required to read paragraphs aloud and answer questions orally.
3. *Silent Reading*—The student is required to read a passage silently and to respond orally to questions asked by the examiner.
4. *Auditory Comprehension*—The student is required to respond to questions orally about paragraphs read aloud by the examiner.
5. *Supplementary Phonics Test*—This subtest measures the student's word-attack skills and phonics knowledge.

Scoring Informaton: There are three derived scores: *instructional level*, *independent level*, and *potential level*. Scores obtained are presented in terms of grade level.

STRENGTHS OF THE SPACHE DIAGNOSTIC READING SCALES

- The latest version of the DRS represents a substantial improvement over the previous version.
- The revised examiner's manual, the training tape cassette, and the guidelines given for testing students who speak nonstandard dialects are all positive features.

WEAKNESSES OF THE SPACHE DIAGNOSTIC READING SCALES

- The definitions of instructional and independent reading levels in the diagnostic reading scales differ substantially from those in ordinary use. Therefore, results from the diagnostic reading scales are of limited value to practitioners who wish to place a student at appropriate levels for reading instructions.
- The comprehension score can be misleading for students with short-term memory problems, which is common with this type of subtest.

WOODCOCK READING MASTERY TESTS—REVISED (WRMT-R)

GENERAL TEST INFORMATION

Author:	Richard W. Woodcock
Publisher:	American Guidance Service
Address of Publisher:	4201 Woodland Rd. Circle Pines, MN 55014-1796
Phone Number of Publisher:	612-786-4343 or 800-328-2560
Fax of Publisher:	612-786-9077

Purpose of Test: To measure several important aspects of reading ability.

Description of Test: The Woodcock Reading Mastery Tests (WMRT-R) is composed of six individually administered subtests. There are two forms of the test, G and H. Form G includes all six subtests while Form H includes only four reading achievement tests.

Type of Test:	Standardized
Administration Time:	40–45 minutes
Type of Administration:	Individual
Who Administers This Test:	Special education teacher, reading specialist, psychologist, and classroom teacher
Age/Grade Levels:	Grades K through 12

Subtest Information: The six subtests found on Form G include the following:

1. *Visual Auditory Learning*—This test requires the student to associate unfamiliar visual stimuli (rebuses) with familiar oral words and to translate sequences of rebuses into sentences.

2. *Letter Identification*—This test measures a student's skill in naming or pronouncing letters of the alphabet. Uppercase and lowercase letters are used.

3. *Word Identification*—This test measures skill in pronouncing words in isolation.

4. *Word Attack*—This test assesses skill in using phonic and structural analysis to read non-sense words.

5. *Word Comprehension*—There are three parts to this section: *Antonyms, Synonyms* and *Analogies*. On the *antonyms* section, the student must read a word and then provide a word that means the opposite. In the *synonyms* section, the student must provide a word with similar meanings to the stimulus words provided. In the *analogies* section, the student must read a pair of words, ascertain the relationship between the two words, read a third word, and then supply a word that has the same relationship to the third word as exists between the initial pair of words read.

6. *Passage Comprehension*—In this subtest, the student must read silently a passage that has a word missing and then tell the examiner a word that could appropriately fill in the blank space. The passages are drawn from actual newspaper articles and textbooks.

Form H does not include the *Visual Auditory Learning* or *Letter Identification*, but does include the following other four subtests:

♦ *Word Identification*

♦ *Word Attack*

WOODCOCK READING MASTERY TESTS—REVISED (WRMT-R)

(continued)

♦ *Word Comprehension*

♦ *Passage Comprehension*

Scoring Information: The three options for interpreting the WRMT-R are designed to provide differing degrees of precision:

1. **Lowest level of interpretation**—Here, the examiner can plot raw score, obtain grade-equivalent and instructional ranges, and observe a student's strengths and weaknesses across the test.

2. **Middle level of interpretation**—At this level, the examiner can refer to norm tables to obtain the total reading score as well as percentile ranks and relative performance indexes (RPIs) for each of the subtests.

3. **Highest level of interpretation**—At the highest level, the examiner uses the norm tables to get exact grade equivalents, age equivalents, a variety of standard scores, confidence bands for relative performance indexes, and percentile rank.

Once the scores have been obtained, Woodcock (1987) describes four levels of interpretive strategies for the WRMT-R in which the examiner can:

1. analyze errors in the responses that a student makes to individual items

2. describe the student's level of development by reporting scores as grade and age equivalents

3. describe the quality of the student's performance by reporting relative performance indexes

4. report the student's standing in a group by reporting percentile ranks or standard scores.

STRENGTHS OF THE WRMT-R

♦ The test is administered in a short period of time.

♦ The test is relatively inexpensive.

♦ There is good reliability and validity data on the test.

♦ A micro computer scoring program is available for both IBM and Apple formats.

♦ Alternate forms of the test allow for test/retest administration.

WEAKNESSES OF THE WRMT-R

♦ It may require numerous administrations for the examiner to make a valid interpretation of a child's results.

♦ Reliability data for many of the grade levels measured by the test are not reported in the manual.

♦ There is no explanation in the manual as to whether or not students with special needs were used in the norming population.

TEST OF READING COMPREHENSION—THIRD EDITION (TORC-3)

GENERAL TEST INFORMATION

Authors:	Virginia L. Brown, Donald D. Hammill, and J. Lee Wiederholt
Publisher:	PRO-ED, Inc.
Address of Publisher:	8700 Shoal Creek Blvd. Austin, TX 78758-6897
Phone Number of Publisher:	512-451-3246 or 800 897-3202
Fax of Publisher:	800-FXPROED

Purpose of Test: The test is intended as a method for assessing the understanding of written language.

Description of Test: The materials in the test kit include an examiner's manual, student booklets, answer sheets, individual and student profile sheets, and separate response forms for several subtests. This current revision of the TORC offers new normative data based on a sample of 1,962 students from 19 states stratified by age, keyed to the 1990 census data, and presented by geographic region, gender, residence, race, ethnicity, and disabling condition.

Type of Test:	Norm-referenced
Administration Time:	30 minutes
Type of Administration:	Individual/group
Who Administers This Test:	Special education teacher, reading specialist, psychologist, and classroom teacher
Age/Grade Levels:	Ages 7 to 18

Subtest Information: There are four general reading comprehension core subtests:

1. *General Vocabulary*—This subtest measures the reader's understanding of sets of vocabulary items that are all related to the same general concept.

2. *Syntactic Similarities*—This subtest measures the reader's understanding of sentence structures that are similar in meaning but syntactically different.

3. *Paragraph Reading*—This subtest measures the reader's ability to answer questions related to story-like paragraphs.

4. *Sentence Sequencing*—This subtest measures the reader's ability to build relationships among sentences both to each other and to a reader-created whole.

There are also four supplemental tests that measure content area vocabulary in mathematics, social studies, and science, and the student's ability to read directions in schoolwork.

Scoring Information: The test provides the following:

♦ Reading Comprehension Quotient: Reflects the student's overall reading comprehension and can be compared to measures of abstract thinking, oral language abilities, and achievement.

♦ Grade Equivalents

♦ Age equivalents

♦ Standard scores

♦ Scaled scores

TEST OF READING COMPREHENSION—THIRD EDITION (TORC-3)

(continued)

STRENGTHS OF THE TORC-3

- ◆ The test is useful in comparing reading comprehension with other conceptual and linguistic abilities.
- ◆ The test is useful for planning remediation and IEPs.

WEAKNESSES OF THE TORC-3

- ◆ Several of the TORC-3 subtests measure abilities seldom taught in classrooms, i.e., Syntactic Similarities.
- ◆ TORC-3 is best used along with other measures of reading skills to arrive at a total evaluation of a child's reading abilities.

DECODING SKILLS TEST (DST)

GENERAL TEST INFORMATION

Authors:	Ellis Richardson and Barbara DiBenedetto
Publisher:	York Press
Address of Publisher:	P.O. Box 504 Timonium, MD 21094
Phone Number of Publisher:	410-560-1557
Fax of Publisher:	410-560-6758

Purpose of Test: The test is designed to assess specific reading disabilities.

Description of Test: The DST gives a clear picture of the reading process and demonstrates the particular areas in which an individual needs help. It provides a diagnostic profile of the decoding skills that are essential to reading comprehension.

Type of Test:	Criterion-referenced
Administration Time:	15–30 minutes
Type of Administration:	Individual
Who Administers This Test:	Special education teacher, reading specialist, psychologist, and classroom teacher
Age/Grade Levels:	Children and adults who are reading at first- through fifth-grade levels

Subtest Information: The DST is composed of three subtests:

- *Basal Vocabulary*—This subtest measures the student's ability to recognize words taught in most basal reading programs.

- *Phonic Patterns*—This subtest assesses the reader's ability to decode words using letter-sound correspondence.

- *Contextual Decoding*—This subtest presents story passages that correspond to first- through fifth-grade reading levels. The student is required to correctly decode words embedded in passages.

Scoring Information: The test provides criterion-referenced scores that can be related directly to the reading curriculum. These scores give a variety of useful information:

- Reading achievement level
- Frustration level
- Phonic pattern knowledge
- Phonic decoding deficiencies
- Oral fluency at various reading levels
- Oral reading levels

STRENGTHS OF THE DST

- The test proves helpful with forming reading groups.
- The test helps evaluators with making program decisions involving a child's decoding skills and possible instructional levels.
- The manual is clearly written.

DECODING SKILLS TEST (DST)
(continued)

WEAKNESSES OF THE DST

- The DST is strictly a decoding test and the inclusion of a cursory measure of comprehension may be misleading in determining the student's instructional level.

- As cited in the manual, this test takes time to administer and score.

- The phonic profile scoring procedures can be time consuming and may require multiple administrations for the evaluator to become familiar with the procedure.

NELSON-DENNY READING TEST (NDRT)

GENERAL TEST INFORMATION

Authors:	James T. Brown, Vivian Vick Fishco, and Gerald Hanna
Publisher:	The Riverside Publishing Company
Address of Publisher:	8420 Spring Lake Drive Itasca, IL 60143-2079
Phone Number of Publisher:	800-323-9540
Fax:	630-467-7192

Purpose of Test: This test is intended to assess a student's achievement and progress in vocabulary, comprehension, and reading rate.

Description of Test: This test is a 136-item, paper-and-pencil reading measure containing two parts.

Type of Test:	Standardized, norm-referenced
Administration Time:	35–45 minutes
Type of Administration:	Individual or group
Who Administers This Test:	Special education teacher, reading specialist, psychologist, and classroom teacher
Age/Grade Levels:	Grades 9 to college

Subtest Information: The test contains two parts as follows:

- *Vocabulary*—This section contains 80 multiple-choice items and assesses a student's vocabulary development.

- *Comprehension*—This section contains seven reading passages and 38 multiple-choice questions and assesses a student's comprehension and reading rate.

Scoring Information: The test provides results in the following manners:

- Percentiles
- Stanines
- Scale Scores

STRENGTHS OF THE NDRT

- The Neslon-Denny is a very good screening assessment measure of potential reading difficulties for secondary level students.
- The measure of reading rate allows this test to be used by evaluators in assessing a student's need for extended time.
- The norms allow for assessing the reading potential of college level students.

WEAKNESSES OF THE NDRT

- The manual is limited in terms of information regarding reliability and validity which is provided in another manual at extra cost.

SPELLING ASSESSMENT

INTERPRETING SPELLING TESTS

Spelling is one of the academic skills often included in the evaluator's test battery of individual achievement tests used in special education assessment.

Spelling ability is viewed by some teachers and school administrators equally with other academic skills. Being a poor speller does not necessarily mean that a child has a learning disorder. However, when poor spelling occurs with poor reading and/or arithmetic, then there is reason for concern. It appears that many of the learning skills required for good spelling are also the ones that enable the students to become good readers.

Many tests assess spelling skills in different ways. For example, the Wide Range Achievement Test-3 uses recall tasks where the student is required to remember and then write the correct spelling of words.

Spelling, like all written language skills, is well suited to work sample analysis because a permanent product is produced. Learning to spell is a developmental process, and young children go through a number of stages as they begin to acquire written language skills.

QUESTIONS TO ASK PRIOR TO ASSESSMENT

There are 3 important questions which should be adressed before one begins to analyze the results of the spelling subtest. These questions are:

Does the child have sufficient mental ability to learn to spell?

This information can be obtained from the school psychologist if an intellectual evaluation was administered. However, if no such test was administered, then a group school abilities index may be present in the child's permanent folder.

Are the child's hearing, speech, and vision adequate?

This information can be obtained through the permanent record folder, information in the nurse's office, or informal screening procedures.

What is the child's general level of spelling ability according to teachers' comments and past evaluations or standardized tests?

Teacher comments and observations about the child's spelling history are very important to show patterns of disability. Also, look at previously administered standardized tests to see if patterns exist throughout the years on such tests.

INFORMATION OBTAINED FROM THE TEACHER PRIOR TO ASSESSMENT

Other information should be obtained from the classroom teacher as well. The teacher can offer some foundational information on the child's patterns. It may be necessary to ask for the following information from the teacher:

- Child's attitude towards spelling in the classroom
- The extent to which the child relies on a dictionary in the classroom
- The extent of spelling errors in classroom written work
- Any patterns of procrastination or avoidance of written work
- Study habits and methods of work in the classroom
- History of scores on classroom spelling tests
- Observable handwriting difficulties
- Any evidence of fatigue as a factor in the child's spelling performance

ERROR ANALYSIS

Once the above questions are considered, then the spelling section of the test should be subjected to an error analysis in terms of the following factors:

- Comparison of the student's ability to spell phonetically regular and irregular words
- Legibility of handwriting
- Defects in letter forms, spacing, alignment, and size
- Control and ability to remain on the line
- Proper use of capitalization
- Style of writing, i.e., script or printing
- Initial consonant sound recognition
- Medial consonant sound recognition
- Final consonant sound recognition
- Reversal of letters in sound parts
- Overuse of phonics
- Recalls the letter and sound symbols quickly and accurately
- Blends the sound parts of words together into whole words
- Child appears to block out or not hear the sounds
- Child's attitude towards spelling
- Evidence of any possible physical disability
- Writing of plural forms and derivatives of given words
- Guessing on the basis of the first letter

When working with a child who is having difficulty in spelling, McLaughlin and Lewis (1990) state that there are certain questions to ask the child to obtain information on his/her coping skills. These are:

1. When writing, how do you tell if you have spelled the word correctly?

2. When you are not sure how to spell a word, what do you do?

3. After you have finished writing, do you read and check what you have written?

4. In checking your writing, what do you do if you find a word that you think may be spelled incorrectly?

The causes of spelling errors in children may be due to either auditory or visual channel deficits. Listed below are examples of each:

Spelling Errors Primarily Due to Auditory Channel Deficits

According to Mann, Suiter and McClung (1979, p. 76), certain spelling errors may be evident in students with certain auditory channel deficits:

- **Auditory discrimination problems or cultural problems**—The child makes incorrect substitution of letters, i.e., t for d, sh for ch.

- **Auditory discrimination problems**—The child confuses vowels, for example, spells bit as bet.

- **Auditory acuity or discrimination problems**—The child does not hear subtle differences in nor discriminate between sounds, and often leaves vowels out of two-syllable words.

- **Auditory–visual association**—The child uses a synonym like house for home in spelling.

- **Auditory–visual associative memory**—The child takes wild guesses with little or no relationship between the letters or words used and the spelling words dictated, such as spelling dog for home or writing phe for home.

Examples of Spelling Errors Due to Visual Channel Deficits

According to Mann, Suiter and McClung (1979, p. 76), certain spelling errors may be evident in students with certain visual channel deficits:

- **Visual memory problems**—The child visualizes the beginning or the ending of words but omits the middle of the words, for example, spells hapy for happy.

- **Visual memory sequence**—The child gives the correct letters but in the wrong sequence; for example, the child writes "the" as teh or hte.

- **Visual discrimination problems**—The child inverts letters, writing "u" for "n," "m" for "w."

- **Visual memory**—The child spells words phonetically that are nonphonetic in configuration, i.e., tuff for tough.

THE SPELLMASTER ASSESSMENT AND TEACHING SYSTEM

GENERAL TEST INFORMATION

Author:	Greenbaum, C.
Publisher:	Pro-Ed
Address of Publisher:	8700 Shoal Creek Boulevard Austin, TX 78758-6897
Phone Number of Publisher:	(512) 451-3246 or 800-897-3202
Fax of Publisher:	800-FXPROED

Purpose of Test: The Spellmaster was developed to assist in the identification of strengths and weaknesses in spelling. It is also a very helpful tool for grouping students according to their current spelling needs.

Description of Test: The Spellmaster is a set of three tests at eight different levels that include specific types of spelling words. There are also entry level tests that can be used to determine the most appropriate level of test to use for a particular student.

Type of Test:	Criterion-referenced
Administration Time:	Varies based on strengths and weaknesses of students' abilities
Type of Administration:	Individual or Group
Who Administers This Test:	Regular Education Teachers, Special Education Teachers, School Psychologists, Educational Evaluators
Age/Grade Levels:	The Spellmaster is designed for use with pupils in kindergarten through grade 8, although it can be used through adult age

Subtest Information:

Diagnostic (8 tests): These tests involve words that use rules that generalize to the spelling of the majority of words in the English language.

Irregular Words (8 tests): These tests involve using words whose spelling violates basic phonic rules.

Homonyms (8 tests): These tests involve words whose spelling can be regular or irregular, but the correct spelling has to do with its meaning.

STRENGTHS OF TEST (According to Taylor, 1997)

◈ Strong ability to pinpoint specific types of spelling errors.

◈ Presents good techniques and activities to remediate spelling problems.

◈ Reflects a very pragmatic approach to testing and teaching spelling.

WEAKNESSES OF TEST (According to Taylor, 1997)

◈ Care needs to be taken to analyze the types of errors made and not simply to group students according to spelling ability.

◈ No evidence that the tests adequately sample spelling skills needed in school.

◈ Test may lack technical adequacy.

TEST OF WRITTEN SPELLING—3 (TWS-3)

GENERAL TEST INFORMATION

Authors:	Stephen C. Larsen and Donald D. Hammill
Publisher:	PRO-ED, Inc.
Address of Publisher:	8700 Shoal Creek Blvd. Austin, TX 78758-6897
Phone Number of Publisher:	512-451-3246 or 800-897-3202
Fax of Publisher:	(800)-FXPROED

Purpose of Test: This test is designed to assess spelling skills across words of different difficulty levels.

Description of Test: Divides spelling of English words into two categories: those that follow orthographic rules (predictable words) and those that do not (unpredictable words).

Type of Test:	Standardized
Administration Time:	15 to 25 minutes
Type of Administration:	Group or individual
Who Administers This Test:	Special education teacher, reading specialist, psychologist, and classroom teacher
Age/Grade Levels:	Ages 6-0 to 18-11.

Subtest Information: The test consists of two subtests:

1. *Predictable Words*—This test contains words that follow the general spelling rules, e.g., spend.

2. *Unpredictable Words*—This test contains words that do not conform to general spelling rules, e.g., campaign.

Scoring Information: Each correct item receives one point. Scores are presented in the following manners:

- ♦ Standard score with a mean of 100
- ♦ Percentile ranks
- ♦ Age equivalents
- ♦ Grade equivalents

STRENGTHS OF THE TWS-3

- ♦ The test manual is clear and concise.
- ♦ The administration and scoring section of the manual details the basal, the ceiling, and the scoring procedures.
- ♦ Reliability estimates indicate that the test can be accepted as a consistent measure of written spelling ability.
- ♦ The test is easily administered.

WEAKNESSES OF THE TWS-3

- ♦ Sample sizes of the studies were limited to 20 students per grade which may be problematic in generalizing results to the entire population.
- ♦ The TWS-3 does not assess all aspects of the spelling process.

WRITTEN LANGUAGE ASSESSMENT

INTERPRETING WRITTEN COMPOSITION

Writing is a highly complex method of expression involving the integration of eye-hand, linguistic, and conceptual abilities. As a result, it is usually the last skill to be mastered by children. While reading is usually considered the receptive form of a graphic symbol system, writing is considered the expressive form of that system. The primary concern in the assessment of composition skills is the content of the student's writing, not its form. Areas of analysis include:

- ◆ organization of the writing
- ◆ vocabulary used to express ideas
- ◆ style in which the composition is written
- ◆ the originality of the ideas expressed

The mechanical aspects of writing also play a role, albeit a secondary one, because a composition's intelligibility can be impaired by mechanical errors. As a result, the evaluator should observe the following prior and during the writing assessment (McLoughlin and Lewis, 1990):

- ◆ How does the student hold the writing implement?
- ◆ Is the student writing with a pen or pencil that is an appropriate size?
- ◆ Does the child exhibit fine motor confusion?
- ◆ Does the student hold the paper in an appropriate direction?
- ◆ Does the student press down when writing?
- ◆ How often does the student erase?
- ◆ How often does the student cross out mistakes?
- ◆ Does the student switch hands while writing?
- ◆ Does the student write with the right or left hand?
- ◆ Does the student break pencil points frequently?
- ◆ What is the child's posture during the assessment?
- ◆ How is the student seated?
- ◆ On what kind of paper is the student writing, i.e., lined, margins?

The term "writing" refers to a variety of interrelated graphic skills, including:

- **composition**—the ability to generate ideas and to express them in acceptable grammar, while adhering to certain stylistic conventions
- **spelling**—the ability to use letters to construct words in accordance with accepted usage

- **handwriting**—the ability to physically execute the graphic marks necessary to produce legible compositions or messages

COMPONENTS OF WRITING

Written composition includes at least three interrelated components: cognitive, linguistic, and stylistic. When these are combined with two additional elements, handwriting and spelling, the result is a comprehensive concept of the entire writing process. Thus the analysis of writing tests can involve the diagnostic interpretation of several areas comprising the writing process. Some of the questions you may want to use in your analysis of the child's writing may include:

Cognitive Questions

- Is the child's writing logical?
- Is the writing coherent?
- Does the child follow proper word sequence?
- Is the passage readily understandable to the reader?
- What is the level of maturity in the child's writing? (i.e., sloppy, disjointed)
- Is the writing lacking in theme?

Linguistic Questions

- Does the child use suitable words?
- Does the child use correct tenses?
- Does the child use plurals correctly?
- Does the writing show agreement between subject and verb?

Stylistic Questions

- Does the child use correct capitalization?
- Does the child use correct punctuation?
- Does the child use the comma correctly?
- Does the child use the period correctly?
- Does the child use quotation marks correctly?

INTERPRETING HANDWRITING

Handwriting refers to the actual motor activity that is involved in writing. Most students are taught manuscript (printing) initially and then move to cursive writing in later grades.

There are those who advocate that only manuscript or only cursive should be taught (Reid & Hresko, 1981). In truth, problems may appear among students in either system. Wiederhold et al. (1978) have suggested a number of areas which may be assessed related to both manuscript and cursive writing. The assessment of manuscript includes:

- ◆ evaluating the position of the hand and paper
- ◆ size of letters
- ◆ the proportion of letters to each other
- ◆ quality of the actual pencil lines
- ◆ the amount and regularity of the slant of the letters
- ◆ letter formation and alignment
- ◆ letter or word spacing
- ◆ speed of production

Cursive writing can be considered according to many of the same qualities, but should also include an evaluation of the way in which letters are connected.

Handwriting skills are usually measured through the use of informal assessment measures, i.e., rating scales, observation measures, and error of handwriting analysis rather than Norm-referenced measures. Given the fact that most measures are informal, it is not normally part of a psychoeducational battery. However, handwriting should always be evaluated and informally assessed if it appears to warrant concern.

DENVER HANDWRITING ANALYSIS (DHA)

GENERAL TEST INFORMATION

Author:	Peggy L. Anderson
Publisher:	Academic Therapy Publications
Address of Publisher:	20 Commercial Blvd. Novato, CA 94949-6191
Phone Number of Publisher:	415-883-3314 or 800-422-7249
Fax of Publisher:	415-883-3720

Purpose of Test: The test provides an informal cursive handwriting evaluation that provides detailed information relating to handwriting instruction.

Description of Test: This test is an informal cursive handwriting evaluation that provides detailed information that relates directly to handwriting instruction and can be used for continuing assessment. The test is a multiple-item, paper-and-pencil test consisting of five areas.

Type of Test:	Criterion-referenced
Administration Time:	20–60 minutes
Type of Administration:	Individual or group
Age/Grade Levels:	Ages 8 through 13

Subtest Information: The test contains five subtests:

- *Near Point Copying*—This subtest assesses a student's ability to copy from a near-point model.

- *Writing the Alphabet*—This subtest assesses a student's ability to properly form all capital and lower case letters of the alphabet when connection is not required.

- *Far Point Copying*—This subtest assesses a student's handwriting skills in the context of copying from a distance.

- *Manuscript-Cursive Transition*—This subtest assesses a student's ability to produce cursive letters that correspond to manuscript letters.

- *Dictation*—This subtest assesses a student's ability to perform an activity which requires writing from dictation.

Scoring Information: The DHA includes three different types of scoring procedures:

- **Subskill Analysis**—This system utilizes a specific task analysis approach in which all individual letter errors are noted and classified under a variety of categories, such as closure, looping, rounding, connection, transition, reversal, poor formation, substitution, omission, and insertion.

- **Performance Analysis**—This system utilizes a more diagnostic approach addressing more general aspects of handwriting and is marked with either pluses (+) or minuses (−). Categories include spatial organization, speed, slant, and appearance.

- **Raw Score Method**—This is a non-task analysis whereby items are scored as either correct or incorrect and the total number of errors is recorded. The results are calculated into mastery levels.

STRENGTHS OF THE DHA

- One of the few informal handwriting measures available.

- The format of the test allows for group administration which is useful for screening large numbers of students.

DENVER HANDWRITING ANALYSIS (DHA)
(continued)

- The test focuses on the age group between 8 and 13, which allows for early identification and remediation of problems in this area.

- It provides the evaluator and the classroom teacher detailed information that relates directly to handwriting instruction.

WEAKNESSES OF THE DHA

- Although weaknesses may exist on the DHA, a review of the literature found no weaknesses reported.

THE PICTURE STORY LANGUAGE TEST (PSLT)

GENERAL TEST INFORMATION

Author:	Helmer R. Myklebust
Publisher:	The Psychological Corporation
Address of Publisher:	555 Academic Court San Antonio, TX 78204-2498
Phone Number of Publisher:	800-211-8378
Fax of Publisher:	800-232-1223
TDD of the Publisher:	800-723-1318

Purpose of Test: The test is designed to determine a child's ability to express ideas through writing.

Description of Test: The test is a multiple-item, pencil-and-paper test in which the examiner asks the student to write the best story he/she can about a picture on an easel.

Type of Test:	Norm-referenced
Administration Time:	20–30 minutes
Type of Administration:	Individual or group
Who Administers This Test:	Special education teacher, classroom teacher
Age/Grade Levels:	Ages 7 to 17

Subtest Information: The writing sample is scored in terms of three aspects of written language: productivity, correctness, and meaning. The three scales of the PSLT correspond to these dimensions:

- *Productivity Scale*—The length of writing sample is used to evaluate the child's productivity. The words in the sample are counted along with the sentences.
- *Syntax Scale*—The purpose of this scale is the evaluation of the child's accuracy in the mechanical spects of writing.
- *Abstract–Concrete Scale*—This scale attempts to assess the content of the child's writing.

Scoring Information: Scores are reported in the following manner:

- Age equivalents
- Percentile ranks
- Stanines

STRENGTHS OF THE PLST

- The test is easy to administer.
- The wide age range makes it a good instrument for measuring the child's progress in writing skills in relation to age.

WEAKNESSES OF THE PLST

- The test is no longer widely used since the newest version of the TOWL has taken its place because of the updated norms.
- Scoring of the writing sample is subjective and lengthy.
- The test's norms are dated.
- Serious questions have been raised about its technical adequacy.

TEST OF EARLY WRITTEN LANGUAGE—2 (TEWL-2)

GENERAL TEST INFORMATION

Author:	Wayne P. Hresko
Publisher:	PRO-ED, Inc.
Address of Publisher:	8700 Shoal Creek Blvd. Austin, TX 78758-6897
Phone Number of Publisher:	512-451-3246 or 800-897-3202
Fax of Publisher:	800-FXPROED

Purpose of Test: The test is intended to:

♦ identify those students who are significantly below their peers in the academic area of writing

♦ identify writing strengths and weaknesses of individual students

♦ document students' progress in written language as a consequence of special intervention programs

♦ serve as a measurement device in research studies pertaining to the academic achievement of young children

Description of Test: The test was developed to assess early writing abilities and covers five areas of writing: transcription, conventions of print, communication, creative expression, and record keeping. The TEWL-2 has a total of 42 items. The starting items vary by age level. An item is graded as 1 if correct and 0 if incorrect. Each item counts equally, although some require more responses or information than others.

Type of Test:	Standardized
Administration Time:	10–30 minutes
Type of Administration:	Individual or group
Who Administers This Test:	Special education teacher, reading specialist, psychologist, and classroom teacher
Age/Grade Levels:	Ages 3 to 7

Subtest Information: The test consists of two subtests:

Basic Writing—This subtest measures the child's ability in such areas as spelling, capitalization, punctuation, sentence construction, and metacognitive knowledge.

Contextual Writing—The subtest measures the child's ability to construct a story when provided with a picture prompt. It measures such areas as story format, cohesion, thematic maturity, ideation, and story structure.

Scoring Information: Scores are presented in four ways:

♦ Standard scores

♦ NCEs (Normal Curve Equivalents)

♦ Age equivalents

♦ Percentiles

STRENGTHS OF THE TEWL-2

♦ The test is one of several recent efforts to provide assessments for the developmental skills and academic abilities of young children.

TEST OF EARLY WRITTEN LANGUAGE—2 (TEWL-2)

(continued)

- The test is useful in assessing and planning educational activities.
- The test is useful for evaluating educational programs designed to promote the writing skills of young children.

WEAKNESSES OF THE TEWL-2

- In reporting the results, the manual's scoring definition and scales look similar to those for IQ, which could lead to misinterpretation of results.
- Additional validity is needed on the test, especially for younger age groups.

TEST OF WRITTEN LANGUAGE—2 (TOWL-2)

GENERAL TEST INFORMATION

Authors:	Donald D. Hammill and Stephen C. Larsen
Publisher:	PRO-ED, Inc.
Address of Publisher:	8700 Shoal Creek Blvd. Austin, TX 78758-6897
Phone Number of Publisher:	512-451-3246 or 800-897-3202
Fax of Publisher:	800-FXPROED

Purpose of Test: The test is intended to identify students with written language disabilities.

Description of Test: This revision of the original TOWL includes two alternate form test booklets A and B, and is organized into three composites: Overall Written Language, Contrived Writing, and Spontaneous Writing. This ten-subtest assessment measure requires the student to write a story about a given theme.

Type of Test:	Standardized, norm-referenced
Administration Time:	40–60 minutes
Type of Administration:	Group or individual
Who Administers This Test:	Special education teacher, classroom teacher
Age/Grade Levels:	Grades 2 to 12

Subtest Information: The TOWL-2 contains 10 subtests. The skills measured by each subtest are as follows:

1. *Vocabulary*—This subtest measures the student's knowledge of word meanings and classes through the writing of meaningful sentences.
2. *Spelling*—This subtest measures the ability to spell dictated words.
3. *Style*—This subtest measures the student's ability to punctuate sentences and capitalize properly.
4. *Logical Sentences*—This subtest measures the student's ability to recognize and correct through rewriting illogicalities existing in stimulus sentences.
5. *Sentence Combining*—This subtest measures the student's ability to incorporate the meaning of several sentences into a comprehensive single sentence containing phrases and clauses.
6. *Thematic Maturity*—This subtest measures the student's ability to write in a logical organized fashion to generate a specific theme, to develop a character's personality, and to incorporate other compositional skills.
7. *Contextual Vocabulary*—This subtest measures the student's ability to use complex sentences that include introductory and concluding clauses.
8. *Syntatic Maturity*—This subtest measures the student's ability to use complex sentences that include introductory and concluding clauses, as well as embedded phrases.
9. *Contextual Spelling*—This subtest measures the student's ability to spell words properly when they appear in a self-generated composition.
10. *Contextual Style*—This subtest measures the student's ability to apply the rules governing punctuation of sentences and capitalization of words when they appear in a written composition.

TEST OF WRITTEN LANGUAGE—2 (TOWL-2)

(continued)

Scoring Information: The examiner may wish to obtain the computer scoring system for the TOWL-2. This system analyzes raw scores and compares information from other tests administered to the student to determine if discrepancies exist. The scores are presented in the following manners:

- ◆ Percentile ranks
- ◆ Standard scores

STRENGTHS OF THE TOWL-2

- ◆ Useful test because it includes methods for evaluating several important components of written language.
- ◆ It incorporates one of the most useful and valuable informal strategies for studying composition—the writing sample.
- ◆ Results are very useful for determing further assessment.

WEAKNESSES OF THE TOWL-2

- ◆ Both reading and writing skills are required; students cannot be given reading assistance.
- ◆ Scoring is time consuming.
- ◆ The tester must be thoroughly familiar with the scoring standards for evaluating both the writing sample and the subtest responses.

TEST OF WRITTEN LANGUAGE—3 (TOWL-3)

GENERAL TEST INFORMATION

Authors:	Donald D. Hammill and Stephen C. Larsen
Publisher:	PRO-ED, Inc.
Address of Publisher:	8700 Shoal Creek Blvd. Austin, TX 78758-6897
Phone Number of Publisher:	512-451-3246 or 800-897-3202
Fax of Publisher:	(800)-FXPROED

Purpose of Test: The test is designed to identify students with written language disabilities.

Description of Test: This test is organized into three composites: Overall Written Language, Contrived Writing, and Spontaneous Writing.

Type of Test:	Standardized, norm-referenced
Administration Time:	Untimed
Type of Administration:	Group or individual
Who Administers This Test:	Special education teacher, classroom teacher
Age/Grade Levels:	Grades 2 to 12

Subtest Information: The TOWL-3 contains 8 subtests. The skills measured by each subtest are as follows:

- *Vocabulary*—This subtest measures the student's knowledge of word meanings and classes through the writing of meaningful sentences.
- *Spelling*—This subtest measures the student's ability to spell dictated words.
- *Style*—This subtest measures the student's ability to punctuate sentences and capitalize properly.
- *Logical Sentences*—This subtest measures the student's ability to recognize and correct through rewriting illogicalities existing in stimulus sentences.
- *Sentence Combining*—This subtest measures the student's ability to incorporate the meaning of several sentences into a comprehensive single sentence containing phrases and clauses.
- *Contextual Conventions*—This subtest measures the student's skills in capitalization, punctuation, and spelling.
- *Contextual Language*—This subtest measures the student's vocabulary, syntax, and grammar.
- *Story Construction*—This subtest measures the student's plot, character development, and general composition.

Scoring Information: The examiner may wish to obtain the computer scoring system for the TOWL-3. This sytem analyzes raw scores and compares information from other tests administered to the student to determine if discrepancies exist. Grade equivalents are also provided.

STRENGTHS OF THE TOWL-3

- Easy items have been added to make the test friendly to poor writers.
- Results are shown to be unbiased relative to gender and race.
- All apects of reliability and validity have been strengthened.

WEAKNESSES OF THE TOWL-3

- Both reading and writing skills are required; students cannot be given reading assistance.

WRITTEN LANGUAGE ASSESSMENT (WLA)

GENERAL TEST INFORMATION

Authors:	J. Jeffrey Grill and Margaret M. Kirwin
Publisher:	Academic Therapy Publications
Address of Publisher:	20 Commercial Blvd. Novato, CA 94949-6191
Phone Number of Publisher:	415-883-3314 or 800-422-7249
Fax of Publisher:	415-883-3720

Purpose of Test: The test is designed to assess written language.

Description of Test: Essay type test offering direct assessment of written language through an evaluation of writing samples that reflect three modes of discourse: Expressive, Instructive, and Creative writing.

Type of Test:	Norm-referenced
Administration Time:	One hour
Type of Administration:	Group
Who Administers This Test:	Special education teacher, classroom teacher
Age/Grade Levels:	Ages 8–18 and older

Subtest Information: None

Scoring Information: Analytic scoring techniques are used to yield scores in General Writing Ability, Productivity, Word Complexity, Readability as well as deriving a Written Language Quotient that is a composite of the four subscores.

STRENGTHS OF THE WLA

- ♦ Can be administered and scored by classroom teachers as well as other educational personnel.
- ♦ Presents real writing tasks in a natural setting.
- ♦ Three types of writing samples cover a wide range of writing skills.

WEAKNESSES OF THE WLA

- ♦ Although weaknesses may exist, a review of the literature found no weaknesses reported.

ARITHMETIC/MATHEMATICS ASSESSMENT

INTERPRETING ARITHMETIC/MATHEMATICS TESTS

Mathematical thinking is a process that begins early in most children. Even before formal education begins, children are exposed to various situations that involve the application of mathematical concepts. As they enter formal schooling, they take the knowledge of what they had previously learned and begin to apply it in a more precise manner.

It is necessary to understand that mathematics and arithmetic are actually two different terms. Although most people use them interchangeably, they have distinct meanings. Mathematics refers to the study of numbers and their relationships to time, space, volume, and geometry, while arithmetic refers to the operations or computations performed.

Mathematics involves many different skills. These include the ability to:

◆ solve problems

◆ recognize how to interpret results

◆ apply mathematics in practical situations

◆ use mathematics for prediction

◆ estimate

◆ understand and perform computations

◆ understand measurement

◆ create and read graphs and charts

All schools, whether regular education or special education, use some form of mathematical assessment. Schools begin the process of learning math skills in kindergarten and proceed throughout the child's formal education. At the college level, mathematics is often a core requirement in many liberal arts schools. In general, next to reading, mathematics is probably the area most frequently assessed in school systems.

Mathematics can be assessed at the individual or group level. Consequently, it is a skill that is stressed and measured by various tests in schools. Mathematics tests often cover a great deal of area. However, according to Ysseldyke and Sylvia (1995), there are three types of classifications involved in diagnostic math tests. Each classification measures certain mathematical abilities.

• *Content*—This consists of Numeration, Fractions, Geometry, and Algebra.

• *Operations*—This consists of Counting, Computation, and Reasoning.

• *Applications*—This consists of Measurement, Reading Graphs and Tables, Money and Budgeting Time, and Problem Solving.

Furthermore, according to the National Council of Supervisors of Mathematics (1978), basic mathematical skills include:

1. Arithmetic computation

2. Problem solving

3. Applying mathematics in everyday situations

4. Alertness to the reasonableness of results

5. Estimation and approximation

6. Geometry

7. Measurement

8. Reading charts and graphs

9. Using mathematics to predict

10. Computer literacy

There are fewer diagnostic math tests than diagnostic reading tests. However, math assessment is more clear-cut. Most diagnostic math tests generally sample similar behaviors.

According to McLoughlin and Lewis (1990), "Mathematics is one of the school subjects best suited for error analysis because students respond in writing on most tasks, thereby producing a permanent record of their work." Also, there is usually one correct answer to mathematics questions and problems, and scoring is unambiguous. Today, the most common use of error analysis in mathematics is assessment of computation skills. Cox (1975, p. 354) differentiates between systematic computation errors and errors that are random or careless mistakes. With systematic errors, students are consistent in their use of an incorrect number fact, operation, or algorithm.

According to Roberts (1968, cited in McLoughlin and Lewis, 1990), there are four identified error types in computational analysis:

- **Incorrect operation**—The student selects the incorrect operation, for example, if the problem requires subtraction, the student performs addition.

- **Incorrect number fact**—The number fact recalled by the student is inaccurate. For example, the student recalls the product of 9×6 as 52.

- **Incorrect algorithm**—The procedures used by the student to solve the problem are inappropriate. The student may skip a step, apply the correct steps in the wrong sequence, or use an inaccurate method.

- **Random error**—The student's response is incorrect and apparently random. For example, the student writes 100 as the answer to 42×6.

Another type of error that the student may encounter is a "slip." When a slip occurs, it is more likely due to a simple mistake rather than a pattern of problems. For example, if a child subtracts $20 - 5$ in eight problems correctly, but for some reason not in the ninth problem, his or her error is probably due to a simple slip rather than a serious operational or processing problem. An error on one problem is not an error pattern. Error patterns can be assessed by analyzing all correct and incorrect answers. When designing a program plan for a particular child in mathematics, it is critical to establish not only what the nature of the problems are, but also the patterns of problems that occur in the child's responses.

Handwriting can play an important role in mathematics. Scoring a math test often involves reading numbers written down on an answer sheet by the student. If a student's handwriting is difficult to interpret or impossible to read, this can create serious problems for the evaluator with respect to obtaining valid scores. When a student's handwriting is not clear on a math test, it is important that the evaluator ask the student to help him or her read the answers. By doing so, the evaluator is analyzing the math skills which need to be assessed rather than spending his or her time trying to decode the student's responses.

According to Mann et al. (1979), problems in arithmetic can be due to visual disorders:

- **Visual discrimination**—The student may not be able to discriminate differences or similarities in size and shape.

- **Visual closure**—The student may not be able to understand sets or groupings.

- **Spatial problems**—The student may not be able to judge with accuracy spatial relationships that deal with distance and quantity.

- **Temporal problems**—The student may have difficulty in learning and telling time.

- **Memory sequence**—The student may exhibit reversals and write E for 3 or a 6 for a 9.

- **Visual motor**—The student may not be able to write numerals.

- **Laterality**—The student may have difficulty relating himself or herself to an object in space, and appear awkward and clumsy in attempts to perform a physical task.

Arithmetic problems may also be due to an auditory disorder (ibid, 262). Two examples of this situation are:

- **Memory sequence and visual scanning**—The student may have difficulty with looking at a series of numerals while counting aloud.

- **Auditory-visual association problems**—The student may not be able to associate a numeral with its auditory referent.

KEY MATH DIAGNOSTIC ARITHMETIC TESTS—REVISED (KEY MATH-R)

GENERAL TEST INFORMATION

Authors:	Austin J. Connolly, William Nachtman, and E. Milo Pritchett
Publisher:	American Guidance Service
Address of Publisher:	4201 Woodland Rd. Circle Pines, MN 55014-1796
Phone Number of Publisher:	612-786-4343 or 800-328-2560
Fax of Publisher:	612-786-9077

Purpose of Test: The Key Math-R is a diagnostic test that assesses mathematical concepts and skills.

Description of Test: The Key Math-R is a point-to and paper-and-pencil test measuring math skills in 14 areas. Two forms of the test are available: Forms A and B. Each form contains 258 items. The materials include a test manual, two easel kits for presentation of test items, and individual record forms for recording responses.

Type of Test:	Norm-referenced, domain-referenced
Administration Time:	Approximately 30–45 minutes
Type of Administation:	Individual
Who Administers This Test:	Special education teacher, classroom teacher
Age/Grade Levels:	Preschool to grade 6

Subtests: The test is broken down into three major areas consisting of 14 subtests:

Basic Concepts—This part investigates basic mathematical concepts and knowledge:

- *Numeration*
- *Rational numbers*
- *Geometry*

Operations—This part consists of basic computation processes:

- *Addition*
- *Subtraction*
- *Multiplication*
- *Division*
- *Mental computation*

Applications—This part focuses on the functional applications use of mathematics necessary to daily life:

- *Measurement*
- *Time*
- *Money*
- *Estimation*
- *Interpretation of data*
- *Problem solving*

KEY MATH DIAGNOSTIC ARITHMETIC TESTS—REVISED (KEY MATH-R)
(continued)

Scoring Information: Scoring involves using percentiles and standard scores. Each subtest has a mean of 10 with a standard deviation of 3, and a standard score with a mean of 100 and a standard deviation of 15 for total test performance. Scores are presented in the following manners:

- Stanines
- Percentiles
- Age equivalents
- Grade equivalents

STRENGTHS OF THE KEY MATH-R

- The test manual guides teachers as to appropriate remediation procedures for students who have mathematics deficiencies.
- The test has a broad range of item content.
- The test has a diversity of item content.
- The test is useful with exceptional children because of the range of norms provided and skills tested.

WEAKNESSES OF THE KEY MATH-R

- Further information is needed about the test's concurrent validity.
- Scoring of the test can be particularly time consuming.
- The test may take a long time to administer and as a result may have to be accomplished in multiple sessions for some students.

TEST OF EARLY MATHEMATICS ABILITY—2 (TEMA-2)

GENERAL TEST INFORMATION

Authors:	Herbert P. Ginsberg & Arthur J. Baroody
Publisher:	PRO-ED, Inc.
Address of Publisher:	8700 Shoal Creek Blvd. Austin, TX 78758-6897
Phone Number of Publisher:	512-451-3246 or 800-897-3202
Fax of Publisher:	800-FXPROED

Purpose of Test: This test is intended to measure the mathematics performance of children. The test's intention is five-fold (Ginsberg, 1990):

1. To identify those children who are significantly behind or ahead of their peers in the development of mathematical thinking.
2. To identify specific strengths and weaknesses in children's mathematical thinking.
3. To allow teachers to design instructional practices appropriate to the needs of individual children.
4. To help teachers document children's progress in learning arithmetic.
5. To serve as a measuring device in research projects.

Description of Test: The TEMA-2 is designed to reflect the mathematical thinking that begins prior to school experiences. The test's informal components include concepts of relative magnitude, counting skills, and calculation skills.

Type of Test:	Criterion-referenced
Administration Time:	With a few exceptions, the TEMA-2 is not a timed test; therefore, no precise time limits are imposed on the children being tested.
Type of Administration:	Individual
Who Administers This Test:	Special education teacher, classroom teacher
Age/Grade Levels:	Ages 3–9

Subtest Information: The test is administered either as a 50-item oral reponse or as a paper-pencil test assessing mathematical abilities in the following domains:

- *Informal Mathematics*—This test domain measures a student's knowledge of concepts of relative magnitude, counting, and calculation
- *Formal Mathematics*—This test domain measures a student's knowledge of conventional facts, calculation, and base-10 concepts.

Scoring Information: The TEMA-2 yields three types of scores:

- Raw score
- Percentiles
- Composite quotient (Mean = 100, SD =15).

STRENGTHS OF THE TEMA-2

- The new manual, *Assessment Probes and Instructional Activities*, can be of great benefit to elementary teachers who want further insight into how their students think mathematically.

WEAKNESSES OF THE TEMA-2

- Does not sufficiently identify the strengths of the student's mathematical thinking.
- Does not sufficiently identify the weaknesses of the student's mathematical thinking.

TEST OF MATHEMATICAL ABILITIES—2 (TOMA-2)

GENERAL TEST INFORMATION

Authors:	Virginia L. Brown, Mary E. Cronin, and Elizabeth McEntire
Publisher:	PRO-ED, Inc.
Address of Publisher:	8700 Shoal Creek Blvd. Austin, TX 78758-6897
Phone Number of Publisher:	512-451-3246 or 800-897-3202
Fax of Publisher:	800-FXPROED

Purpose of Test: The test measures a child's attitudes towards mathematics, and identifies that child's strengths and weaknesses in mathematics skill development.

Description of Test: The test comprises five paper-pencil subtests that assess various areas of mathematical ability.

Type of Test:	Criterion-referenced
Administration Time:	Not timed
Type of Administration:	Individual or group
Who Administers This Test:	Special education teacher, classroom teacher
Age/Grade Levels:	Ages 8.0 to 18.11

Subtest Information: The test consists of four core subtests and one supplemental subtest:

- *Vocabulary*—In this subtest, students are presented with mathematical terms, which they are asked to define briefly as they are used in a mathematical sense.

- *Computation*—In this subtest, students are presented with computational problems consisting of basic operations and involving manipulation of fractions, decimals, money, percentages, etc.

- *General Information*—In this subtest, the student is read questions by the examiner involving basic general knowledge and must reply orally. This subtest is usually administered individually.

- *Story Problems*—In this subtest, the student reads brief story problems that contain extraneous information and must extract the pertinent information required to solve the problem. Work space is provided for calculation.

- *Attitude Towards Math (supplemental)*—In the subtest, the child is presented with various statements about math attitudes and must respond with "agree," "disagree," or "don't know."

Scoring Information: The TOMA-2 yields the following:

- Math quotient with a mean of 100
- Age equivalents
- Percentile ranks
- Standard scores
- Grade equivalents

STRENGTHS OF THE TOMA-2

- The new manual can be of great benefit to elementary teachers who want further insight into how their students think mathematically.

TEST OF MATHEMATICAL ABILITIES—2 (TOMA-2)
(continued)

♦ The TOMA-2 can help educators answer the following questions:

Where should a student be placed in a curriculum?

What are the student's expressed attitudes towards mathematics?

Do the student's attitudes, vocabulary, and level of general math information differ markedly from those of a group of age peers?

WEAKNESSES OF THE TOMA-2

♦ Students need both reading and writing skills to complete the TOMA-2.

♦ Further information about the test's validity is necessary.

THE STEENBURGEN DIAGNOSTIC-PRESCRIPTIVE MATH PROGRAM AND QUICK MATH SCREENING TEST (STEENBURGEN)

GENERAL TEST INFORMATION

Author:	Fran Steenburgen Gelb
Publisher:	Academic Therapy Publications
Address of Publisher:	20 Commercial Blvd. Novato, CA 94949-6191
Phone Number of Publisher:	415-883-3314 or 800-422-7249
Fax of Publisher:	415-883-3720

Purpose of Test: This test is designed to assess a student's computational skills.

Description of Test: This math testing program assesses 55 computational skills and spans grades 1 through 6. It includes two types of tests: the Quick Math Screening Test and the Prescriptive Tests. The author suggests that the screening test, one item per skill, be used by a teacher to identify the skill deficiencies of a student. In addition, the author recommends that the screening test be used as a pretest and posttest for monitoring the amount that a student learns. The prescriptive tests, 10 items per skill, are intended as drill exercises for students after they receive instruction on the skills.

Type of Test:	Criterion-referenced
Administration Time:	10–20 minutes
Type of Administration:	Group
Who Administers This Test:	Special education teacher, classroom teacher
Age/Grade Levels:	Ages 6 through 11

Subtest Information: There are no formal subtests. However, tests are broken down into two levels:

- Level I—Grades 1–3
- Level II—Grades 4–6

Scoring Information: Tests are easy to score and the results can be plotted on a profile sheet that shows a graphic representation of a student's progress from pre- to posttest.

STRENGTHS OF THE STEENBURGEN

- The worksheets are printed attractively and the author has granted permission to duplicate these skill tests on an as-needed basis.
- The test can be used as a quick screening measure of specific math skills.

WEAKNESSES OF THE STEENBURGEN

- The omissions created in this program by its use of single items to assess mastery of a skill has led to serious criticisms.
- This test neither allows for assessment by degree of difficulty within a skill nor for assessment of specific error patterns, which the prescriptive portion of the test claims to ameliorate,
- There is no supporting evidence that guarantees that students may be assessed for varying degrees of mastery within a skill by teachers' implementation of the Steenburgen Diagnostic-Prescriptive Math Program.

ENRIGHT DIAGNOSTIC INVENTORY OF BASIC ARITHMETIC SKILLS (ENRIGHT)

GENERAL TEST INFORMATION

Author:	Brian E. Enright
Publisher:	Curriculum Associates, Inc.
Address of Publisher:	5 Esquire Road, No. Billerica, MA 01862-2589
Phone Number of Publisher:	800-225-0248
Fax of Publisher:	800-366-1158

Purpose of Test: The test is designed to assess basic mathematical computational skills.

Description of Test: The test assesses 144 basic computational skills to provide a sequential assessment of computational skills and an analysis of errors.

Type of Test:	Criterion-referenced
Administration Time:	15–30 minutes
Type of Administration:	Individual or group
Who Administers This Test:	Special education teacher, classroom teacher
Age/Grade Levels:	Grades 1 to 6

Subtest Information: The test has no formal subtests but is a comprehensive measure of a child's math computational skills. The 144 computational skills are assessed through the use of several tests including:

1. *Range Placement Test*—This screening test measures a student's computational skills in addition, subtraction, multiplication, and division of whole numbers as well as fractions and decimals. The purpose of this test is to determine a starting point for assessing a wide range of basic computational skills.

2. *Skill Placement Test*—The results of the Range Placement Test determine which specific skill test the student will be given. This test determines the student's competency within a specific sequence of skills.

3. *Skill Test*—The examiner then determines which skill test will be administered by the student's first error and an analysis is made of the student's error patterns. This information helps the teacher determine the error pattern style the student is using to derive answers. This information can then be used to develop a remedial program.

Scoring Information: The test provides objective standardization scores. It also provides the evaluator with the grade level at which basic math computation skills are commonly taught, an overall assessment of the student's computational skills, and an analysis of error patterns which are useful in planning and development of remedial instruction.

STRENGTHS OF THE ENRIGHT

- The test provides a sequential assessment of a student's computational skills.
- The test is very useful for classroom teachers and diagnosticians.
- The test results are useful in planning remedial instruction.
- The test record booklet format allows for the longitudinal study of a child's math development over the years.

WEAKNESSES OF THE ENRIGHT

- The test does not assess overall mathematical skills, only computation.
- The test may be cumbersome to administer.

Comprehensive Achievement Assessment

Some achievement tests are considered comprehensive because they focus on several skill areas at one time. Unlike a single focus test (e.g., Gray Oral Reading, Key Math, Denver Handwriting Analysis, etc.) these comprehensive measures offer the examiner a thorough evaluation of a student's overall achievement ability. Having a variety of academic skills in one test rather than several different measures may not only save money, but in many cases can provide a total test score which reflects a student's overall academic achievement. This score, like a full scale IQ, can be used for purposes of ability/achievement discrepancy comparisons. These tests also provide scores for a variety of skills normed on the same population which helps in generalizing results. Using several different tests which are all standardized on different populations may make comparisons between skill areas difficult and not as reliable.

BRIGANCE DIAGNOSTIC INVENTORY OF BASIC SKILLS

GENERAL TEST INFORMATION

Author: Albert Brigance

Publisher: Curriculum Associates, Inc.

Address of Publisher: 5 Esquire Road, No.
                                 Billerica, MA 01862-2589

Phone Number of Publisher: 800-225-0248

Fax of Publisher: 800-366-1158

Purpose of Test: The test is designed to measure academic readiness and reading, language arts, and math skills.

Description of Test: The test is presented in a plastic ring binder that is designed to be laid open and placed between the examiner and the student. A separate student booklet provided for the students' answers is designed so that the skills range from easy to difficult; thus, the teacher can quickly ascertain the skills level the student has achieved.

Type of Test: Criterion-referenced

Administration Time: Specific time limits are listed on many tests; others are untimed.

Type of Administration: Individual or group

Who Administers This Test: Special education teacher, Classroom teacher, Psychologist

Age/Grade Levels: Grades K through 6. It is also used for academic assessment of older students functioning below sixth-grade academic levels.

Subtest Information: There are four subtest areas including 143 pencil-and-paper or oral response tests:

- *Readiness*—The skills assessed include color naming; visual discrimination of shapes, letters, and short words; copying designs; drawing shapes from memory; drawing a person; gross motor coordination; recognition of body parts; following directional and verbal instructions; fine-motor self-help skills; verbal fluency; sound articulation; personal knowledge; memory for sentences; counting; alphabet recitation; number naming and comprehension; letter naming; and writing name, numbers, and letters.

- *Reading*—This test evaluates word recognition, oral reading and comprehension, oral reading rate, word analysis (auditorily and while reading), meaning of prefixes, syllabication, and vocabulary.

- *Language Arts*—This test assesses cursive handwriting, grammar and mechanics, spelling, and reference skills.

- *Mathematics*—This test assesses rote counting, writing numerals in sequence, reading number words, ordinal concepts, numeral recognition, writing to dictation, counting in sets, Roman numerals, fractions, decimals, measurement (money, time, calendar, linear/liquid/weight measurement, temperature), and two- and three-dimensional geometric concepts.

Scoring Information: The scores are presented in the following manners:

- Grade equivalents
- Age equivalents

BRIGANCE DIAGNOSTIC INVENTORY OF BASIC SKILLS

(continued)

STRENGTHS OF THE BRIGANCE

- It helps determine what a student has or has not learned.
- It contains suggestions for specific instructional objectives.
- It can help with referral decisions.
- This test is considered to be one of the most comprehensive elementary grade-level, criterion-referenced instruments.
- The Brigance is also viewed as being well suited to determining mastery of very specific teaching objectives.
- The test manual states that results of the Brigance should be considered in conjunction with evaluation of the student's classroom performance, classroom observation, and scrutiny of actual curricular goals.

WEAKNESSES OF THE BRIGANCE

- Guidelines on where to begin testing are imprecise.
- No data is offered on reliability.
- There is no description of norms for 10 of the subtests.
- There are no suggested standards of mastery for 65% of the tests.
- Not appropriate for making decisions that compare children against one another, or for class or reading group placement.
- This test has no norm to validate the sequence, difficulty level, or percent correct criteria for items within tests. Hence, the Brigance inventory is stated to be faulty in determining a student's grade level performance on the tested skill.

KAUFMAN TEST OF EDUCATIONAL ACHIEVEMENT (KTEA)

GENERAL TEST INFORMATION

Authors:	Alan S. Kaufman & Nadeen L. Kaufman
Publisher:	American Guidance Service
Address of Publisher:	4201 Woodland Rd. Circle Pines, MN 55014-1796
Phone Number of Publisher:	612-786-4343 or 800-328-2560
Fax of Publisher:	612-786-9077

Purpose of Test: The test is intended to screen students on global achievement skills to determine the need for follow-up testing and evaluation.

Description of Test: The test includes a brief achievement battery, two parallel forms of an educational achievement battery, and a design that facilitates diagnostic interpretation in addition to standard score data.

Type of Test:	Norm-referenced, standardized
Administration Time:	60–75 minutes
Type of Administration:	Individual
Who Administers This Test:	Special education teacher, Classroom teacher, Psychologist
Age/Grade Levels:	Grades 1–12

Subtest Information: The test contains five subtests:

1. *Reading decoding*—This subtest presents words visually for the student to read aloud to the examiner.

2. *Mathematics applications*—This subtest presents story-type problems printed on easel pages. The student can use a pencil and paper to figure out his or her answer but must answer orally.

3. *Spelling*—This subtest is presented as a typical spelling test.

4. *Reading comprehension*—This subtest presents sentences and passages for the student to read silently and respond to orally.

5. Mathematics computation-This subtest includes 60 math problems presented in the student's answer booklet.

Scoring Information: Scores are presented in the following manners:

- Percentiles
- Standard scores
- Age equivalents
- Grade equivalents

STRENGTHS OF THE KTEA

- The KTEA appears to be a well standardized, reliable measure with some innovative features that could make it the measure of choice for analyzing academic strengths and weaknesses.
- The KTEA provides valid scores for the basic achievement areas covered in school.

WEAKNESSES OF THE KTEA

- Final assessment of the validity of the measure must await a more complete study by independent investigators.
- The test lacks a breakdown of scores for the ethnic groups included in the standardization sample.

PEABODY INDIVIDUAL ACHIEVEMENT TEST—REVISED (PIAT-R)

GENERAL TEST INFORMATION

Author:	Frederick C. Markwardt, Jr.
Publisher:	American Guidance Service
Address of Publisher:	4201 Woodland Rd. Circle Pines, MN 55014-1796
Phone Number of Publisher:	612-786-4343 or 800-328-2560
Fax of Publisher:	612-786-9077

Purpose of Test: The test is designed to measure academic achievement.

Description of Test: The PIAT-R is used in special education for identifying academic deficiencies. It is made up of six subtests. The most typical response format on the PIAT-R is multiple choice. The student is shown a test plate with four possible answers and asked to select the correct response.

Type of Test:	Norm-referenced, standardized
Administration Time:	50–70 minutes
Type of Administration:	Individual
Who Administers This Test:	Special education teacher, Classroom teacher, Psychologist
Age/Grade Levels:	Level 1 grades K–1, Level 2 grades 2–12

Subtest Information: The following lists and describes the test's six subtests:

1. *General information*—This subtest has 100 questions that are open-ended and presented orally. They measure the student's factual knowledge related to science, social studies, humanities, fine art, and recreation.

2. *Reading Recognition*—There are 100 items. Items 1–16 are multiple choice and measure prereading skills. Items 17–100 measure decoding skills and require the student to read orally words that are individually presented.

3. *Reading Comprehension*—This subtest consists of 82 items and measures the student's ability to draw meaning from printed sentences.

4. *Spelling*—Items 1–15 are multiple choice tasks that assess reading skills. Items 16–100 require the student to select from four possible choices the correct spelling of a word read orally by the examiner.

5. *Written Expression*—This subtest has 2 levels. Level 1 consists of 19 copying and dictation items that are arranged in order of ascending difficulty. In level 2 the child is presented with one or two picture plates and given 20 minutes to write a story about the picture.

6. *Mathematics*—In this subtest the student is asked the question orally and must select the correct response from four choices. Questions cover topics ranging from numerical recognition to trigonometry.

Scoring Information: A variety of scores are available, including:

♦ Grade equivalents

♦ Age equivalents

♦ Standard scores

♦ Percentile ranks

PEABODY INDIVIDUAL ACHIEVEMENT TEST—REVISED (PIAT-R)

(continued)

STRENGTHS OF THE PIAT-R

♦ The revision is broader in scope and contains more items than the original test.

♦ The test manual presents evidence to support content, concurrent, and construct validity.

♦ The test is useful for the assessment of school performance across a range of academic subjects.

WEAKNESSES OF THE PIAT-R

♦ The test does not produce results specific enough to provide direction for instructional planning.

♦ The test assesses some skills with tasks that are dissimilar to typical classroom activities.

WECHSLER INDIVIDUAL ACHIEVEMENT TEST (WIAT)

GENERAL TEST INFORMATION

Author:	The Psychological Corporation
Publisher:	The Psychological Corporation
Address of Publisher:	555 Academic Court San Antonio, TX 78204-2498
Phone Number of Publisher:	800-211-8378
Fax of Publisher:	800-232-1223
TDD of the Publisher:	800-723-1318

Purpose of Test: This test is designed to assess the educational achievement of children and adolescents.

Description of Test: The WIAT is made up of eight subtests. The test format includes easels and paper-and-pencil tasks.

Type of Test:	Norm-referenced
Administration Time:	30–75 minutes
Type of Administration:	Individual
Who Administers This Test:	Special education teacher, Classroom teacher, Psychologist
Age/Grade Levels:	Ages 5 to 19

Subtest Information: The test consists of eight individually administered subtests:

1. *Basic Reading*—This subtest measures decoding and sight-reading ability.
2. *Mathematics Reasoning*—This subtest encompasses major curriculum objectives in problem solving, geometry, measurement, and statistics.
3. *Spelling*—This subtest assesses the student's encoding and spelling ability.
4. *Reading Comprehension*—This subtest taps skills that include comprehension of detail, sequence, cause-and-effect relationships, and inference.
5. *Numerical Operations*—This subtest tests the student's ability to write dictated numerals; to solve basic addition, subtraction, multiplication, and division problems; to solve problems with whole numbers, fractions, and decimals; and to solve algebraic equations.
6. *Listening Comprehension*—This subtest measures the student's levels of comprehension, ranging from understanding of details to making inferential conclusions.
7. *Oral Expression*—This subtest assesses the student's ability to name targeted words, describe scenes, give directions, and explain steps in sequential tasks.
8. *Written Expression*—This subtest consists of a free writing task. It affords the assessment of idea development and organization as well as capitalization and punctuation.

Scoring Information: The test provides the following:

- Age and grade-based standard score information
- Age and grade-based composite score information
- Percentile Ranks
- Stanines
- Age and grade equivalents
- Hand or computer scoring materials

WECHSLER INDIVIDUAL ACHIEVEMENT TEST (WIAT)
(continued)

STRENGTHS OF THE WIAT

- The WIAT is the only achievement battery standardized with the Wechsler Intelligence Scale for Children-Third Edition (WISC-III).

- The test meets regulatory requirements for assessing or reevaluating children and adolescents.

- The manual includes the scope and sequence of objectives and how they relate to curricula.

- The test manual provides guidelines for creating curriculm-related IEPs.

WEAKNESSES OF WIAT

- Cultural bias may be present on some subtests.

- The test provides limited assessment of kindergarten and first grade students because it covers such a wide range. Therefore, as with any achievement test, the scores are more valid in the middle of the age range than at the extremes.

- The three subtests involved in Oral Expression measure very different skills. As a result, the total oral expression score may not be as useful with certain students.

WIDE RANGE ACHIEVEMENT TEST—3 (WRAT-3)

GENERAL TEST INFORMATION

Author:	Gary S. Wilkinson
Publisher:	Jastak Associates/Wide Range Inc.
Address of Publisher:	Jastak Associates/Wide Range Inc. P.O. Box 3410 Wilmington, DE 19804-0250
Phone Number of Publisher:	800-221-9728
Fax of Publisher:	302-652-1644

Purpose of Test: The WRAT-3 is a screening instrument for the identification of students' possible strengths and weaknesses in specific academic areas.

Description of Test: This new edition of the Wide Range Achievement Test has returned to a single-level format. The test contains a Blue and a Tan form that can be used in a pretest/posttest format, test-retest format, or administered together in a combined test format.

Type of Test:	Norm-referenced
Administration Time:	Each form of the WRAT-3 takes aproximately 15–30 minutes to administer. However, age, ability, and behavioral style of the student will vary the length of the test administration.
Type of Administration:	Primarily individual although certain portions of the test can be administered to small groups (Spelling and Math)
Who Administers This Test:	Special education teacher, Classroom teacher, Psychologist
Age/Grade levels:	Ages 5–75

Subtest Information: The three subtests contained on both the BLUE and TAN forms are:

1. *Reading*—This subtest involves decoding where the child is asked to recognize and rename letters and pronounce words in isolation.

2. *Spelling*—This subtest of written spelling asks the child to write his/her name, letters, and words from dictation.

3. *Arithmetic*—This is a subtest of mathematical computation where the child is asked to count, read numbers, identify number symbols, solve oral problems, and perform written computation within a defined time limit.

Scoring Information: The WRAT-3 offers several types of scores for each subtest but no total test or summary score. The results from the WRAT-3 are provided in the following ways:

- Standard scores
- Grade scores
- Percentiles

STRENGTHS OF THE WRAT-3

- This test makes for a very useful screening instrument because of the short administration time and specific areas measured.
- The test is quick and reliable.
- The test is reasonably valid in measuring achievement in its subtest areas.
- The written spelling subtest is an excellent test and one of the few available in this area.

WIDE RANGE ACHIEVEMENT TEST—3 (WRAT-3)
(continued)

WEAKNESSES OF THE WRAT-3

- ♦ This test is often referred to as tedious.

- ♦ The test only provides a few items at each level which can make interpreting diagnostic patterns of strengths and weaknesses less reliable.

- ♦ The reading subtest measures word recognition only, so additional achievement testing is often needed to test other reading skills like comprehension.

- ♦ The mathematics subtest measures computational math only, so additional testing is often needed to test other mathematics skills like applications and word problems.

TEST OF ACADEMIC ACHIEVEMENT SKILLS—READING, ARITHMETIC, SPELLING, AND LISTENING COMPREHENSION (TAAS-RASLC)

GENERAL TEST INFORMATION

Author:	Morison F. Gardner, EdD
Publisher:	Psychological and Educational Publications
Address of Publisher:	PO Box 520 Hydesville, CA 95547-0520
Phone Number of Publisher:	800-523-5775
Fax of Publisher:	800-447-0907

Purpose of Test: This test measures a child's reading, arithmetic, and spelling skills.

Description of Test: The TAAS-RASLC is an excellent tool for diagnosing learning disabilities when used in combination with other standardized tests.

Type of Test:	Norm-referenced
Administration Time:	15–25 minutes; scoring time is approximately 15 minutes
Type of Administration:	Individual
Who Administers This Test:	Special education teacher, Classroom teacher, Psychologist
Age/Grade Levels:	Ages 4–12

Subtest Information: The test contains four subtests:

- *Reading*—The child is required to identify upper and lower case letters and individual words.

- *Listening Comprehension*—The child is required to comprehend story content from listening to words, sentences, and paragraphs.

- *Arithmetic*—The child is required to identify numbers, determine numbers before and after (sequence), compute word problems, and compute various problems presented visually.

- *Spelling*—From auditory cues, the child is required to write letters of the alphabet and words.

Scoring Information: Scores are presented in the following manner:

- Age equivalents
- Percentiles
- Standard scores
- Stanines

STRENGTHS OF THE TAAS-RASLC

- This test can furnish the examiner with results that could determine a child's readiness for kindergarten.
- The test results can be used to determine necessary remediation in the academic areas measured by the test.
- The Listening Comprehension subtest can aid examiners in determining how a child will learn from verbal instructions, verbal directions, and from lectures.

WEAKNESSES OF THE TAAS-RASLC

- Although weaknesses may exist on the TAAS-RACSCC, a review of the literature found no weaknesses reported.

NORRIS EDUCATIONAL ACHIEVEMENT TEST (NEAT)

GENERAL TEST INFORMATION

Author:	Jane Switzer
Publisher:	Western Psychological Services
Address of Publisher:	12031 Wilshire Blvd. Los Angeles, CA 90025
Phone Number of Publisher:	310-478-2061 or 800-648-8857
Fax of Publisher:	310-478-7838

Purpose of Test: The test is designed to assess basic academic skills in reading, spelling, writing achievement, and math.

Description of Test: The NEAT is available in two parallel forms, A and B, each separately normed and validated. This makes the test especially useful for IEP reviews, progress assessments, and other evaluations that involve retesting.

Type of Test:	Norm-referenced
Administration Time:	30 minutes
Type of Administration:	Individual
Who Administers This Test:	Special education teacher, Classroom teacher, Psychologist
Age/Grade Levels:	Preschool to grade 12

Subtest Information: The NEAT is composed of six subtests:

- *Readiness*
- *Word Recognition*
- *Spelling*
- *Arithmetic*
- *Oral Reading and Comprehension*
- *Written Language*

Scoring Information: The test provides results in the following manner:

- Percentile ranks
- Standard scores
- Age equivalents
- Grade equivalents

STRENGTHS OF THE NEAT

- The test is easy to administer.
- The test offers a quick screening of basic academic skills.
- The test's tasks are familiar to students.

WEAKNESSES OF THE NEAT

- Due to the the newness of the test, further studies are necessary to assess its validity and reliability.

Section 6

PERCEPTUAL MEASURES

THE LEARNING PROCESS

The perceptual evaluation is theoretically based upon the concept of the *learning process.* When we evaluate a child's perceptual abilities, we are looking to see if there is a deficit in some area of the learning process that may be slowing down the processing of information, thereby interfering in the child's ability to receive, organize, memorize or express information. Severe deficits in the learning process can have adverse affects upon a child's ability to function in the classroom.

In order to understand how learning takes place, we must first understand the process by which information is received and the manner in which it is processed and expressed. In very simple terms, the learning process can be described in the following way:

- **Input of information**

- **Organization of information**

- **Expression of information**

Information is received in some manner and is filtered through a series of internal psychological processes. As information progresses along this "assembly line," it is given meaning and organized in some fashion and then expressed through a variety of responses.

Modalities or Channels

In order to understand how learning takes place, we must first understand the specific parts that make up the learning process. There are six *modalities* or *channels* (avenues through which information is received):

1. *Auditory Modality*—the delivery of information through sound

2. *Visual Modality*—the delivery of information through sight

3. *Tactile Modality*—the delivery of information through touch

4. *Kinesthetic Modality*—the delivery of information through movement

5. *Gustatory Modality*—the delivery of information through taste

6. *Olfactory Modality*—the delivery of information through smell

Process Areas

Information is delivered to the senses through one or several of the above channels. Once received, the information goes through a series of processes that attempt to give meaning to the material received. There are several processes that comprise the learning process:

- **Reception**—the initial receiving of information

- **Perception**—the initial organization of information

- **Association or Organization**—relating new information to other information and giving meaning to the information received

- **Memory**—the storage or retrieval process that facilitates the associational process to give meaning to information or help in relating new concepts to other information that might have already been learned. This process involves short-term, long-term, and sequential memory.

- **Expression**—the output of information through vocal, motoric, or written responses

In chart form, the learning process may look like this:

	RECEPTION (initial receiving of information)	PERCEPTION (initial organizing of information)	ASSOCIATION (relating new information to other information)	MEMORY (short-term, sequential, and long-term)	EXPRESSION (vocal, written, or motoric)
PROCESSES					
Modalities or Channels					
Auditory	Auditory Reception	Auditory Perception	Auditory Association	Auditory Memory	Auditory Vocal/Motoric
Visual	Visual Reception	Visual Perception	Visual Association	Visual Memory	Visual Vocal/Motoric
Tactile	Tactile Reception	Tactile Perception	Tactile Association	Tactile Memory	Tactile Vocal/Motoric
Kinesthetic	Kinesthetic Reception	Kinesthetic Perception	Kinesthetic Association	Kinesthetic Memory	Kinesthetic Vocal/Motoric
Gustatory	Gustatory Reception	Gustatory Perception	Gustatory Association	Gustatory Memory	Gustatory Vocal/Motoric
Olfactory	Olfactory Reception	Olfactory Perception	Olfactory Association	Olfactory Memory	Olfactory Vocal/Motoric

Skills are usually taught using all six modalities in nursery school to grade 1. By grade 2, most teachers teach through approximately four of the modalities with a greater emphasis on visual and auditory input. By the upper elementary grades, this can shift to skill development through the use of only two modalities, visual and auditory. This generally remains the souce of informational input in most classrooms until possibly college, where information is sometimes presented through only one modality, auditory (lectures only). Children should be taught using *multisensory approaches* (the input of information through a variety of receptive mechanisms, i.e., seeing, hearing, touching, etc.) whenever possible since retention of information is enhanced by increased sensory input.

OBJECTIVES OF PERCEPTUAL EVALUATION

Now that we have some understanding of how the learning process functions, we can explore the objectives of the perceptual evaluation. The objectives are as follows:

♦ To help determine the child's *stronger and weaker modality* for learning. Some children are visual learners, some are auditory, and some learn best through any form of input. However, if a child is a strong visual learner in a class where the teacher relies on auditory lectures, then it is possible that his or her ability to process information may be hampered. The evaluation may give us this information, which is very useful when making practical recommendations to teachers about how to best present information to assist the child's ability to learn.

♦ To help determine a child's *stronger and weaker process areas*. A child having problems in memory and expression will fall behind the rest of his or her class very quickly. The longer these processing difficulties continue, the greater the chance for secondary emotional problems to develop (emotional problems resulting from continued frustration with the ability to learn).

♦ To develop *a learning profile* that can help the classroom teacher understand the best way to present information to the child and therefore increase his or her chances of success.

♦ Along with other information and test results, to help determine if the child's learning process deficits are suitable for a regular class or so severe that he or she may require a more *restrictive educational setting* (an educational setting or situation best suited to the present needs of the student other than a full-time regular class placement, i.e., resource room, self-contained class, special school, etc.).

Whatever perceptual battery the special educator chooses, it should be one that covers enough skill areas to make an adequate diagnosis of process and modality strengths and weaknesses. Following you will find some of the areas that need to be measured in choosing a series of visual perception tests.

VISUAL PERCEPTION ASSESSMENT

Visual perception is considered to be one of the more important specific ability areas in early assessment because of the assumed relationship between visual perception deficits and reading performance. The following are assessment area skills most often associated with visual perception:

- **Visual coordination**—the ability to follow and track objects with coordinated eye movements

- **Visual discrimination**—the ability to differentiate visually the forms and symbols in one's environment

- **Visual association**—the ability to organize and associate visually presented material in a meaningful way

- **Visual long-term memory**—the ability to retain and recall general and specific long-term visual information

- **Visual short-term memory**—the ability to retain and recall general and specific short-term visual information

- **Visual sequential memory**—the ability to recall in correct sequence and detail prior visual information

- **Visual vocal expression**—the ability to reproduce vocally prior visually presented material or experiences

- **Visual motoric expression** (visual motor integration)—the ability to reproduce motorically prior visually presented material or experiences

- **Visual figure ground discrimination**—the ability to differentiate relevant stimuli (the figure) from irrelevant stimuli (the background)

- **Visual spatial relationships**—the ability to perceive the relative positions of objects in space

- **Visual form perception** (visual constancy)—the ability to discern the size, shape, and position of visual stimuli

DIAGNOSTIC SYMPTOMS FOR VISUAL PERCEPTUAL DISABILITIES

There are many symptoms that may indicate problems in a certain perceptual area. Some of these are observable, while others are discovered through intakes and testing. What follows is a list of symptoms that may reflect perceptual disabilities in a variety of visual areas.

Visual-Motor Channel Disability

- Exhibits poor motor coordination.

- Is awkward motorically—frequent tripping, stumbling, bumps into things, has trouble skipping, jumping.

- Demonstrates restlessness, short attention span, perseveration.

- Exhibits poor handwriting, artwork, drawing.
- Exhibits reversals of b,d,p,q,u,n when writing beyond a chronological age of 7 or 8 years.
- Inverts numbers (17 for 71); reverses as well.
- Gives correct answers when teacher reads test, but can't put answers down on paper.
- Exhibits poor performance in group achievement tests.
- Appears brighter than test scores indicate.
- Demonstrates poor perception of time and space.

Visual-Receptive Process Disability

- Fails to understand what is read.
- Is unable to give a simple explanation of the contents of a picture.
- Is unable to categorize pictures.

Visual-Association Disability

- Is unable to tell a story from pictures; can only label objects in the pictures.
- Is unable to understand what he or she reads.
- Fails to handle primary workbook tasks.
- Needs auditory cues and clues.

Manual-Expressive Disability

- Has poor handwriting and drawing.
- Communicates infrequently with gestures.
- Is poor at "acting out" ideas, feelings.
- Is clumsy, uncoordinated.
- Plays games poorly; can't imitate other children in games.

Visual-Memory Disability

- Misspells frequently, even after undue practice.
- Misspells his or her own name frequently.
- Can't write alphabet, numbers, computation facts.
- Identifies words one day and fails to the next.

The following are a series of tests that are used to assess visual perceptual disabilities.

DEVELOPMENTAL TEST OF VISUAL MOTOR INTEGRATION— FOURTH EDITION (VMI-4)

GENERAL TEST INFORMATION

Author:	Keith E. Beery
Publisher:	PRO-ED, Inc.
Address of Publisher:	8700 Shoal Creek Blvd. Austin, TX 78758-6897
Phone Number of Publisher:	512-451-3246 or 800-897-3202
Fax of Publisher:	800-FXPROED

Purpose of Test: This test is designed to assess visual perception and motor coordination, and is used to screen for visual-motor problems. The author indicates that the primary purpose of the VMI-4 is to help prevent learning and behavioral problems through early screening identifications.

Description of Test: This test is intended for use primarily with pre-kindergarten children and those enrolled in the early grades. The short form of the VMI-4 uses 18 geometric figures to assess visual motor integration in children 3 to 8 years of age. The long form uses 27 geometric figures to assess functioning in examinees 3 to 18 years of age.

Type of Test:	Standardized
Administration Time:	10–15 minutes
Type of Administration:	Individual or group
Who Administers This Test:	Psychologists, special educators, speech and language therapists
Age/Grade Levels:	Ages 3 to 18; grades preschool to 12th

Subtest Information: The VMI-4 has no subtests. The 27 geometric figures that make up this test are weighed in terms of their developmental difficulty.

Scoring Information: Scores are presented in the following manners:

 ♦ Standard scores with a mean of 10 and a standard deviation of 3

 ♦ Percentile ranks

 ♦ Age equivalents

STRENGTHS OF THE VMI-4

 ♦ The VMI-4 can be used to provide assessors with information on how well students copy geometric shapes.

 ♦ The test has high reliability.

WEAKNESSES OF THE VMI-4

 ♦ Due to the newness of the test, further studies are necessary to assess its validity and reliability.

BENDER VISUAL MOTOR GESTALT TEST (BVMGT)

GENERAL TEST INFORMATION

Author:	Lauretta Bender
Publisher:	The American Orthopsychiatric Association Inc.
Address of Publisher:	19 W. 44th Street Suite 1616 New York, NY 10036
Phone Number of Publisher:	212-564-5930
Fax of Publisher:	212-564-6180

Purpose of Test: The test is designed to measure perceptual motor skills. It intends to determine visual-motor gestalt functioning in children, neurological maturation, and organic brain defects.

Description of Test: The test consists of a set of nine stimulus cards, which the student is asked to reproduce on a blank piece of paper, one figure at a time.

Type of Test:	Standardized
Administration Time:	10 minutes for an individual, 15–25 minutes for group administration
Type of Administration:	Individual or group
Who Administers This Test:	Psychologists, special educators, speech and language therapists
Age/Grade Levels:	4 to 12 years using the Koppitz Scoring System, 5 to 14 using the Watkins Scoring System, and 15 to 50 years using the Pascal and Suttell Scoring System

Subtest Information: There are no subtests for this instrument.

Scoring Information: Scoring using any of these systems mentioned previously is detailed, but breaks down to several specific classifications of errors:

1. *Rotation,* which involves the rotation of the figure or any part by 45 degrees or more
2. *Perseveration,* which involves increase, continuation, or prolongation of the number of units in the design
3. *Distortion of shape,* which involves destruction of the total figure, substitution of circles for dots, substitution of distinct angles for curves, or total lack of curves where they should exist, extra angles, or missing angles
4. *Integration,* which involves failure to connect properly the two parts of a figure; failure to cross two lines or crossing them in an incorrect place; omissions or addition of units; or the loss of overall shape.

STRENGTHS OF THE BVMGT

- The test is quick and reliable.
- The test is easy to administer.
- The test provides developmental data on a child's perceptual maturity.
- Group administration is a time saver.
- The test is effective as a screening instrument when combined with other tests.

BENDER VISUAL MOTOR GESTALT TEST (BVMGT)
(continued)

WEAKNESSES OF THE BVMGT

- The norms provided cannot be used to gauge the performance of individuals because of the extremely small sample size, ambiguity of the samples, and overall lack of information about the nature of the groups.

- The test scoring systems still require some subjectivity.

- Projective interpretations of the test results are questionable because of the absence of objective scoring criteria.

MARIANNE FROSTIG DEVELOPMENTAL TEST OF VISUAL PERCEPTION (DTVP)

GENERAL TEST INFORMATION

Author: Marianne Frostig, in collaboration with Welty Lefever and John R. B. Whittlessey

Publisher: PRO-ED, Inc.

Address of Publisher: 8700 Shoal Creek Blvd.
Austin, TX 78758-6897

Phone Number of Publisher: 512-451-3246 or 800-897-3202

Fax of Publisher: 800-FXPROED

Purpose of Test: The test is designed to measure specific visual perceptual abilities and to screen for visual perceptual difficulties at early ages.

Description of Test: The DTVP is a pencil-and-paper test of visual perception. The test materials consist of an examiner's manual and monograph, test booklets in which the students record their answers, demonstration cards, and plastic scoring keys. Evaluators must provide colored pencils (red, blue, green, and brown) and a pencil with no eraser for each student.

Type of Test: Standardized

Administration Time: 30–45 minutes for individual administration, and 40-60 minutes for group administration

Type of Administration: Individual or group

Who Administers This Test: Psychologists, special educators, speech and language therapists

Age/Grade Levels: Ages 3–8

Subtest Information: The tasks are arranged in increasing order of difficulty in five areas:

- *Eye Motor Coordination*—This task consists of 16 items that require the child to draw lines between increasingly narrow boundaries. These may include straight, curved, or angled lines.

- *Figure Ground*—This task consists of 8 items in which the child is required to distinguish and then outline embedded figures between intersecting shapes.

- *Constancy of Shape*—This task consists of 17 items in which the child must discriminate common geometric shapes presented in diferent shapes, sizes, positions, and textures from other similar shapes.

- *Position in Space*—This task consists of 8 items in which the child must distinguish between figures in an identical position and those in a reversed or rotated position.

- *Spatial Relations*—This task consists of 8 items in which the child is asked to copy simple forms and patterns by joining dots.

Scoring Information: Scores are presented in the following manners:

- Age levels

- Scaled scores—The scaled scores on the five subtests are added to obtain a total test score. When this is divided by the student's age, the total score yields a perceptual quotient. Scaled scores range from 0–20, with 10 as an average, and 8 or below indicating need for concern.

- Perceptual Quotient (PQ)—overall total test score

MARIANNE FROSTIG DEVELOPMENTAL TEST OF VISUAL PERCEPTION (DTVP)
(continued)

STRENGTHS OF THE DTVP

- This test yields a good evaluation of hand-eye coordination and visual perception in young children.
- This test is useful as a screening instrument for evaluating groups of children.
- The test instructions are well presented and easy to understand.

WEAKNESSES OF THE DTVP

- Only geometric forms and shapes are used, no numbers or letters.
- The test reliability is low.
- The test validity is low.

MOTOR FREE PERCEPTUAL TEST—REVISED (MVPT-R)

GENERAL TEST INFORMATION

Authors: Ronald Colarusso and Donald D. Hammill

Publisher: Academic Therapy Publications

Address of Publisher: 20 Commercial Blvd.
Novato, CA 94949-6191

Phone Number of Publisher: 415-883-3314 or 800-422-7249

Fax of Publisher: 415-883-3720

Purpose of Test: The test measures visual-perceptual processing ability. The MVPT-R is especially useful with those students who may have learning, cognitive, motor or physical disabilities.

Description of Test: The test consists of a test-item book with design plates, a manual, and a scoring protocol. The child is required to point to the correct answer among four alternatives for forty items arranged into five subtests.

Type of Test: Standardized, norm-referenced

Administration Time: 10–15 minutes

Type of Administration: Individual

Who Administers This Test: Psychologists, special educators, speech and language therapists

Age/Grade Levels: Ages 4.0 to 11.11

Subtest Information: The test is arranged into five tasks used to assess visual perception:

- *Spatial Relationships*—The student must select the drawing in which the stimulus figure is reproduced. The choices may be smaller, bigger, darker, or turned to the side.

- *Visual Discrimination*—The student must select the drawing that is different from the other three.

- *Figure Ground*—The student must select the correct response by locating the drawing in which the stimulus figure is embedded.

- *Visual Closure*—The student must select the drawing that, if completed, would be identical to the stimulus drawing.

- *Visual Memory*—After viewing a design for five seconds, having it removed, and being shown samples from which to choose, the student must select the response similar to the stimulus.

Scoring Information: The MVPT-R only provides a total test score. The total test consists of a Perceptual Age score and a Perceptual Quotient.

STRENGTHS OF THE MVPT-R

- The test is easy to administer.
- The test is not excessively time-consuming.
- The test is a useful diagnostic tool that helps to determine which area of visual perception may be a problem for a particular student.
- The test employs a useful method of reporting scores.
- The test's directions are clear and simple.

WEAKNESSES OF THE MVPT-R

- There is still some question surrounding the perceptual categories presented by the authors. They tend to be loosely defined and confusing.
- Due to the newness of the revision, further reliability and validity studies are necessary.

AUDITORY PERCEPTION ASSESSMENT

Auditory perception has long been a concern for special educators because of its relationship to speech and language development. The areas that are part of auditory perception are listed below:

- **Auditory discrimination**—the ability to differentiate auditorily the sounds in one's environment.

- **Auditory association**—the ability to organize and associate auditorily presented material in a meaningful way.

- **Auditory long-term memory**—the ability to retain and recall general and specific long-term auditory information.

- **Auditory short-term memory**—the ability to retain and recall general and specific short-term auditory information.

- **Auditory sequential memory**—the ability to recall in correct sequence and detail prior auditory information.

- **Auditory vocal expression**—the ability to reproduce vocally prior auditorily presented material or experiences.

- **Auditory motoric expression**—the ability to reproduce motorically prior auditorily presented material or experiences.

DIAGNOSTIC SYMPTOMS FOR AUDITORY PERCEPTUAL DISABILITIES

As previously indicated, a major objective of a perceptual evaluation is to identify those areas that may have a direct impact on a child's ability to adequately process information and that may possibly interfere in his or her academic achievement. What follows is a list of symptoms that may reflect perceptual disabilities in a variety of auditory areas.

Auditory Vocal Channel Disability

- Appears less intelligent than IQ tests indicate.

- Does many more things than one would expect: puts puzzles together, fixes broken objects, and so on.

- Appears to have a speech problem.

- May emphasize wrong syllables in words.

- May sequence sounds oddly.

- May use "small words" incorrectly.

- Appears not to listen or comprehend.

- Watches teachers' or adults' faces intently, trying to grasp words.

- Offers little in group discussions; appears shy.

♦ Answers in one-word responses.

♦ Follows directions better after he or she is shown rather than told.

♦ Has difficulty in learning rote-memory tasks such as alphabet, number combinations, addresses, and phone numbers.

Auditory Receptive Process Disability

♦ Fails to comprehend what he or she hears.

♦ Exhibits poor receptive vocabulary.

♦ Fails to identify sounds correctly.

♦ Fails to carry out directions.

Auditory Association Disability

♦ Fails to enjoy being read to.

♦ Has difficulty comprehending questions.

♦ Raises hand to answer question, but gives foolish response.

♦ Is slow to respond; takes a long time to answer.

♦ Has difficulty with abstract concepts presented auditorily.

♦ Demonstrates poor concept formation in verbal responses.

♦ Relies heavily on picture clues.

Verbal Expressive Disability

♦ Mispronounces common words.

♦ Uses incorrect word endings and plurals.

♦ Omits correct verbal endings.

♦ Makes grammatical or syntactical errors that do not reflect those of his or her parents.

♦ Has difficulty blending sounds.

Auditory Memory Disability

♦ Does not know address or phone number.

♦ Fails to remember instructions.

♦ Has difficulty memorizing nursery rhymes or poems.

♦ Has difficulty remembering the alphabet.

♦ Has dificulty counting.

♦ Fails to learn multiplication, addition, or subtraction facts.

GOLDMAN-FRISTOE-WOODCOCK TEST OF AUDITORY DISCRIMINATION (GFW)

GENERAL TEST INFORMATION

Authors: Ronald Goldman, Macalyne Fristoe, and Richard W. Woodcock

Publisher: American Guidance Service

Address of Publisher: 4201 Woodland Rd,
Circle Pines, MN 55014-1796

Phone Number of Publisher: 612-786-4343 or 800-328-2560

Fax of Publisher: 612-786-9077

Purpose of Test: The test is designed to provide a measure of speech/sound discrimination ability.

Description of Test: The test is a two-part test in which the examiner presents a test plate containing four drawings to the subject. The subject responds to a stimulus word (presented via audio cassette to ensure standarized presentation) by pointing to one of the drawings on the plate.

Type of Test: Norm-referenced

Administration Time: 20–30 minutes

Type of Administration: Individual

Who Administers This Test: Psychologists, special educators, speech and language therapists

Age/Grade Levels: Ages 4 to 70

Subtest Information: The test has three parts:

- *Training Procedure*—During this time, the examinee is familiarized with the pictures and the names that are used on the two subtests.

- *Quiet Subtest*—In this subtest, the examinee is presented with individual words in the absence of any noise. This subtest provides a measure of auditory discrimination under ideal conditions.

- *Noise Subtest*—In this subtest, the examinee is presented with individual words in the presence of distracting background noise on the tape. This subtest provides a measure of auditory discrimination under conditions similar to those encountered in everyday life.

Scoring Information: Scores are presented in the following manners:

- Percentiles
- Standard Scores with a mean of 50 and a standard deviation of 10 on each subtest

STRENGTHS OF THE GFW

- More reliability and validity data are given for this test than for most other discrimination tests.
- The test is applicable to a wide age range.
- The test is easy to administer.
- The test manual provides clear instruction.

WEAKNESSES OF THE GFW

- For some students the pace of the auditory presentation may be too rapid.

LINDAMOOD AUDITORY CONCEPTUALIZATION TEST (LACT)

GENERAL TEST INFORMATION

Authors:	Charles Lindamood and Patricia Lindamood
Publisher:	The Riverside Publishing Company
Address of Publisher:	8420 Brynmawr Avenue Chicago, Illinois 60631
Phone Number of Publisher:	800-323-9540
Fax of Publisher:	630-467-7192

Purpose of Test: The test measures an individual's ability to discriminate one speech sound from another and to perceive the number, order, and sameness or difference of speech sounds in sequence.

Description of Test: The test is a 40-item test in which the subject arranges colored blocks, each symbolizing one speech sound in a row, to represent a sound pattern spoken by the examiner.

Type of Test:	Criterion-referenced
Administration Time:	10 minutes
Type of Administration:	Individual
Who Administers This Test:	Psychologists, special educators, speech and language therapists
Age/Grade Levels:	Pre-school to adult

Subtest Information: There are no formal subtests but the test is divided into four parts:

- *Pre-check*—This five-item subtest is designed to examine a child's knowledge of various concepts, i.e., same/different, first/last.
- *Category I, Part A*—This subtest consists of 10 items in which the student is asked to identfy certain isolated sounds and determine whether they are the same or different.
- *Category I, Part B*—This subtest requires the student to identify sounds in isolation, sameness or difference, and in their order.
- *Category II*—This subtest consists of a list of 12 items in which the student must change sound patterns when sounds are added, omitted, substituted, shifted, or repeated.

Scoring Information: Scores are presented in the following manner:

- Grade levels

STRENGTHS OF THE LACT

- The test's lack of reading symbols enhances the examiner's opportunity to evaluate auditory perception skills.
- The Pre-check section is very useful because it allows for a quick assessment of the student's knowledge of the basic skills required to take the test.
- The test can be used with a wide range of students.

WEAKNESSES OF THE LACT

- Children with limited intellectual ability may find the instructions confusing.
- Scoring is difficult to interpret.
- The *Consumers Guide to Tests in Print* rates the norms, reliability, and validity as unacceptable.

TESTS OF AUDITORY PERCEPTUAL SKILLS—REVISED (TAPS-R)

GENERAL TEST INFORMATION

Author:	Morrison F. Gardner
Publisher:	Psychological and Educational Publications
Address of Publisher:	PO Box 520 Hydesville, CA 95547-0520
Phone Number of Publisher:	800-523-5775
Fax of Publisher:	800-447-0907

Purpose of Test: The test measures a subject's ability to perceive auditory matter. It is useful for diagnosing students who have auditory difficulties and/or language problems that could be the basis for learning problems.

Description of Test: This is a multiple-item response test consisting of seven subtests.

Type of Test:	Standardized
Administration Time:	Approximately 5–10 minutes
Type of Administration:	Individual
Who Administers This Test:	Psychologists, special educators, speech and language therapists
Age/Grade Levels:	Ages 4–13

Subtest Information: The test is divided into seven subtests:

- *Auditory Number Memory-Digits Forward*—This subtest measures a child's rote memory of nonsensical auditory matter.

- *Auditory Number Memory-Digits Reversed*—This subtest requires the child's ability to hear the sounds of digits forward and to repeat them in reverse.

- *Auditory Sentence Memory*—This subtest measures a child's ability to remember for immediate recall not only rote auditory matter but also auditory matter in sequence, thus measuring two processes.

- *Auditory Word Memory*—This subtest measures a child's ability to understand and interpret what he or she perceives by ear.

- *Auditory Word Discrimination*—This subtest measures a child's ability to discriminate paired one- and two-syllable words with phonemically similar consonants, cognates, or vowel differences.

- *Auditory Processing (Thinking and Reasoning)*—This subtest measures a student's ability to use common sense and ingenuity in solving common thought problems and avoids as much as possible what a subject has learned from "formal" education and from the home.

Scoring Information: The scores are presented in the following manners:

- Standard scores
- Stanines
- Percentiles

STRENGTHS OF THE TAPS-R

- This test is useful in the diagnosing of students who have auditory difficulties.
- The test is useful in diagnosing language problems that could be the basis for learning problems.

WEAKNESSES OF THE TAPS-R

- Given the newness of the test, more research is necessary to assess its validity and reliability.

WEPMAN TEST OF AUDITORY DISCRIMINATION—SECOND EDITION (ADT-2)

GENERAL TEST INFORMATION

Authors:	Joseph M. Wepman and William M. Reynolds
Publisher:	Western Psychological Services
Address of Publisher:	12031 Wilshire Blvd. Los Angeles, CA 90025
Phone Number of Publisher:	310-478-2061 or 800-648-8857
Fax of Publisher:	310-478-7838

Purpose of Test: This test measures children's ability to hear spoken English accurately, and is designed specifically to discriminate between commonly used phonemes in the English language.

Description of Test: The mode of presentation is the same for all editions of the test. The test consists of 40 word pairs of similar sounding words, or contrasts of similar words. The child has to say if the word pairs read aloud are the "same" or "different."

Type of Test:	Standardized
Administration Time:	15–20 minutes
Type of Administration:	Individual
Who Administers This Test:	Psychologists, special educators, speech and language therapists
Age/Grade Levels:	Ages 4 to 8

Subtest Information: There are no subtests on this instrument.

Scoring Information: This test provides scores in the folowing manners:

- ♦ Standard scores
- ♦ Percentiles

STRENGTHS OF THE ADT-2

- ♦ The test has a simple administration procedure.
- ♦ The test is useful for preschool and kindergarten screening.
- ♦ The test-retest reliability is high.
- ♦ The test is easy to score and interpret.

WEAKNESSES OF THE ADT-2

- ♦ Children with attentional problems may have difficulty attending to task.
- ♦ Very young children may not understand the concept of "same" or "different."

COMPREHENSIVE ASSESSMENT
OF PERCEPTUAL ABILITIES

Besides the assessment measures already discussed under visual and auditory perception, there are many comprehensive measures of perceptual ability. These tests are sometimes referred to as *multi-process tests* (tests that contain a variety of subtests used to measure many perceptual areas). Examiners usually administer a comprehensive perceptual test when a total overview of the child's learning process is needed. Such a test provides the examiner with a thorough picture of how the child receives, organizes, and expresses information. Most comprehensive perceptual tests cover a variety of perceptual areas and provide the examiner with modality and process strengths and weaknesses. With this information, the examiner is able to develop a more comprehensive plan to remediate the areas of the learning process that directly impair the child's ability to process information.

There are many comprehensive perceptual tests on the market today. Which one the examiner chooses is a personal choice. However, keep in mind that many of these comprehensive tests involve very long administration sessions as well as lengthy and sometimes complicated scoring procedures. Nevertheless, the results of these measures and the practical applications of the results far outweigh the time required to give and score the test. Following is a review of some available comprehensive perceptual tests.

BRUININKS-OSERETSKY TEST OF MOTOR PROFICIENCY

GENERAL TEST INFORMATION

Author:	Robert Bruininks
Publisher:	American Guidance Service
Address of Publisher:	4201 Woodland Rd. Circle Pines, MN 55014-1796
Phone Number of Publisher:	612-786-4343 or 800-328-2560
Fax of Publisher:	612-786-9077

Purpose of Test: This test is used to assess the motor skills of able-bodied students as well as of students with serious motor dysfunctions and developmental disabilities.

Description of Test: This test is a 46-item physical performance and paper-and-pencil assessment measure containing eight subtests. The examiner observes and records the student's performance on certain tasks, and the student is given a booklet in which he completes cutting and paper-and-pencil tasks.

Type of Test:	Standardized
Administration Time:	Complete battery takes 45–60 minutes; short form takes 15–20 minutes
Type of Administration:	Individual
Who Administers This Test:	Psychologists, special educators, speech and language therapists
Age/Grade Levels:	Ages 4.5 to 14.5

Subtest Information: The test consists of eight subtests in three areas:

1. *Gross Motor Development*
   - Running speed and agility
   - Balance
   - Bilateral coordination
   - Strength (arm, shoulder, abdominal, and leg)
2. *Gross and Fine Motor Development*
   - Upper-limb coordination
3. *Fine Motor Development*
   - Response speed
   - Visual-motor control
   - Upper-limb and speed dexterity

Scoring Information: Scores are presented in the follwing manners:
   - Age-based standard scores
   - Percentile ranks
   - Stanines
   - Age equivalents (for the complete battery only)

STRENGTHS OF THE BRUININKS-OSERETSKY TEST OF MOTOR PROFICIENCY
   - The test is relatively inexpensive.

BRUININKS-OSERETSKY TEST OF MOTOR PROFICIENCY
(continued)

- The short form is very useful for testing large numbers of students because of its ease of administration and short test time.
- The manual is clearly written.

WEAKNESSES OF THE BRUININKS-OSERETSKY TEST OF MOTOR PROFICIENCY

- Before the test can be useful as a diagnostic scale for children, additional standardization work must be done in the U.S.
- The test requires a great deal of space.
- The test includes complex scoring procedures.

DETROIT TESTS OF LEARNING APTITUDES—FOURTH EDITION (DTLA-4)

GENERAL TEST INFORMATION

Author: Donald D. Hammill

Publisher: PRO-ED, Inc.

Address of Publisher: 8700 Shoal Creek Blvd.
Austin, TX 78758-6897

Phone Number of Publisher: 512-451-3246 or 800-897-3202

Fax of Publisher: 800-FXPROED

Purpose of Test: The test is designed to measure "general" intelligence and discrete ability areas.

Description of Test: The DTLA-4 is a multiple-item, oral-response, paper-pencil battery of 10 subtests. The test provides the examiner with a profile of the student's perceptual abilities and deficiencies.

Type of Test: Standardized

Administration Time: 50–120 minutes

Type of Administration: Individual

Who Administers This Test: Psychologists, special educators, speech and language therapists

Age/Grade Levels: Ages 6-0 to 17-11

Subtest Information: The latest edition of this test contains 10 subtests which are grouped into three domains. Within each domain there are two sub-areas called composites. Listed below are the subtests included in each domain:

LINGUISTIC DOMAIN

1. *Verbal Composite*—This composite tests the student's knowledge of words and their use. The subtests making up this composite are listed below:
   - Basic Information
   - Reversed Letters
   - Sentence Imitation
   - Story Construction
   - Word Opposites
   - Word Sequences

2. *Nonverbal Composite*—This composite does not involve reading, writing, or speech. The subtests making up this composite are listed below:
   - Design Reproduction
   - Design Sequences
   - Story Sequences
   - Symbolic Relations

ATTENTIONAL DOMAIN

1. *Attention-Enhanced Composite*—This composite emphasizes concentration, attending, and short-term memory. The tests that make up this composite are listed below:
   - Design Reproduction
   - Design Sequences
   - Reversed Letters
   - Sentence Imitation
   - Story Sequences
   - Word Sequences

2. *Attention-Reduced Composite*—This composite emphasizes long-term memory. The subtests that make up this composite are listed below:
   - Basic Information
   - Story Construction
   - Symbolic Relations
   - Word Opposites

MOTORIC DOMAIN

1. *Motor-Enhanced Composite*—This composite emphasizes complex manual dexterity. The subtests that make up this composite are:

   ❖ Design Reproduction   ❖ Reversed Letters
   ❖ Design Sequences   ❖ Story Sequences

2. *Motor-Reduced Composite*—This composite requires very little motor involvement. The subtests that make up this composite are:

   ❖ Basic Information   ❖ Symbolic Relations
   ❖ Picture Fragments   ❖ Word Opposites
   ❖ Sentence Imitation   ❖ Word Sequences
   ❖ Story Construction

The following table lists and describes the 10 subtests that comprise the above-mentioned domains:

Subtest	Ability Measured	Description
1. Word Opposites	Vocabulary	Examiner says a word and examinee responds with a word that means just the opposite.
2. Design Sequences	Visual Discrimination and Memory	Examinee is shown series of designs for five seconds. Picture is then removed from view and examinee is then given a group of cubes that have designs on all sides. Examinee then arranges cubes to reproduce previously shown design sequence.
3. Sentence Imitation	Grammar	Examiner says a sentence and examinee repeats it verbatim.
4. Reversed Letters	Order-Recall, Auditory	Examiner says a series of letter names. Examinee then writes each letter in a small box reversing the letters' presentation order.
5. Story Construction	Story Telling	Examinee makes up three stories about three different topics. Stories are scored for thematic content.
6. Design Reproduction	Drawing from memory	Examiner shows a design for five seconds. Once it is removed from view the examinee draws the design from memory.
7. Basic Information	Everyday fact knowledge	Subject responds to questions concerning commonly known facts.
8. Symbolic Relations	Reasoning, Visual	Examinee is shown a visual problem involving geometric or line drawings and is then asked to point to the correct answer which is embedded among six pictured possibilities.
9. Word Sequences	Repeating Words	Examiner says a series of unrelated and isolated words to the examinee who then repeats the series.
10. Story Sequences	Organizing meaningful segments	Examiner shows a series of cartoon-like pictures to the examinee who then indicates the meaningful order of the pictures by placing numbered chips in boxes below the pictures.

DETROIT TESTS OF LEARNING APTITUDES—FOURTH EDITION (DTLA-4)

(continued)

Scoring Information: Three types of derived scores are available for the subtests and composites:

- Standard scores
- Percentiles
- Age equivalents

STRENGTHS OF THE DTLA-4

- This new version of the test still offers the examiner some worthwhile scales for examining various abilities in learning disabled or neurologically impaired subjects.
- The test provides some potentially valuable information about diverse abilities.

WEAKNESSES OF THE DTLA-4

- The test should not be regarded as a substitute for some of the better developed measures of intelligence.

ILLINOIS TEST OF PSYCHOLINGUISTIC ABILITIES (ITPA)

GENERAL TEST INFORMATION

Author:	S.A. Kirk, J.J. McCarthy, and W.D. Kirk
Publisher:	University of Illinois Press
Address of Publisher:	43 East Gregory Drive Champaign, Illinois 61820
Phone Number of Publisher:	217-333-0950
Fax of Publisher:	217-244-8082

Purpose of Test: The test intends to measure a child's ability to receive, organize, and express information from the environment.

Description of Test: This instrument is a 300-item test assessing a student's cognitive and perceptual abilities. The test measures these abilities in three areas: psycholinguistic processes, communication, and levels of organization. The test kit includes an examiner's booklet, two picture books, tiles with designs, picture strips, and an audiocassette for a supplemental test.

Type of Test:	Standardized
Administration Time:	60–90 minutes
Type of Administration:	Individual
Who Administers This Test:	Psychologists, special educators, speech and language therapists
Age/Grade Levels:	Ages 2–10

Subtest Information: The ITPA consists of 10 subtests and two optional supplementary subtests. They are:

- *Auditory Reception*—This subtest evaluates the child's ability to derive meaning from verbally presented material.
- *Visual Reception*—This subtest evaluates the child's ability to match concepts presented visually.
- *Visual Memory*—This subtest evaluates the child's ability to reproduce a sequence of non-meaningful figures from memory.
- *Auditory Sequential Memory*—This subtest evaluates the child's short-term memory for digits.
- *Auditory Association*—This subtest evaluates the child's ability to complete verbal analogies presented by the examiner.
- *Visual Association*—This subtest evaluates the child's ability to relate associated concepts.
- *Visual Closure*—This subtest evaluates the child's ability to recognize a pictured object when partially hidden from view by extraneous stimuli.
- *Grammatical Closure*—This subtest evaluates the child's ability to complete verbal statements presented by the examiner.
- *Verbal Expression*—This subtest evaluates the child's ability to express concepts relating to familiar objects presented by the examiner.
- *Manual Expression*—This subtest evaluates the child's ability to demonstrate the use of objects through pantomime.

The two supplementary tests are listed below:

- *Auditory Closure*—This subtest evaluates the child's ability to listen and then respond verbally to sounds omitted in words presented by the examiner.
- *Sound Blending*—This subtest evaluates the child's ability to to blend sounds.

ILLINOIS TEST OF PSYCHOLINGUISTIC ABILITIES (ITPA)

(continued)

Scoring Information: Scores are presented in the following manners:

- Age levels
- Scaled scores
- Psycholinguistic Age Level score

STRENGTHS OF THE ITPA

- Directions for administration and scoring the test are simple.
- The limitation of language on certain visual tests allows for a more accurate diagnosis of visual perceptual difficulties.

WEAKNESSES OF THE TEST

- Language interference on several subtests is questionable in light of what the subtest is said to measure.
- The results for minorities must be considered due to the limitations of the normative sample.
- Test administration is time-consuming.
- Several of the stimulus pictures are outdated and may affect reliability and validity of the results.

WOODCOCK-JOHNSON PSYCHOEDUCATIONAL BATTERY—REVISED (WJ-R)

GENERAL TEST INFORMATION

Author:	Richard W. Woodcock and Mary Bonner Johnson
Publisher:	The Riverside Publishing Company
Address of Publisher:	8420 Brynmawr Avenue Chicago, Illinois 60631
Phone Number of Publisher:	800-323-9540
Fax of Publisher:	630-467-7192

Purpose of Test: Applications of the battery include individual identification of deficits associated with disabilities, diagnosis of specific weaknesses that may interfere with related aspects of development, occupational and instructional selection and placement, individual program planning guidance, production and prediction of future performance, evaluation of individual growth, evaluation of programs, research, and psychometric training.

Description of Test: This test is the first major individual instrument that includes measures of cognitive ability, academic achievement, and scholastic interest to be standardized on the same norming sample. A complex instrument with many facets and a wide range, it is an individual cognitive and achievement test.

Type of Test:	Norm-referenced
Administration Time:	Part one, 60–90 minutes; Part II, 30–45 minutes; Part III, 15–30 minutes
Who Administers This Test:	Psychologists, special educators, speech and language therapists
Age/Grade Levels:	Ages 3 to 80

Subtest Information: The test is divided into two sections, Cognitive and Achievement. The *Cognitive Battery* comprises the following subtests:

COGNITIVE BATTERY

- *Memory for Names*—In this subtest the student is shown a picture of a "space creature" and is told its name. The individual must then identify from a group of nine pictures the creature just introduced. A new creature is introduced on each item, and the individual must identify the new creature, as well as those from all previous items.

- *Memory for Sentences*—In this subtest the student must repeat phrases and sentences exactly as spoken by a model.

- *Visual Matching*—In this subtest the student is required to locate and circle the two identical numbers in a row of six numbers.

- *Incomplete Words*—In this subtest the student hears words with one or more phonemes missing and must identify the complete word.

- *Visual Closure*—In this subtest the student is required to name a drawing or picture that has been distorted, has missing lines or areas, or is partially covered by a superimposed pattern.

- *Picture Vocabulary*—In this subtest the student identifies pictures of objects, either by pointing to the object named or by naming the object presented.

- *Analysis-Synthesis*—In this subtest the student is required to analyze the presented components of an incomplete logic puzzle and to determine the missing components.

WOODCOCK-JOHNSON PSYCHOEDUCATIONAL BATTERY—REVISED (WJ-R)
(continued)

The *Supplemental Battery* of the Cognitive tests is made up of the following subtests:

- *Visual-Auditory Learning*—This test measures the individual's ability to associate new visual symbols (rebuses) with familiar words and to translate a series of symbols into verbal sentences.

- *Memory for Words*—The individual is required to repeat lists of unrelated words in correct sequence.

- *Cross Out*—The individual is given a page containing rows of 3 drawings, with 20 drawings per row. He or she marks the five drawings in a row that are identical to the first drawing in the row.

- *Sound Blending*—The individual must integrate and say whole words after hearing parts (syllables or phonemes) of the word.

- *Picture Recognition*—This test requires the individual to recognize a subset of previously presented pictures within a field of distracting pictures.

- *Oral Vocabulary*—This test has two parts, Synonyms and Antonyms. Synonyms requires the individual to state a word similar in meaning to the word presented. Antonyms requires the subject to state a word that is opposite in meaning to the word presented.

- *Concept Formation*—The individual must identify the rules for concepts when shown illustrations of both instances of the concept and noninstances of the concept.

- *Delayed Recall/Memory for Names*—This test requires the individual to identify (after one to eight days) the space creatures presented in *Memory for Names*.

- *Delayed Recall/Visual-Auditory Learning*—This test requires the individual to recall (after 1 to 8 days) the words associated with the symbols (rebuses) presented in *Visual-Auditory Learning*.

- *Numbers Reversed*—The individual must repeat series of random numbers in exact reverse order.

- *Sound Patterns*—This test requires the individual to state whether pairs of complex sound patterns, presented by tape, are the same or different.

- *Spatial Relations*—The individual must select from a series of shapes the component parts needed to make a given whole shape.

- *Listening Comprehension*—The individual listens to a short passage and must supply the last word in order to complete the passage sensibly.

- *Verbal Analogies*—This test requires the individual to complete phrases with words that indicate appropriate verbal analogies.

The subtests that make up the *Achievement Battery* are listed below:

ACHIEVEMENT BATTERY

- *Letter-Word Identification*—On the first test items, the student is shown a colored drawing and must match it to one of a series of smaller line drawings. Next, when shown a letter, the student must say its name. On more difficult items, the student is asked to pronounce real words.

- *Passage Comprehension*—Early items present several colored drawings and a phrase that describes one of the drawings; the student points to the drawing corresponding to the phrase. Next, the student silently reads a passage of one or more sentences. In each passage is a blank space where one word has been omitted. The student's task is to say a word that correctly completes the sentence.

157

WOODCOCK-JOHNSON PSYCHOEDUCATIONAL BATTERY—REVISED
(WJ-R)
(continued)

- *Calculation*—The student is given pages that contain computation problems and asked to write the answer to each. Beginning items are simple number facts and basic operations. Also included are problems requiring manipulation of fractions and more advanced calculations using algebra, geometry, trigonometry, and calculus.

- *Applied Problems*—The student solves word problems. In the beginning items, the tester reads a question while the student looks at a drawing. On later items, the student is shown the word problem that the tester reads aloud. Answers are given orally on this subtest, but the student may use pencil and paper for computation.

- *Dictation*—Items for young children include making marks, drawing lines, and writing individual letters. With older students, the test takes on a dictation format. Included are spelling items where the tester dictates a word, capitalization items, and punctuation items where the student writes the symbol for a punctuation mark. Usage items require knowledge of plural forms, comparatives, and superlatives.

- *Writing Samples*—This subtest is made up of a series of brief writing prompts to which the student responds. Early items require only one-word answers. On later items, students must write a complete sentence. Prompts vary in specificity and complexity. For example, in some items, the student must write a sentence describing a drawing; in others, a phrase must be expanded.

- *Science*—The tester reads questions aloud, and the student replies orally. Drawings accompany some of the questions. Items sample general scientific knowledge, including aspects of biology, physics, and chemistry.

- *Social Studies*—Using the same format as the *Science* subtest, this measure assesses social sciences such as geography, political science, and economics.

- *Humanities*—Again, the same format as the *Science* subtest is used to evaluate knowledge of art, music, and literature.

The *Supplemental Battery* of the Achievement test is made up of the following subtests:

- *Word Attack*—The student is presented with nonsense words to read aloud. A pronunciation key is provided for the tester.

- *Reading Vocabulary*—The subtest is divided into two parts, Synonyms and Antonyms. The student reads a word aloud and then must supply either a word that means the same or one that has an opposite meaning.

- *Quantitative Concepts*—The student responds to oral questions concerning mathematics concepts. Items sample skills such as counting, understanding quantitative vocabulary, reading numerals, defining mathematical terms and symbols, and solving computational problems. Visuals accompany most test items.

- *Proofing*—The student is shown a sentence or sentences with one error. After reading the passage silently, the student must locate the error and tell how to correct it. The tester may tell the student an occasional word but not an entire sentence. Like the *Dictation* subtest, this subtest contains items that assess punctuation and capitalization, spelling, and usage.

- *Writing Fluency*—Students are given seven minutes to write sentences. Students write to a series of prompts, each of which contains a drawing and three words. Sentences must describe the picture using the words provided.

WOODCOCK-JOHNSON PSYCHOEDUCATIONAL BATTERY—REVISED
(WJ-R)
(continued)

Scoring Information: Scores are presented in the following manners:

- Age equivalents
- Grade equivalents
- Standard scores
- Percentile ranks
- Relative Mastery Index

STRENGTHS OF THE WJ-R

- The strengths of the test are primarily in the originality of many tasks, in the technical expertise and sophistication involved in the test construction, and in the psychometric properties of the battery.
- This test is a multifaceted tool for the assessment of cognitive achievement and scholastic interests.
- This test's subtests show validity.
- The test is a useful measure for the assessment of school performance across a wide range of academic areas and ages.

WEAKNESSES OF THE WJ-R

- Obtaining scores is complex.
- Profile interpretation is cumbersome.
- The interpretation process is complicated by the sheer number of scores and profiles produced.
- The time required to score the test can be lengthy if scores other than age or grade scores are desired.

TEST OF GROSS MOTOR DEVELOPMENT (TGMD)

GENERAL TEST INFORMATION

Author:	Dale A. Ulrich
Publisher:	PRO-ED, Inc.
Address of Publisher:	8700 Shoal Creek Blvd. Austin, TX 78758-6897
Phone Number of Publisher:	512-451-3246 or 800-897-3202
Fax of Publisher:	800-FXPROED

Purpose of Test: The TGMD assesses common motor skills. The primary uses of this test are listed below:

- ◆ To identify children who are significantly behind their peers in gross motor skill development and should be eligible for special education services in physical education
- ◆ To assist in the planning of an instructional program in gross motor skill development
- ◆ To assess individual student progress in gross motor development
- ◆ To evaluate the gross motor program
- ◆ To serve as a measurement instrument in research involving gross motor development

Description of Test: This is a multiple-item, task-performance test consisting of two subtests. The examiner records observations in a student record book. The TGMD allows examiners to administer one test in a relatively brief time and gather data for making important educational decisions.

Type of Test:	Standardized
Administration Time:	15 minutes
Type of Administration:	Individual
Who Administers This Test:	Psychologists, special educators, speech and language therapists
Age/Grade Levels:	Ages 3 to 10

Subtest Information: The test is divided into the following two subtests:

- • *Locomotion*—This subtest measures the run, gallop, hop, leap, horizontal jump, skip, and slide skills that move a child's center of gravity from one point to another.
- • *Object Control*—This subtest measures the two-hand strike, stationary bounce, catch, kick, and overhand throw skills that include projecting and receiving objects.

Scoring Information: The Scores are presented in the following manners:

- ◆ Perceptual ages
- ◆ Standard scores

STRENGTHS OF THE TGMD

- ◆ The test has solid reliability and validity
- ◆ The test demonstrates strong ability to differentiate between children with and without disabilities

WEAKNESSES OF THE TGMD

- ◆ Information is needed in the manual on the relationship of the TGMD to other measures of motor development.
- ◆ The *Consumers Guide to Tests in Print* gives an unacceptable overall rating for the TGMD.

SLINGERLAND SCREENING TESTS FOR IDENTIFYING CHILDREN WITH SPECIFIC LANGUAGE DISABILITY

GENERAL TEST INFORMATION

Author:	Beth H. Slingerland
Publisher:	Educators Publishing Service, Inc.
Address of Publisher:	31 Smith Place Cambridge, MA 02138
Phone Number of Publisher:	800-225-5750
Fax of Publisher:	617-547-0412

Purpose of Test: This test is primarily designed to provide a group testing format for identifying children at risk for academic failure. Additionally, the test is designed to identify children having difficulty in academic areas, rather than to identify linguistically handicapped children.

Description of Test: This test is not a test of language but rather a test of various auditory, visual, and motor skills related to specific academic areas. It is a multiple-item, verbally presented, paper-and-pencil examination containing eight subtests.

Type of Test:	Informal diagnostic
Aministration Time:	60–80 minutes for Forms A, B, and C; 110–130 minutes for Form D
Type of Administration:	Individual or group
Who Administers This Test:	Psychologists, special educators, speech and language therapists
Age/Grade Levels:	Grades 1 to 6

Subtest Information: Each subtest focuses on curriculum-related skills. They are as follows:

- *Far Point Copying*—This subtest requires the student to copy a printed paragraph from far points to probe visual perception and graphomotor responses. The subtest assesses visual motor skills related to handwriting.

- *Near Point Copying*—This subtest requires the student to copy a printed paragraph from near points in order to probe visual perception and graphomotor responses. The subtest assesses visual motor skills related to handwriting.

- *Visual Perception Memory*—This subtest requires the student to recall and match printed words, letters, and numbers presented in brief exposure with a delay before responding. This subtest assesses visual memory skills related to reading and spelling.

- *Visual Discrimination*—This subtest requires the student's immediate matching of printed words and eliminates the memory component of *Visual Perception Memory*. The subtest assesses basic visual discrimination without memory or written response.

- *Visual Kinesthetic Memory*—This subtest requires the student's delayed copying of words, phrases, letters, designs, and number groups presented with brief exposure. The subtest assesses the combination of visual memory and written response, which is necessary for written spelling.

- *Auditory Kinesthetic Memory*—This subtest requires the student to write groups of letters, numbers, and words to dictation after a brief delay with distraction. This subtest combines auditory perception and memory with written response.

- *Initial and Final Sounds*—This subtest requires the student to write the initial phoneme and later to write the final phoneme of groups of spoken words. This subtest assesses auditory discrimination and sequencing related to basic phonics with a written response.

- *Auditory/Visual Integration*—This subtest requires the student's delayed matching of spoken words, letters, or number groups. This subtest assesses visual discrimination related to word recognition.

There are *four different forms* of this test (Forms A, B, C, and D). Some of the forms contain subtests other than those already mentioned:

- *Following Directions*—This subtest requires the student to give a written response from a series of directions given by the examiner. It assesses auditory memory and attention with a written response.

- *Echolalia*—This subtest requires the student to listen to a word or phrase given by the examiner and to repeat it four or five times. As an individual auditory test, it assesses auditory kinesthetic confusion related to pronunciation.

- *Word Finding*—This subtest requires the child to fill in a missing word from a sentence read by the examiner. As an individual auditory test, it assesses comprehension and the ability to produce a specific word on demand.

- *Story Telling*—This subtest requires the child to retell a story previously read by the examiner. As an individual auditory test, it assesses auditory memory and verbal expression of content material.

STRENGTHS OF THE SLINGERLAND

- This is a very useful test for those who need a test to screen for academic problems.
- The test uses skills related to classroom tasks.
- This is one of the few group tests designed for disability screening for treatment purposes.
- This test can be used to predict reading problems.

WEAKNESSES OF THE SLINGERLAND

- There is a lack of information concerning the test's reliability and validity.
- The author states that standardized national norms would destroy the usefulness of the tests. As a result, it is a diagnostic test with subjective scoring criteria.
- Because of its lack of normative data, this test may be a problem for more inexperienced evaluators because of the general scoring rules and the generalization of the results to classroom recommendations.

AN OVERVIEW OF LANGUAGE, PSYCHOLOGICAL & SOCIAL, AND ADAPTIVE MEASURES

The primary areas in which students are assessed that have been addressed so far include:

- intellectual ability and potential

- overall academic achievement strengths and weaknesses

- perceptual abilities

This chapter provides a brief overview of the other areas of assessment that would be primarily used by other professionals on the team, i.e., speech/language therapist, psychologist. These areas include:

- expressive and receptive language

- classroom and school behavior

- emotional development

- social development

Keep in mind that when the suspected disability is related to a medically related condition (e.g., sensory deficit, orthopedic impairment, blindness), assessment information from physicians or other medical practitioners needs to be included as well. A global assessment approach utilizing a combination of measures should be used in any given area, and the assessment team should clearly understand that each area encompasses more than one ability.

SPEECH AND LANGUAGE ASSESSMENT

Speech and language are related, but they are not the same thing. According to Blackhurst and Berdine (1981, p. 111), "Speech is the physical process of making the sounds and sound combinations of a language. Language is much more complex than speech; speech production is one of its components. Language is essentially the system according to which a people agree to talk about or represent environmental events. Once a group of people agree on a system for representing objects, events, and the relationships among objects and events, the system can be used to communicate all their experiences. The language system consists of words and word combinations."

Whereas the meaning of language is contained in its words and word combinations, it is speech that permits the transmission of meaning. Speech sounds are not meaningful in themselves, of course. They acquire meaning only if the speaker or listener knows their relationship to real events. To state it very simply, speech sounds are a medium for carrying messages.

Language is an integral part of our everyday functioning. At a minimum, we use language for problem solving, communicating, and expressing knowledge. Therefore, when problems in language become evident, they can affect individuals in many different ways.

In school, children need language in order to function in the classroom. Without language, a child would have serious disadvantages when compared to other students. A student with difficulties in language may not be able to express to teachers, parents, or peers all that he or she knows. Such problems can result in lower levels of self esteem, low achievement, confusion, helplessness, and frustration.

Because language plays such a critical role in a child's development, most schools have a speech or language pathologist to help students who are having difficulties with these areas. Speech and language pathologists are specially trained professionals who, working with other professionals throughout the school, gather data and assess the language functioning of individual students.

According to Bloom and Lahey (1978), language processes can be broken down into three general categories. These are:

LANGUAGE PROCESSES

1. **Form**—When special educators speak of form, they normally are speaking of three interconnected concepts. These are:

   - **Phonology.** This refers to the knowledge a student has of sounds in language.

   - **Morphology.** This refers to the smallest meaningful unit of language and involves the stringing together of sounds.

   - **Syntax.** This refers to the rules used in combining words to make a sentence.

2. **Content**—This refers to the importance of meaning. It involves knowledge of vocabulary, relationships between words, and time and event relationships.

3. **Use**—This refers to the pragmatic functions of language in varying contexts. It sees the individual as an active communicator whose words and sentences are intentionally selected in relation to the effect the speaker wishes to have on a listener.

INTERPRETING SPEECH AND LANGUAGE TESTS

According to the IDEA, a speech and language impairment can be defined as "a communication disorder such as stuttering, a language impairment, or a voice impairment that adversely affects a child's educational performance." [34 CFR sec 300.7 (b)(11)]

Simply stated, a child with a speech disorder may have difficulties with any of the following:

♦ producing sounds properly

♦ speaking in a normal flow

♦ speaking with a normal rhythm

♦ using his or her voice in an effective way

Children with language disorders may exhibit the following:

♦ difficulty in comprehending questions and following commands (receptive language)

♦ difficulty in communicating ideas and thoughts (expressive language)

There are numerous tests which one can give to assess speech and language disorders. According to Wallace et al. (1992, p. 252), "some provide a comprehensive view of all language functioning while others measure specific components of linguistic performance (e.g., phonology, linguistic structure or semantics)."

When doing an assessment for speech and language, it is imperative that the evaluator understand that many diagnostic tests can be insensitive to the subtleties of ongoing functional communication (Swanson and Watson, 1989, p. 5). Consequently, in order to do a thorough and complete speech and language evaluation, one should include obtaining a language sample that seeks to show how the individual performs in a real-life communication setting.

Speech and language evaluations are normally done by the speech and language pathologists in the school. However, teachers and parents also play an instrumental role in this evaluation. Through interviews and observations, a student's teacher and the child's parents can gather and give valuable input to the overall assessment. As a result, both teachers and parents should become familiar with developmental language milestones. Listed below are the milestones for ages birth to five years.

DEVELOPMENTAL MILESTONES

Birth to 6 months

♦ First form of communication is crying.

♦ Babies also make sounds of comfort, such as coos and gurgles.

♦ Babbling soon follows as a form of communication.

♦ Vowel sounds are produced.

♦ No meaning is attached to the words heard from others.

6 to 12 months

♦ The baby's voice begins to rise and fall while making sounds.

♦ Child begins to understand certain words.

♦ Child may respond appropriately to the word "no" or own name.

♦ Child may perform an action when asked.

♦ Child may repeat words said by others.

12 to 18 months

♦ Child has learned to say several words with appropriate meaning.

♦ Child is able to tell what he or she wants by pointing.

♦ Child responds to simple commands.

18 to 24 months

♦ There is a great spurt in the acquisition and use of speech at this stage.

♦ Child begins to combine words.

♦ Child begins to form words into short sentences.

2 to 3 years

♦ At this age, the child talks.

♦ Child asks questions.

♦ Child has vocabulary of about 900 words.

♦ Child participates in conversation.

♦ Child can identify colors.

♦ Child can use plurals.

♦ Child can tell simple stories.

♦ Child begins to use some consonant sounds.

3 to 4 years

♦ Child begins to speak more rapidly.

♦ Child begins to ask questions to obtain information.

♦ Sentences are longer and more varied.

♦ Child can complete simple analogies.

4 to 5 years

♦ Child has an average vocabulary of over 1500 words.

♦ Child's sentences average 5 words in length.

- ◆ Child is able to modify speech.

- ◆ Child is able to define words.

- ◆ Child can use conjunctions.

- ◆ Child can recite poems and sing songs from memory.

In conclusion, by comparing the child's receptive and expressive language levels to his or her mental age, we can differentiate between a language problem and a developmental delay. IQ tests that are language based can be problematic, because a child with a language problem will do poorly, regardless of his or her overall intelligence. There is no shortcut to a thorough, effective language assessment. The skills being tested must be thoroughly understood, and the results of testing carefully considered, before an appropriate strategy of language intervention can be formulated (Blackhurst and Berdine, 1981, p. 125).

PEABODY PICTURE VOCABULARY TEST—III (PPVT-III)

GENERAL TEST INFORMATION

Author: Lloyd M. Dunn and Leota M. Dunn, with Kathleen T. Williams

Publisher: American Guidance Service

Address of Publisher: 4201 Woodland Rd.
                                   Circle Pines, MN 55014-1796

Phone Number of Publisher: 612-786-4343 or 800-328-2560

Fax of Publisher: (612)-786-9077

Purpose of Test: The test is intended as a measure of listening comprehension for spoken words in standard English and a screening test of verbal ability.

Description of Test: The test is offered in two parallel forms, IIIA and IIIB, for reliable testing and retesting. Items consist of pictures arranged in a multiple-choice format. To administer an item, the evaluator shows a plate in the test easel and says a corresponding stimulus word. The child or adult responds by pointing to one of the pictures.

Type of Test: Norm-referenced

Administration Time: 10–12 minutes

Type of Administration: Individual

Who Administers This Test: Speech and language therapists, special education evaluators, psychologists

Age/Grade Levels: Ages 2 to 90+

Subtest Information: This test is not divided into subtests.

Scoring Information: Scores are presented in the following manner:

- Standard score
- Percentile rank
- Stanine
- Age equivalent

STRENGTHS OF THE PPVT-III

- The test has a wide range of use.
- The test scoring system is objective and rapid.
- The test has a quick administration time.
- The test has clear, black-and-white line drawings.
- No reading or writing is required of the examinee.
- The test has expanded adult norms through the age of 90.

WEAKNESSES OF THE PPVT-III

- Given the newness of the test, further study is required to determine the limitations, if any, of its validity and reliability.

TEST FOR AUDITORY COMPREHENSION OF LANGUAGE—REVISED
(TACL-R)

GENERAL TEST INFORMATION

Author:	Elizabeth Carrow-Woolfolk
Publisher:	The Riverside Publishing Company
Address of Publisher:	8420 Spring Lake Drive
	Itasca, Illinois 60143-2079
Phone Number of Publisher:	800-323-9540
Fax of Publisher:	630-467-7192

Purpose of Test: The test is designed to measure a child's auditory comprehension of language, determine the developmental level, and provide diagnostic information regarding those areas of language comprehension that present difficulty to the child.

Description of Test: This is a multiple-item response test assessing auditory understanding of word classes and relations, grammatical morphemes, and elaborated sentence constructions.

Type of Test:	Norm-referenced
Administration Time:	10–20 minutes
Type of Administration:	Individual
Who Administers This Test:	Speech and language therapists, special education evaluators, psychologists
Age/Grade Levels:	Ages 3.9 to 10

Subtest Information: There are three subtests:

1. *Word Classes and Relations*—This subtest contains 40 items composed of nouns, verbs, modifiers, and word relations. It measures mastery of vocabulary and concepts needed by children in preschool, kindergarten, and the elementary grades.

2. *Grammatical Morphemes*—This subtest contains 40 items composed of short simple sentences that measure grammatical morphemes, including prepositions, pronouns, noun inflections, verb inflections, noun-verb agreement, and derivational suffixes.

3. *Elaborated Sentences*—This subtest contains 40 items composed of complex sentences that vary on a number of dimensions. It tests a student's competence with sentences with interrogatives, active and passive voice, direct and indirect objects, and coordination, subordination, and embedding of contextual elements.

Scoring Information: Scores are presented in the following manner:

- Percentile ranks
- Standard scores
- Age equivalents

STRENGTHS OF THE TACL-R

- This test has high reliability.
- This test has high validity.
- The test manual offers a variety of normative comparisons.

WEAKNESSES OF THE TACL-R

- Impulsive children may obtain lower scores if they fail to look at each picture carefully.
- Children with attention difficulties may perform poorly if they fail to attend to the wording of each item. Consequently, scores for some children may not be a reflection of language competency.

BOEHM TEST OF BASIC CONCEPTS—REVISED (BTBC-R)

GENERAL TEST INFORMATION

Author: Ann E. Boehm

Publisher: The Psychological Corporation

Address of Publisher: 555 Academic Court
San Antonio, TX 78204-2498

Phone Number of Publisher: 800-211-8378

Fax of Publisher: 800-232-1223

TDD of Publisher: 800-723-1318

Purpose of Test: This test is designed to measure children's mastery of the concepts that are fundamental both to understanding verbal instruction and for early school achievement.

Description of Test: The test consists of a 50-item, paper-and-pencil, multiple-choice picture test arranged in increasing order of difficulty. The relational concepts measured on the test include size, direction, position in space, quantity, and time—concepts commonly found in preschool and primary instructional materials. There are two alternate forms of this test: C and D. The materials for the Boehm-R include individual student test booklets and the examiner's manual.

Type of Test: Norm-referenced

Administration Time: 30–40 minutes

Type of Administration: Individual and group

Who Administers This Test: Speech and language therapists, special education evaluators, psychologists

Age/Grade Level: Grades K to 2

Subtest Information: There are no subtests in this test.

Scoring Information: Scores are presented in the following manner:

- Percentile ranks
- Normal curve equivalents

STRENGTHS OF THE BTBC-R

- The administration of this test is straightforward and well explained in the manual.
- People being examined seem to enjoy the test.
- This test is designed to assess attainment of certain concepts that are used extensively in primary-grade curriculum materials.
- The test's standardization sample is impressive in terms of the number of subjects used in the norming population.

WEAKNESSES OF THE BTBC-R

- Some sections of the manual may be difficult to follow for evaluators unfamiliar with the test.
- The test's reliability is not well established.

COMPREHENSIVE RECEPTIVE AND EXPRESSIVE VOCABULARY TEST (CREVT)

GENERAL TEST INFORMATION

Author: Gerald Wallace and Donald D. Hammill

Publisher: PRO-ED, Inc.

Address of Publisher: 8700 Shoal Creek Blvd.
Austin, TX 78758-6897

Phone Number of Publisher: 512-451-3246 or 800-897-3202

Fax of Publisher: 800-FXPROED

Purpose of Test: This test is designed to measure both oral and receptive vocabulary. It is also useful in identifying students who are significantly below their peers in oral vocabulary proficiency.

Description of Test: This test is a two subtest measure based on current theories of vocabulary development. Two equivalent forms are available and full-color photos are used on the receptive vocabulary subtest. The kit includes examiner's manual, photo album picture book, and record forms.

Type of Test: Standardized

Administration Time: 20–30 minutes

Type of Administration: Administered individually

Who Administers This Test: Speech and language therapists, special education evaluators, psychologists

Age/Grade Levels: Ages 4.0 to 17.11

Subtest Information: There are two subtests in this measure:

- *Receptive Vocabulary*—This subtest is a variation of the familiar "point-to-the-picture-of-the-word-I-say" technique. It is made up of 10 plates, each of which contains 6 pictures. All of the pictures on the plate relate to a particular theme.

- *Expressive Vocabulary*—This subtest uses the "define-the-word-I-say" format. The format of this 25-item subtest encourages and requires the student to converse in detail about a particular stimulus word.

Scoring Information: The scores are presented in the following manners:

- Standard scores
- Percentiles
- Composite scores

STRENGTHS OF THE CREVT

- The test is easy to score.
- The subtests are easy to administer.
- Test items are proven to be unbiased.
- All words tested on the CREVT are appropriate for school age sample and related to familiar concepts.

WEAKNESSES OF THE CREVT

- Given the newness of the test, more research is necessary to assess its validity and reliability.

GOLDMAN-FRISTOE TEST OF ARTICULATION

GENERAL TEST INFORMATION

Author:	Ronald Goldman and Macalyne Fristoe
Publisher:	American Guidance Service
Address of Publisher:	4201 Woodland Rd. Circle Pines, MN 55014-1796
Phone Number of Publisher:	612-786-4343 or 800-328-2560
Fax of Publisher:	612-786-9077

Purpose of Test: The purpose of this test is to provide a systematic approach to the evaluation of articulation of speech sounds.

Description of Test: The first part of the test contains 23 phonemes and 12 blends that are tested in words. The subject names pictures and answers questions to provide 44 responses at this level. The second part of the test determines whether or not those same sounds are used correctly in sentences by the subject.

Type of Test:	Norm-referenced
Administration Time:	10–20 minutes
Type of Administration:	Individual
Who Administers This Test:	Speech and language therapists, special education evaluators, psychologists
Age/Grade Levels:	Ages 2 and over

Subtest Information: The test comprises three subtests:

- *Sounds in Words*—This subtest is a picture naming task in which the child is shown pictures of familiar objects and is asked to name or answer questions about them.

- *Sounds in Sentences*—This subtest assesses spontaneous sound production used in connected speech.

- *Stimulability Subtest*—This subtest assesses the child's ability to correctly produce a previously misarticulated sound when asked to watch and listen to the examiner's production of the sound.

Scoring Information: Scores are presented in the following manner:

- Percentile ranks

STRENGTHS OF THE GOLDMAN-FRISTOE

- The test is easy to administer.
- No reading is required of the student.
- Full-colored test pictures hold the child's interest.
- The test easily elicits spontaneous responses.

WEAKNESSES OF THE GOLDMAN-FRISTOE

- Reliability data are inadequately reported.
- Validity data are lacking.

KAUFMAN SURVEY OF EARLY ACADEMIC AND LANGUAGE SKILLS (K-SEALS)

GENERAL TEST INFORMATION

Author:	Alan S. Kaufman and Nadeen L. Kaufman
Publisher:	American Guidance Service
Address of Publisher:	4201 Woodland Rd. Circle Pines, MN 55014-1796
Phone Number of Publisher:	612-786-4343 or 800-328-2560
Fax of Publisher:	612-786-9077

Purpose of Test: The test is intended as a measure of children's language, preacademic skills, and articulation.

Description of Test: The K-SEALS surveys both expressive and receptive vocabulary in an organized and systematic fashion. Children must identify objects, actions, numbers, letters, and words via expressive (communicating ideas and thoughts) and receptive (comprehending questions and following commands) formats.

Type of Test:	Norm-referenced
Administration Time:	15–25 minutes
Type of Administration:	Individual
Who Administers This Test:	Speech and language therapists, special education evaluators, psychologists
Age/Grade Levels:	Ages 3.0 to 6.11

Subtest Information: The K-SEALS features three subtests:

- *Vocabulary Subtest*—The child identifies, by gesture or name, pictures of objects or actions and points to or names objects based on verbal descriptions of their attributes.
- *Numbers, Letters, and Words*—The child selects or names numbers, letters, or words; counts and indicates knowledge of number concepts; and solves number problems.
- *Articulation Survey*—The child pronounces the names of common objects or actions and is assessed for correctness of pronunciation

Scoring Information: The scores are presented in the following manners:

- Standard scores with a mean of 100 and a standard deviation of 15
- Percentile ranks
- Age equivalents

STRENGTHS OF THE K-SEALS

- The test surveys both expressive and receptive vocabulary.
- The test has good reliability.
- The test manual is easy to read.
- Administration and scoring of the test is not complex.

WEAKNESSES OF THE K-SEALS

- As of the printing of this publication, Buros did not contain a writeup on this test.
- Due to the newness of the test, further studies are necessary to assess its validity and reliability.

TEST OF ADOLESCENT AND ADULT LANGUAGE— THIRD EDITION (TOAL-3)

GENERAL TEST INFORMATION

Authors:	Virginia Brown, Donald Hammill, Stephen Larson, J. Lee Wiederholt
Publisher:	PRO-ED, Inc.
Address of Publisher:	8700 Shoal Creek Blvd. Austin, TX 78758-6897
Phone Number of Publisher:	512-451-3246 or 800-897-3202
Fax of Publisher:	800-FXPROED

Purpose of Test: The test is designed to determine the student's areas of relative strength and weakness across language abilities.

Description of Test: The test consists of 10 composite scores. The subtests assess oral, written, receptive, and expressive language abilities.

Type of Test:	Standardized
Administration Time:	60–180 minutes
Type of Administration:	Individual and group
Who Administers This Test:	Speech and language therapists, special education evaluators, psychologists
Age/Grade Levels:	Ages 12–25

Subtest Information: The test consists of the following composites:

- *Listening*—assesses student's ability to understand the spoken language of other people.
- *Speaking*—assesses student's ability to express one's ideas orally.
- *Reading*—assesses student's ability to comprehend written messages.
- *Writing*—assesses student's ability to express thoughts in graphic form.
- *Spoken Language*—assesses student's ability to listen and speak.
- *Written Language*—assesses student's ability to read and write.
- *Vocabulary*—assesses student's ability to understand and use words in communication.
- *Grammar*—assesses student's ability to understand and generate syntactic structures.
- *Perceptive Language*—assesses student's ability to comprehend both written and spoken language.
- *Expressive Language*—assesses student's ability to produce written and spoken language.

Scoring Information: The scores are presented in the following manners:

- Composite Quotient with a mean of 100 and a standard deviation of 15
- Standard scores
- Percentiles

STRENGTHS OF THE TOAL-3

- The test is carefully developed and has a comprehensive system for assessing selected adolescent and adult languages.

TEST OF ADOLESCENT AND ADULT LANGUAGE—
THIRD EDITION (TOAL-3)
(continued)

♦ Scores allow for the clear differentiation between groups known to have language problems and those known to have normal language.

♦ Reliability is high.

♦ Items do not appear to be biased.

WEAKNESSES OF THE TOAL-3

♦ Due to the newness of the test, more convincing evidence is needed before users can be confident in scores, interpretations, and applications.

TEST OF EARLY LANGUAGE DEVELOPMENT—SECOND EDITION
(TELD-2)

GENERAL TEST INFORMATION

Authors:	Wayne P. Iliesko, D. Kim Reid, and Donald D. Hammill
Publisher:	PRO-ED, Inc.
Address of Publisher:	8700 Shoal Creek Blvd. Austin, TX 78758-6897
Phone Number of Publisher:	512-451-3246 or 800-897-3202
Fax of Publisher:	800-FXPROED

Purpose of Test: This test is designed to measure the early development of oral language in the areas of receptive and expressive language, syntax, and semantics.

Description of Test: The TELD-2 screens children for language deficiency. It is designed for normal children but can be administered to special populations after making proper adjustments in administering the test and establishing different norms.

Type of Test:	Norm-referenced
Administration Time:	20 minutes
Type of Administration:	Administered individually
Who Administers This Test:	Speech and language therapists, special education evaluators, psychologists
Age/Grade Levels:	Ages 2.0 to 7.11

Subtest Information: There are no subtests on this measure.

Scoring Information: The scores are presented in the following manners:

- ◆ Standard scores
- ◆ Percentiles
- ◆ Normal Curve Equivalents
- ◆ Age Equivalents

STRENGTHS OF THE TELD-2

- ◆ The test is well grounded in theory, and measures form and content of language development.
- ◆ Syntax, morphology, and semantics are measured in receptive as well as expressive modes.
- ◆ Content validity of the test has been adequately established.
- ◆ The manual is well written.
- ◆ Useful examples for establishing basals and ceilings are provided in the manual.

WEAKNESSES OF THE TELD-2

- ◆ The test lacks evidence in support of its construct validity.
- ◆ Small sample sizes and lack of representation for all age levels in the norming population may be a cause of concern in generalizability.
- ◆ The method of scoring diminishes the diagnostic value of the language-related data collected.

TEST OF LANGUAGE DEVELOPMENT—PRIMARY 2 (TOLD-P:2)

GENERAL TEST INFORMATION

Authors:	Phyllis L. Newcomer and Donald D. Hammill
Publisher:	PRO-ED, Inc.
Address of Publisher:	8700 Shoal Creek Blvd. Austin, TX 78758-6897
Phone Number of Publisher:	512-451-3246 or 800-897-3202
Fax of Publisher:	800-FXPROED

Purpose of Test: This test is used for the following purposes:

♦ to identify children who are significantly below their peers in language proficiencies

♦ to determine children's specific strengths and weaknesses in language skills

♦ to document children's progress in language as a consequence of special intervention programs

♦ to measure language in research studies

Description of Test: The TOLD-P:2 uses a two-dimensional linguistic model involving linguistic systems (listening and speaking) and linguistic features (phonology, syntax, and semantics). The seven subtests of the TOLD-P:2 sample each component of the model.

Type of Test:	Norm-referenced
Administration Time:	30–60 minutes
Type of Administration:	Individual
Who Administers This Test:	Speech and language therapists, special education evaluators, psychologists
Age/Grade Levels:	Ages 4.0 to 8.11

Subtest Information: The test consists of the following subtests:

Subtest	Specific Ability	Language Area Measured
Picture Vocabulary	understanding words	Semantics
Oral Vocabulary	defining words	Semantics
Grammatic Understanding	understanding sentence structures	Syntax
Sentence Imitation	generating proper sentences	Syntax
Grammatic Completion	morphological usage	Syntax
Word Discrimination	noticing sound differences	Phonology
Word Articulation	saying words correctly	Phonology

Scoring Information: The scores are presented in the following manners:

♦ Percentile ranks

♦ Standard scores

♦ Composite scores

TEST OF LANGUAGE DEVELOPMENT—PRIMARY 2 (TOLD-P:2)

(continued)

STRENGTHS OF THE TOLD-P:2

♦ The TOLD-P:2 is well designed in terms of utilizing established psychometric criteria for reliability and criterion-related validity.

♦ The test is a useful measure for investigating the oral language skills of young children.

♦ The test is very useful in identifying areas where the child is proficient and areas that require further evaluation.

WEAKNESSES OF THE TOLD-P:2

♦ The construct validity (theoretical basis) of the TOLD-2 may be considered weak. The author's rationale for the majority of the subtests is that these types of subtests have been used on other language tests.

♦ No information is provided about inclusion of students identified as disabled in the sample which may create problems with generalizability.

TEST OF LANGUAGE DEVELOPMENT—INTERMEDIATE 2 (TOLD-I:2)

GENERAL TEST INFORMATION

Author: Phyllis L. Newcomer and Donald D. Hammill

Publisher: PRO-ED, Inc.

Address of Publisher: 8700 Shoal Creek Blvd.
Austin, TX 78758-6897

Phone Number of Publisher: 512-451-3246 or 800-897-3202

Fax of Publisher: 800-FXPROED

Purpose of Test: This test is used to:

♦ identify children who are significantly below their peers in language proficiencies

♦ determine children's specific strengths and weaknesses in language skills

♦ document children's progress in language as a consequence of special intervention programs

♦ measure language in research studies

Description of Test: Like the TOLD-P:2, this test offers measures of receptive and expressive syntax and semantics. However, phonology measures are not included.

Type of Test: Norm-referenced

Administration Time: 40 minutes

Type of Administration: Individual

Who Administers This Test: Speech and language therapists, special education evaluators, psychologists

Age/Grade Levels: Ages 8.6 to 12.11

Subtest Information: The test consists of the following subtests:

Subtest	Specific Ability	Language Area Measured
Sentence Combining	constructing sentences	Syntax
Vocabulary	understanding word relationships	Semantics
Word Ordering	constructing sentences	Syntax
Generals	knowing abstract relationships	Semantics
Grammatic Comprehension	recognizing grammatical sentences	Syntax
Malapropisms	correcting ridiculous sentences	Semantics

Scoring Information: The scores are presented in the following manners:

♦ Percentile ranks

♦ Standard scores

♦ Composite scores

TEST OF LANGUAGE DEVELOPMENT—INTERMEDIATE 2 (TOLD-I:2)

(continued)

STRENGTHS OF THE TOLD-I:2

- The test is a useful measure for investigating the oral language skills of older children.
- The test is very useful in identifying areas where the child is proficient and areas that require further evaluation.
- The test has solid reliability.

WEAKNESSES OF THE TOLD-I:2

- The test results are not sufficiently specific to direct instructional planning.
- No information is provided about the handicapping conditions or home languages of students in the sample which may be problematic in generalizability.

PSYCHOLOGICAL AND SOCIAL ASSESSMENT

BEHAVIORAL, EMOTIONAL, AND SOCIAL DEVELOPMENT

When a referral is made on a child for a suspected disability, a behavioral and emotional assessment is a normal part of the psychoeducational evaluation. Behavioral and emotional measures are usually administered and reported on by the school psychologist. When doing a psychoeducational assessment of a child in a school, one critical component to address is the child's behavior, since behavior can have a serious impact on his or her learning processes. For example, a child with problems staying on task or focusing may have the intelligence to do math or social studies, but consistently gets low grades because he or she cannot sit still in order to complete the assignments given by the teacher.

Behaviors which are not appropriate in school can occur for many different reasons. Some include:

◆ attention deficit problems

◆ mental illness

◆ environmental factors at home

◆ problems with teachers of certain classes

When behaviors are believed to be a contributing factor to a child's problems in school, a variety of methods can be used for assessment. Because there are so many different possibilities as to why a child is acting inappropriately in school, it is critical to do a thorough behavioral assessment. By doing this, reasons for future placement in special education programs and the nature of the appropriate services will be more easily accomplished.

Assessing Problem Behavior

A behavioral assessment is often done when parents, teachers, or any other individuals working with a child feel there are possible concerns involving a child's emotional, social, or behavioral issues. The purpose of a behavioral assessment is to gain an awareness of what environmental factors, if any, are influencing the behavior that the child is exhibiting. In order to do a complete and thorough evaluation of behavior, it is critical that the following situations are assessed:

◆ Observation of a specific situation: Here, an observation of the child is done during a specified time, such as lunch time, at recess, or during show and tell.

◆ Observation in various settings like the classroom, the playground, and during band.

◆ Observation at different times during the day, such as morning, afternoon, and/or evening

When doing the above observations, information about the child becomes much more comprehensive. Collectively, the observations should provide the following:

♦ The nature of the most frequently seen behaviors

♦ Information which can be related to the types of services the child may need

♦ Information to help with intervention plans and instructional goals for the child

♦ Baseline information against which progress can be measured once intervention begins

Besides observations, interviews become a very important part of doing a behavioral assessment. Both parents and the child should be interviewed in order to gain insight into the nature and history of the child's difficulties. It is important to interview the child because the evaluator needs to know whether or not the child has any awareness that there is a concern about his or her behaviors, and the degree to which the child may be willing to change.

Assessing Emotional and Social Development

Assessment of emotional and social development is not an easy task. Throughout the course of a given day, children are involved in many different situations with many different people. It is not like assessing math or reading whereby we can simply compare numbers of a given child to national norms and make conclusions based on the quantifiable data. With a child, he or she may act completely differently with one person than another. Assessment of a child's behaviors involves knowledge about the following:

♦ The degree to which he or she believes that personal behaviors make a difference in his or her life

♦ His or her tolerance for frustration

♦ General activity level

♦ How the child views him- or herself

♦ How the child responds emotionally to situations

♦ How much conflict he or she is experiencing

There are many different instruments available to assess a child's emotional and social functioning. According to Salvia and Ysseldyke (1995), these include:

• **Rating Scales:** These scales allow questions to be asked in a standardized way and to be accompanied by the same stimulus materials, and they provide a standardized set of response options.

• **Projective Tests:** These tests ask students to respond to vague or ambiguous stimuli such as inkblots (Rorschach test), draw pictures (Draw a House-Tree-Person), or express themselves through the use of puppets, dolls, or telling stories (Thematic Apperception Test).

• **Personality Inventories:** These tests assess behavior patterns and characteristics of a student.

• **Personality Questionnaires:** These tests predict personality and mental health outcome.

While information gathered through all of these instruments may be very helpful, they are not without criticism. Due to the subjective nature of some of these tests and measures, many consider them to be lacking in validity and reliability, creating much controversy about their use.

WHAT YOU NEED TO KNOW ABOUT IN-SCHOOL COUNSELING

Although there may be staff members who believe a child may need in-school counseling, it is the role of the school psychologist to make this recommendation. It is important to understand the basis for such a recommendation and the criteria used by the psychologist to make such a recommendation. Special educators may pick up certain characteristics during an assessment through responses or observation that might make them consider contributing issues, i.e., tension and anxiety, other than learning problems. When this occurs, it would be very useful to discuss these concerns with the psychologist so that he or she may incorporate them into recommendations for the student.

When Is In-School Counseling Necessary?

In-school counseling is a free service to children enrolled in a public school district. A child may be referred for counseling by a teacher, guidance counselor, principal, parent, or even through self-referral. In-school counseling can be voluntary or recommended as a related service which may be the case on an IEP. This related service becomes necessary when a general pattern exists in which the child exhibits one or more of the following behaviors:

♦ An inability to learn on a consistent basis that cannot be explained by intellectual capability, hearing and vision status, or physical health anomalies

♦ An inability or unwillingness to develop or maintain satisfactory interpersonal relationships with peers, teachers, parents, or other adults

♦ Extreme over-reactions to minimally stressful situations over a prolonged period of time

♦ A general pervasive mood of sadness or depression

♦ A tendency toward somatic complaints, pains, or excessive fears associated with home, school, or social situations

♦ Lack of knowledge and skill acquisition in academic and social behaviors not attributed to intellectual capability, hearing and vision status, and physical health anomalies

♦ Observable periods of diminished verbal and motor activity (moods of depression or unhappiness)

The pattern of behaviors should be evaluated as to the frequency, duration, and intensity of the symptoms. Specific symptoms that might indicate the need for a consultation with the school psychologist and possible in-school counseling might involve patterns of behaviors including:

♦ academic underachievement

♦ social isolation or withdrawal

♦ excessive latenesses

♦ excessive absences

♦ frequent trips to the nurse

♦ negativism

♦ open defiance to authority or rules

♦ highly distractible

♦ poor social relationships

♦ feelings of hopelessness

♦ verbal aggression

♦ confrontational behavior

♦ inappropriate classroom behaviors

♦ impulsive behavior

♦ rigid behavior patterns

♦ anxious and worried, excessive fears and phobias

♦ easily frustrated even when confronted with a simple task

♦ resistance to change

Catching inappropriate and unhealthy patterns of behavior quickly can reduce the child's tension, anxiety, and negative reactions.

Questions About In-School Counseling

If a child is recommended for in-school counseling, then that child's parent should be provided with as much information as possible about this related service. Being informed can greatly reduce the misconceptions and resistance parents may have. Counseling has a better chance of working if the child sees that the parents are positive and supportive about the process.

Often times parents will turn to teachers to gain information about the in-school counseling process. As a teacher, you may be asked to answer the following questions about the individual providing the counseling:

♦ What are the qualifications of the counselor?

♦ What is the counselor's experience with the child's age group?

♦ What is the counselor's experience with the child's specific problem areas?

♦ What are the goals of counseling?

♦ What is the average length of a session?

♦ What classes will the student have to miss in order to go to counseling?

♦ Will the parents be involved in the sessions, either alone or with the child?

♦ Will the parents be contacted on a regular basis by the counselor?

♦ What are the rules of confidentiality?

♦ Will records be kept of the sessions?

♦ Will there be any indication of counseling placed on the child's permanent record card or folder?

CHILDREN'S APPERCEPTION TEST (CAT)

GENERAL TEST INFORMATION

Authors:	Leopold Bellak and Sonya Sorel Bellak
Publisher:	C.P.S. Incorporated
Address of the Publisher:	P.O. Box 83 Larchmont, NY 10538
Phone Number of the Publisher:	914-833-1633
Fax of Publisher:	914-833-1633

Purpose of Test: The test is intended to probe a child's fears in a variety of everyday situations including play situations, interpersonal problems in the classroom, fantasies about being an adult, oral themes, reaction to physical handicaps or castration fears, competitiveness with others, body image ideas, fears of physical illness, bathroom reactions, and so on.

Description of Test: This test uses a story-telling technique for personality evaluation. It employs pictures of animal figures in a variety of situations because it is assumed that children will be more comfortable expressing their feelings with pictures of animals than humans.

Administration Time:	Untimed
Type of Administration:	Individual
Who Administers This Test:	Psychologist
Age/Grade Levels	Ages 5 to 10

Subtest Information: There are no subtests.

Scoring Information: The test has no objective scoring.

STRENGTHS OF THE CAT

- Good indicator of the presence of psychological needs
- Easy to administer
- Very popular test within school systems as part of a psychological battery

WEAKNESSES OF CAT

- Issues of validity and reliability
- Very subjective interpretation by examiner
- Nonverbal students will have difficulty with this test

GOODENOUGH-HARRIS DRAWING TEST (GHDT)

GENERAL TEST INFORMATION

Author:	Florence L. Goodenough and Dale B. Harris
Publisher:	The Psychological Corporation
Address of Publisher:	555 Academic Court San Antonio, TX 78204-2498
Phone Number of Publisher:	800-211-8378
Fax of Publisher:	800-232-1223
TDD of the Publisher:	800-723-1318

Purpose of Test: The test is designed to measure intellectual maturity—the ability to form concepts of an abstract character—or to screen for children who may have emotional disorders.

Description of Test: The test comprises a formal system of administering and scoring human figure drawings to screen children for intellectual maturity as well as emotional problems. Practitioners can detect children who are at risk of having an emotional disturbance by comparing the scores obtained on their figure drawings with the scores from a normative sample.

Type of Test:	Standardized
Type of Administration:	Individual or group
Administration Time:	15–20 minutes
Who Administers This Test:	Psychologist and special education teacher
Age/Grade Levels:	Ages 3 to 15.11, but the preferred ages are 3 to 10 years

Subtest Information: This test does not contain subtests.

Scoring Information: The GHDT is composed of two scales, MAN and WOMAN. Twelve ranked drawings are provided for each of the scales; the respondent's drawings are compared to the ranked ones. Performance may be scored by a short holistic method with quality scale cards or by a more detailed method. Each drawing may also be scored for the presence of up to 73 characteristics specified in the Test Manual.

STRENGTHS OF THE GHDT

- The test's reliability is relatively high.
- The test manual provides a clear description of the scoring system. The record form is clear and efficient.
- The test is psychometrically sound as well as easily and objectively quantified.

WEAKNESSES OF THE GHDT

- Because of the subjective nature of the test and the drawings involved, there are issues concerning the validity of this test.

DRAW-A-PERSON: SCREENING PROCEDURE FOR EMOTIONAL DISTURBANCE (DAP: SPED)

GENERAL TEST INFORMATION

Authors:	Jack A. Naglieri, Timothy J. McNeish, and Achilles N. Bardos
Publisher:	PRO-ED, Inc.
Address of Publisher:	8700 Shoal Creek Boulevard Austin, TX 78758-6897
Phone Number of Publisher:	512-451-3246 or 800-897-3202
Fax of Publisher:	800-FXPROED

Purpose of Test: The test is designed as a nonverbal screening measure for identifying children and adolescents who may have emotional or behavioral disorders.

Description of Test: The test contains a formal system of administering and scoring human figure drawings to screen children for emotional problems. Practitioners can detect children who are at risk of having an emotional disturbance by comparing the scores obtained on their figure drawings with the scores from normative sample.

Type of Test:	Standardized
Type of Administration:	Individual or group
Administration Time:	15 minutes
Who Administers This Test:	Psychologist
Age/Grade Levels:	Ages 6 to 17, but the preferred ages are 3 to 10 years

Subtest Information: The test has no subtests.

Scoring Information: The DAP:SPED scoring system is composed of two types of criteria, or items. With the first type, eight dimensions of each drawing are scored. With the second type, each drawing is rated according to 47 items specified in the Test Manual.

STRENGTHS OF THE DAT:SPED

- The test reliability is relatively high.
- The test manual provides a clear description of the scoring system. The record form is clear and efficient.
- he test is psychometrically sound as well as easily and objectively quantified.

WEAKNESSES OF THE DAT:SPED

- Because of the subjective nature of the test and the drawings involved, there are issues concerning the validity of this test.
- This test should never be used alone for decision-making processes.

RORSCHACH PSYCHODIAGNOSTIC TEST

GENERAL TEST INFORMATION

Author:	Hermann Rorschach
Publisher:	Hans Huber
	14 Bruce Park Avenue
	Toronto, Ontario
	M4P 2S3
	416-482-6339
	Distributed by The Psychological Corporation
Address of Publisher:	555 Academic Court
	San Antonio, TX 78204-2498
Phone Number of Publisher:	800-211-8378
Fax of Publisher:	800-232-1223
TDD of the Publisher:	800-723-1318

Purpose of Test: The test intends to evaluate personality through the use of projective techniques.

Description of Test: The test is a ten-card oral response projective personality test in which the subject is asked to interpret what he or she sees in ten inkblots.

Type of Test:	Non-standardized
Type of Administration:	Individual
Administration Time:	Untimed
Who Administers This Test:	Psychologist
Age/Grade Levels:	Ages 3 and older

Subtest Information: The test has no subtests.

Scoring Information: The scoring procedure is elaborate and detailed, focusing on many variables. Only a well-trained examiner should administer and score this instrument.

STRENGTHS OF THE RORSCHACH

- With proper scoring the test can yield valuable information about the emotional state of a person.
- The test is easy to administer.
- Directions are simple and easily understood for administration and taking it.

WEAKNESSES OF THE RORSCHACH

- The test is very difficult to score because of the many variables involved in the scoring procedure.
- Because of the subjective nature of the test and the drawings involved, there are issues concerning the validity of this test.

THE POLITTE SENTENCE COMPLETION TEST (PSCT)

GENERAL TEST INFORMATION

Author:	Alan Politte
Publisher:	Psychologists and Educators Incorporated
Address of Publisher:	PO Box 513 Chesterfield, MO 63006
Phone Number of Publisher:	314-576-9127
Fax of Publisher:	314-878-3090

Purpose of Test: The test is designed to assess personality functioning. It is used for clinical counseling and academic guidance.

Description of Test: The test is a 35-item, paper-and-pencil test measuring personality. Items are sentence stems that the subject completes.

Type of Test:	Non-standardized
Type of Administration:	Individual or group
Administration Time:	15 minutes
Who Administers This Test:	Psychologist
Age/Grade Levels:	Grades 1 to 12

Subtest Information: The test has no subtests.

Scoring Information: The Politte is not an instrument that provides a score for the student. Rather, the results are based on clinical interpretation.

STRENGTHS OF THE PSCT

♦ The test is easy to administer.

♦ The test is useful for clinical interpretation of personality.

♦ The test has relatively short administration time.

WEAKNESSES OF THE PSCT

♦ Because of the subjective nature of the test and the drawings involved, there are issues concerning its validity.

♦ This test should never be used alone for decision-making processes.

THEMATIC APPERCEPTION TEST CHILDREN AND ADULTS (TAT)

GENERAL TEST INFORMATION

Author:	Henry A. Murray
Publisher of the Test:	Harvard University Press
Address of Publisher:	79 Garden Street Cambridge, MA 02138
Phone Number of the Publisher:	617-495-2600
Fax of Publisher:	617-495-2600

Purpose of Test: This test is intended to reveal to the trained interpreter some of the dominant drives, emotions, sentiments, complexes, and conflicts of a personality.

Description of Test: The test comprises a series of 20 pictures about which the individual being tested is instructed to tell stories, usually with a beginning, middle, and end. During this process the story is coded for evaluating certain emotional and behavioral characteristics.

Type of Test:	Non-standardized
Type of Administration:	Individual
Administration Time:	Untimed
Who Administers This Test:	Psychologist
Age/Grade Levels:	Ages 14 and over

Subtest Information: The test has no subtests.

Scoring Information: The test has no objective scoring.

STRENGTHS OF THE TAT

♦ The test is a good indicator of the presence of psychological needs.

♦ The test is easy to administer.

♦ The test is a very popular test within school systems as part of a psychological battery because of the easy administration and the quality of information which can be obtained.

WEAKNESSES OF TAT

♦ Because of the subjective nature of the test and the drawings involved, there are issues concerning the validity of this test.

♦ This test should never be used alone for decision-making processes.

♦ Nonverbal students will have difficulty with this test because of the test's verbal nature.

CONNERS' PARENT AND TEACHER RATING SCALES (CPRS/CTRS)

GENERAL TEST INFORMATION

Author:	C. Keith Conners
Publisher:	Multi-Health Systems Incorporated
Address of the Publisher:	908 Niagra Falls Boulevard North Tonawanda, NY 14120-2060
Phone Number of the Publisher:	800-456-3003
Fax of Publisher:	888-540-4484

Purpose of Test: The test is designed to measure hyperactivity and other patterns of a child's behavior.

Description of Test: This test is a paper-pencil or computer administered instrument used to evaluate problem behaviors of children as reported by the child's teacher, parents, or alternate care giver.

Type of Test:	Standardized
Administration Time:	Untimed
Type of Administration:	Individual
Who Administers This Test:	Psychologist, special education teacher, classroom teacher, parent
Age/Grade Levels:	The Conners' Parent Rating Scale can help identify behavior problems in children 3 to 17 years of age. The Conners' Teacher Rating Scale provides measures for identifying a variety of behavioral problems in children 4 to 12 years old.

Subtest Information: There are four forms available:

- *Conners' Teacher Rating Scale* (CTRS)—Here the person providing the information about the child is the teacher. This scale is utilized for children 3 to 17 years of age.

- *Conners' Teacher Rating Scale-39*—Here the person providing the information about the child is the teacher. This scale is utilized for children 4 to 12 years of age.

- *Conners'/Parent Rating Scales-93*—Here the person providing the information about the child is the parent. This scale is utilized for children 6 to 14 years of age.

- *Conners'/Parent Rating Scale-48*—Here the person providing the information about the child is the parent. This scale is utilized for children 3 to 17 years of age.

These forms measure a variety of behavioral characteristics grouped into several scales:

- Conduct Problems
- Hyperactivity
- Inattentive-Passive
- Anxious-Passive
- Asocial
- Daydream Attention Problems
- Emotional Overindulgent
- Anxious-Shy
- Conduct disorders

CONNERS' PARENT AND TEACHER RATING SCALES (CPRS/CTRS)
(continued)

- Hyperactive-Immature
- Learning Problems
- Obsessive Compulsive
- Psychosomatic
- Restless-Disorganized
- Anxiety
- Impulsive-Hyperactive

Scoring Information: Standard scores allow the examiner to compare the student's score on each scale with the normed population.

STRENGTHS OF THE CPRS/CTRS

- The instrument has been used by professionals for over twenty years.
- This test is a thorough measure of a student's behavioral characteristics because of the number of questions rated.

WEAKNESSES OF THE CPRS/CTRS

- The test standardization sample is not well described, which may be problematic for generalizability.
- The test has not been updated to measure more current definitions of ADD and ADHD.

KINETIC-HOUSE-TREE-PERSON DRAWINGS (K-H-T-P)

GENERAL TEST INFORMATION

Author: Robert C. Burns

Publisher: Western Psychological Services

Address of the Publisher: 12031 Wilshire Blvd.
Los Angeles, CA 90025

Phone Number of the Publisher: 310-478-2061 or 800-648-8857

Fax of Publisher: 310-478-7838

Purpose of Test: The test assesses personality disturbances in children ages 3 and older and reveals not only pathology and emotional disturbance but also developmental characteristics.

Description of Test: The student is asked to draw a house, a tree, and a person in action using one page of paper for each.

Type of Test: Nonstandardized

Administration Time: Untimed

Type of Administration: Individual

Who Administers This Test: Psychologist

Age/Grade Levels: Children and adolescents

Subtest Information: The test has no subtests.

Scoring Information: There is no objective scoring for this test. The test is evaluated through the use of diagnostic criteria.

STRENGTHS OF THE K-H-T-P

- The test is easy to administer.
- The test is non-threatening because the objects being drawn by the child are familiar.

WEAKNESSES OF THE K-H-T-P

- Because of the subjective nature of the test and the drawings involved, there are issues concerning the validity of this test.
- This test should never be used alone for decision-making processes.

ATTENTION DEFICIT DISORDERS EVALUATION SCALE—REVISED (ADDES)

GENERAL TEST INFORMATION

Author:	Stephen B. McCarney
Publisher of the Test:	Hawthorne Educational Services
Address of the Publisher:	800 Gray Oak Drive Columbia, MO 65201
Phone Number of the Publisher:	800-542-1673
Fax of Publisher:	800-442-9509

Purpose of Test: The test is intended as an evaluation tool for the diagnosis of Attention Deficit Disorder, with or without hyperactivity (ADD/ADHD).

Description of Test: There are two versions of this test: The Home Version, completed by parents, has 46 items that assess certain ADD behaviors in the home; and the School Version has 60 ADD-related items that teachers must rate along a five-point scale.

Type of Test:	Norm-referenced rating scale
Administration Time:	15 minutes
Type of Administration:	Individual for parents and teachers
Who Administers This Test:	Psychologist
Age/Grade Levels:	4 to 18 years

Subtest Information: The two forms of this test measure the following:

- Inattention
- Impulsivity
- Hyperactivity

SCORING INFORMATION

- Standard scores

STRENGTHS OF THE ADDES

- The test Computerized Quick Scoring Program makes scoring of both versions efficient and convenient.
- The test proves very helpful to evaluators in planning IEP development because of the amount of information obtained.
- This test has the largest normative sample of any ADD rating scale.

WEAKNESSES OF THE ADDES

- Given the newness of the test, further studies are needed to determine reliability and validity.

ADAPTIVE BEHAVIOR ASSESSMENT

ASSESSING ADAPTIVE BEHAVIOR

The assessment of adaptive behavior is a very important part of the overall assessment process. Adaptive behavior refers to the effectiveness or degree with which individuals meet the standards of personal independence and social responsibility expected for age and cultural groups (Grossman, 1983, p.1). When doing an evaluation of adaptive behavior, there are a number of areas in which the examiner should focus. These areas include:

- Communication
- Community use
- Self-direction
- Health and safety
- Functional academics
- Self-care
- Home living
- Social skills
- Leisure
- Work

Understanding adaptive behavior is very important when working with or assessing the mentally retarded population. Adaptive behavior is a required area of assessment when a classification of mental retardation is being considered for a student. Under IDEA, it specifies "deficits in adaptive behavior" as one of the two characteristics necessary for a student to be classified as mentally retarded (the other being "significantly subaverage general intellectual functioning") [34 CFR sec 300.7 (b)(5)].

There are many different ways in which an evaluator can measure adaptive behavior. Because it is often used to assess those with lower levels of intellectual functioning, the student being evaluated may not have to take part directly in the evaluation. The way many of these diagnostic assessment instruments work is that the examiner records information collected from a third person who is familiar with the student (e.g., parent, teacher, direct service provider). Probably the greatest problem with doing an assessment on adaptive behavior is the fact that many of the scales and tests do not have high validity and reliability. Also, there are serious concerns about the cultural bias of the tests. Consequently, great care must be taken when selecting the most appropriate measure for an individual student. With respect to minority students, it should also be noted that is imperative to develop an understanding of what types of behavior are considered adaptive (and thus appropriate) in the minority culture before making diagnostic judgments about the particular functioning of a student.

AAMR ADAPTIVE BEHAVIOR SCALE—RESIDENTIAL AND COMMUNITY—2 (ABS-RC-2)

GENERAL TEST INFORMATION

Authors:	Kazuo Nihira, Henry Leland, and Nadine Lambert
Publisher:	PRO-ED, Inc.
Address of Publisher:	8700 Shoal Creek Blvd. Austin, TX 78758-6897
Phone Number of Publisher:	512-451-3246 or 800-897-3202
Fax of Publisher:	800-FXPROED

Purpose of Test: The test is designed to determine an individual's strengths and weaknesses among adaptive domains and factors.

Description of Test: The test is intended for persons with disabilities in residential and community settings. It measures various domain areas and is available as a kit or on software for administration and scoring.

Type of Test:	Norm-referenced
Administration Time:	15–30 minutes
Type of Administration:	Individual
Who Administers This Test:	Psychologist, special education teacher, classroom teacher
Age/Grade level:	Ages 18 to 80

Subtest Information: The test has no subtests.

Scoring Information: The test provides the following:

- Percentiles
- Standard Scores

STRENGTHS OF THE ABS:RC-2

- It is one of the few tests available as a measure for persons with disabilities in the area of adaptive behaviors and factors.
- Many different factors are considered; this is helpful for evaluation.

WEAKNESSES OF THE ABS:RC-2

- The test is difficult to evaluate.
- Scoring the test is time consuming.

AAMR ADAPTIVE BEHAVIOR SCALE—SCHOOL (ABS-S:2)

GENERAL TEST INFORMATION

Authors:	Nadine Lambert, Kazuo Nihira, and Henry Leland
Publisher:	PRO-ED, Inc.
Address of Publisher:	8700 Shoal Creek Blvd. Austin, TX 78758-6897
Phone Number of Publisher:	512-451-3246 or 800-897-3202
Fax of Publisher:	800-FXPROED

Purpose of Test: The test is designed to assess the current functioning of children being evaluated for evidence of mental retardation, for evaluating adaptive behavior characteristics of children with autism, and for differentiating children with behavior disorders.

Description of Test: There are 16 subscores that are measured using this test. The test includes an examiner's manual, examiner booklets, computer scoring systems, and profile summary forms.

Type of Test:	Norm-referenced
Type of Administration:	Individual
Administration Time:	15–30 minutes
Who Administers This Test:	Psychologist, special education teacher, classroom teacher
Age/Grade Levels:	Ages 3 to 18.11

Subtest Information: The scale is divided into two parts:

Part I focuses on personal independence and is designed to evaluate coping skills considered to be important to independence and responsibility in daily living. The skills within Part I are grouped into nine behavior domains:

1. Independent Functioning
2. Physical Development
3. Economic Activity
4. Language Development
5. Numbers and Time
6. Prevocational/Vocational Activity
7. Self Direction
8. Responsibility
9. Socialization

Part II of the scale contains content related to social adaptation. The behaviors in Part II are assigned to seven domains:

1. Social Behavior
2. Conformity
3. Trustworthiness
4. Stereotyped and Hyperactive Behavior
5. Self-Abusive Behavior
6. Social Engagement
7. Disturbing Interpersonal Behavior

197

Scoring Information: The test provides scores in the following manners:

- Raw scores
- Percentiles

STRENGTHS OF THE ABS-2

- The scale has an excellent standardization sample and is appropriate for use with a wide variety of individuals.
- The scale's psychometric qualities are good.
- It has been and remains one of the best available scales for assessment of adaptive behavior.

WEAKNESSES OF THE ABS-2

- The test requires further validity research, especially regarding construct validity.

THE ADAPTIVE BEHAVIOR EVALUATION SCALE—REVISED (ABES-R)

GENERAL TEST INFORMATION

Author:	Stephen B. McCarney
Publisher of the Test:	Hawthorne Educational Services
Address of the Publisher:	800 Gray Oak Drive Columbia, MO 65201
Phone Number of the Publisher:	800-542-1673
Fax of Publisher:	800-442-9509

Purpose of Test: The test is used as a measure of adaptive behavior in the identification of students who are mentally retarded, behaviorally disordered, learning disabled, vision or hearing impaired, and physically handicapped students.

Description of Test: The ABES-R consists of 105 items assessing adaptive behaviors that are not measured by academic skill testing, but are necessary for success in an educational setting.

Type of Test:	Norm-referenced
Administration Time:	20–25 minutes
Type of Administration:	Individual
Who Administers This Test:	Psychologist, special education teacher, classroom teacher
Age/Grade Level:	Norms are for students from grades K–12

Subtest Information: The test contains 10 adaptive skill areas:

1. Communication Skills
2. Self Care
3. Home Living
4. Social Skills
5. Community Use
6. Self Direction
7. Health and Safety
8. Functional Academics
9. Leisure
10. Work Skills

SCORING INFORMATION:

♦ Standard scores
♦ Percentiles

STRENGTHS OF THE ABES-R

♦ This test is a good measure of adaptive behavior for the identification of students with intellectual disabilities.
♦ The test comes with an Adaptive Behavior Intervention Manual which may be useful in developing a student's IEP.

WEAKNESSES OF THE ABES-R

♦ The test's interpretive materials only address students with mental retardation.
♦ The test's literature offers no profiles to show how the mentally retarded may differ from those with behavioral or learning handicaps.

DEVELOPMENTAL ASSESSMENT FOR THE SEVERELY HANDICAPPED (DASH)

GENERAL TEST INFORMATION

Author:	Mary Kay Dykes
Publisher:	PRO-ED, Inc.
Address of Publisher:	8700 Shoal Creek Blvd. Austin, TX 78758-6897
Phone Number of Publisher:	512-451-3246 or 800-897-3202
Fax of Publisher:	800-FXPROED

Purpose of Test: To provide a discrete profile of a child's functioning levels of skills across socioemotional, language, sensorimotor, activities of daily living, and preacademic areas.

Description of Test: This assessment system is a developmentally sequenced, fine-grained, behaviorally defined criterion-referenced measure of current and developing skills in five skill domains—sensorimotor, language, preacademic, activities of daily living, and social-emotional. The instrument may be useful in identifying and measuring very discrete changes in behavior in very low-functioning individuals in order to pinpoint skills and facilitate training within the IEP process.

Type of Test:	Performance rating
Administration Time:	120–180 minutes
Type of Administration:	Individual
Who Administers This Test:	Psychologist, special education teacher, classroom teacher
Age/Grade Levels:	Individuals functioning within the developmental range of birth to 8 years

Subtest Information: The DASH consists of five pinpoint scales which assess performance in the following:

♦ Language
♦ Sensorimotor Skills
♦ Activities of Daily Living
♦ Preacademic Skills
♦ Social/Emotional Skills

Each of the five scales contains several hundred items for that area of performance analysis arranged by developmental age.

Scoring Information: The test is an observational performance rating scale; therefore, there is no objective scoring.

STRENGTHS OF THE DASH

♦ Provides multiple examples of behavior at young age ranges.
♦ Provides a scoring method to measure the conditions under which behavior occurs.

WEAKNESSES OF THE DASH

♦ Performance rating observational rating scales can be affected by subjective, biased reporting which may dilute the results.
♦ No training is provided for observers in order to operationalize the observable behaviors.

VINELAND ADAPTIVE BEHAVIOR SCALE (VABS)

GENERAL TEST INFORMATION

Authors:	Sara S. Sparrow, David A. Balla, and Domenie V. Cicchetti
Publisher:	American Guidance Service
Address of Publisher:	4201 Woodland Rd. Circle Pines, MN 55014-1796
Phone Number of Publisher:	612-786-4343 or 800-328-2560
Fax of Publisher:	612-786-9077

Purpose of Test: The test intends to provide a general assessment of adaptive behavior.

Description of Test: The VABS assesses the social competence of handicapped and nonhandicapped individuals. It requires that a respondent familiar with the behavior of the individual in question answer behavior orientation questions posed by a trained examiner. There are three versions of this test including the Interview Edition—Survey Form, Interview Edition—Expanded Form, and the Classroom Edition.

Type of Test:	Norm-referenced
Administration Time:	20–60 minutes
Type of Administration:	Individual
Who Administers This Test:	Psychologist, social worker, special education teacher with training in individual assessment and test interpretation
Age/Grade Levels:	Birth to 18.11 and low functioning adults, ages 3 through 12.11

Subtest Information: All of the versions measure the following domains:

- *Communication,* which contains the subdomains of receptive, expressive, and written communication
- *Daily Living Skills,* which contains the subdomains of personal, domestic, and community daily living skills
- *Socialization,* which contains the subdomains of interpersonal relationships, play and leisure time, and coping skills
- *Motor Skills,* which contains the subdomains of gross and fine motor skills

Scoring Information: The test provides the following:

- Standard scores
- Percentile ranks
- Age equivalents
- Domain and Adaptive Behavior Composite

STRENGTHS OF THE VINELAND

- The test is a useful tool for the assessment of adaptive behavior.
- The test has adequate validity and reliability.

WEAKNESSES OF THE VINELAND

- The test requires a great deal of training to properly administer the semi-structured parent interview.
- The manual restricts administration of the interview editions to a psychologist, social worker, or other professional with a graduate degree and specific training in individual assessment and test interpretation.

LIGHT'S RETENTION SCALE (LRS)

GENERAL TEST INFORMATION

Author:	H. Wayne Light
Publisher:	Academic Therapy Publications
Address of Publisher:	20 Commercial Blvd. Novato, CA 94949-6191
Phone Number of Publisher:	415-883-3314 or 800-422-7249
Fax of Publisher:	415-883-3720

Purpose of Test: This test aids the school professional in determining whether a student would benefit from grade retention.

Description of Test: This test is a rating scale designed as a counseling tool for use by school professionals, in conjunction with parents, to determine if an elementary or secondary student would benefit from repeating a school grade.

Type of Test:	Survey
Administration Time:	10–15 minutes
Type of Administration:	Individual
Who Administers This Test:	Psychologist, special education teacher, classroom teacher
Age/Grade Levels:	Grades K–12

Subtest Information: While there are no formal subtests, the LRS evaluates 19 specific areas of concern such as age, motivation, and behavioral problems, using a rating scale designed to be completed during parent conferences along with the teacher.

Scoring Information: Each of the 19 criteria is evaluated on a scale of 1 to 5 and the total score is used as a guide to help determine if grade retention is appropriate.

STRENGTHS OF THE LRS

 ♦ The LRS manual is a very useful document for teachers as a source of information on the topic of school retention.

 ♦ The test may be useful for schools in the development of retention policies.

 ♦ The LRS encourages evaluators to consider a broad range of factors that determine retention rather than basing decisions solely on factors such as immaturity or low achievement.

WEAKNESSES OF THE LRS

 ♦ There are conceptual and technical problems in the definitions of the areas being measured.

 ♦ There may be issues of validity and reliability that need further exploration.

Section 8

AN OVERVIEW OF EARLY CHILDHOOD HEARING IMPAIRED, OCCUPATIONAL & PHYSICAL THERAPY, AND BILINGUAL TESTS

EARLY CHILDHOOD ASSESSMENT

Early intervention is rapidly becoming an area of study for many special educators. Both undergraduate and graduate schools are beginning to stress the importance of early intervention assessment and education. Many states are becoming increasingly aware of the importance of early intervention for children. The idea of helping children before they get to elementary school with whatever concerns they may be facing has educational, social, and political implications. Whatever the reasons for the initiation of early intervention in a given state, it has become apparent that it is a very important part of the special education process.

It is important to keep in mind that the parents of very young children who are suspected of having a disability will be anxious and in search of answers from educational professionals. When potential problems occur at such an early age, parents need answers that will inform them as to the diagnosis of the problem, the prognosis of the child's development in later years, and remediation and intervention strategies that will help their child. Therefore, it is important for special educators to be familiar with early childhood evaluation instruments that will begin the process of assessment by diagnosing the child's potential strengths and weaknesses. From this information, a team of professionals can then prepare intervention recommendations for the parent.

One of the problems with early intervention assessment is that many special educators have limited, if any, training with the birth to five-year-old population. Consequently, although there are a number of tests to measure intellectual development, speech and language delays, and behavioral norms, few educators are well versed in knowledge of these assessment instruments.

Bagnato, Neisworth and Munson (1997) list six standards of assessment materials for use with young children:

- **Authenticity:** Does the assessment focus on actual child behavior in real settings?

- **Convergence:** Does the assessment rely on more than one source of information?

203

- **Collaboration:** Does the assessment involve cooperation and sharing, especially with parents?

- **Equity:** Does the assessment accommodate special sensory, motor, cultural, or other needs rather than penalize children who have such needs?

- **Sensitivity:** Does the assessment include sufficient items for planning lessons and detecting changes?

- **Congruence:** Was the assessment developed and field tested with children similar to those being assessed?

It is important for special educators to be familiar with early childhood evaluation instruments. Such instruments contribute information to the assessment process by diagnosing the child's strength and weakness areas. From this information, a team of professionals can then prepare intervention recommendations for the parent.

BAYLEY SCALES OF INFANT DEVELOPMENT—2ND EDITION (BSID-II)

GENERAL TEST INFORMATION

Author:	Nancy Bayley
Publisher:	The Psychological Corporation
Address of Publisher:	555 Academic Court San Antonio, TX 78204-2498
Phone Number of Publisher:	800-211-8378
Fax of Publisher:	800-232-1223
TDD of the Publisher:	800-723-1318

Purpose of Test: This test is designed to assess the developmental functioning of infants.

Description of Test: This individually administered test has three subscales: the Mental Scale, the Motor Scale, and the Behavior Rating Scale. The items in the Mental and Motor scales are mixed together; thus, examiners are required to identify which items go on each scale and tally them separately. The Behavior Rating Scale is completed after the Mental and Motor scales have been administered. This second edition has more than 100 new items created to apply to the expanded age range. The test includes the examiner's manual, stimulus booklet, Mental Scale record forms, Motor Scale record forms (with tracing design sheet), Behavior Rating Scale record forms, visual stimulus cards, map, and all necessary manipulatives.

Type of Test:	Norm-referenced
Administration Time:	Under 15 months, 25–30 minutes; over 15 months, up to 60 minutes
Type of Administration:	Individual
Who Administers This Test:	Psychologist
Age/Grade levels:	Ages 1–42 months

Subtest Information: The test comprises three subtests:

1. The *Mental Developmental Index (MDI)* assesses a variety of abilities including:
   - Sensory/perceptual acuity, discriminations, and responses
   - Acquisition of object constancy
   - Memory, learning, and problem solving
   - Vocalization, beginning of verbal communication
   - Basis of abstract thinking
   - Habituation
   - Mental Mapping
   - Mathematical concept formation

2. The *Psychomotor Developmental Index (PDI)* assesses a variety of abilities including:
   - Degree of body control
   - Large muscle coordination
   - Finer manipulatory skills of the hands and fingers
   - Dynamic movement
   - Postural imitation
   - Stereognosis

3. The **Behavior Developmental Index (BDI)** is a separate scale made up of its own items and assesses qualitative aspects of the child's test-taking behavior and allows an examiner to rate:

- Arousal
- Attention
- Orientation
- Engagement
- Emotional regulation
- Motor quality

Scoring Information: The test provides a mean of 100 and a standard deviation of 15 and offers the following scores:

- Mental Developmental Index (MDI)
- Physical Developmental Index (PDI)
- Behavior Developmental Index (BDI)

STRENGTHS OF THE BSID-II

- The scales' norms are representative in terms of race, ethnicity, geographic region, parental education, and sex.
- The BSID-II is a well standardized and very comprehensive test of infant development.
- The BSID-II is a very popular test used by early intervention clinicians.
- Data are provided in the manual for the following groups: children who were born prematurely, have the HIV antibody, were prenatally drug exposed, were asphyxiated at birth, are developmentally delayed or have frequent otitis media, are autistic, or have Down's Syndrome.

WEAKNESSES OF THE BSID-II

- The test demands a great deal on the part of the examiner with respect to administration and interpretation.
- The BSID-II is comprehensive and appropriate; however, there is limited evidence of the test's criterion-related and construct validity.

PRESCHOOL LANGUAGE SCALE—3 (PLS-3)

GENERAL TEST INFORMATION

Authors:	Irla Lee Zimmerman, Violette G. Steiner, and Roberta L. Evatt
Publisher:	The Psychological Corporation
Address of Publisher:	555 Academic Court San Antonio, TX 78204-2498
Phone Number of Publisher:	800-211-8378
Fax of Publisher:	800-232-1223
TDD of the Publisher:	800-723-1318

Purpose of Test: This test is designed to isolate areas of strength and weakness with regard to language facility.

Description of Test: This test is designed in a format of three sections: Auditory Comprehension, Verbal Ability, and Articulation. The test consists of pictures and items that each child must point to or explain. The level depends upon the child's developmental level at the time of testing. This test may be used as a criterion-referenced test for older children functioning within the range of behaviors assessed by PLS-3 and, with suggested modifications, for children with physical or hearing impairments. The test includes an examiner's manual, picture book, and record forms.

Type of Test:	Norm-referenced, criterion-referenced
Administration Time:	30 minutes
Type of Administration:	Individual
Who Administers This Test:	Special education teacher, psychologist, speech/language therapist
Age/Grade Levels:	Birth to 6.11

Subtest Information: The test includes two separate scales:

1. *Auditory Comprehension Scale*—The scale requires nonverbal responses, such as pointing to a picture that the examiner has named.

2. *Expressive Communication Scale*—In this section items are presented that require the child to name or explain the items. The difficulty varies depending on the child's developmental level during the time of testing.

The items on the test assess the following areas in both the receptive and expressive modes:

- ◆ Vocabulary
- ◆ Concepts of quality
- ◆ Concepts of quantity
- ◆ Space and time
- ◆ Morphology
- ◆ Syntax
- ◆ Integrative thinking skills

PRESCHOOL LANGUAGE SCALE—3 (PLS-3)
(continued)

Scoring Information: This test provides scores in the following manner:

♦ Standard scores

♦ Percentile ranks

♦ Language age-equivalents

STRENGTHS OF THE PLS-3

♦ This test may be useful to a preschool teacher who wishes to identify a pattern of strengths and weaknesses in a child's conceptual and auditory abilities.

♦ The test offers a comprehensive assessment of receptive and expressive language in young children.

♦ The test meets general federal and state guidelines, including IDEA legislation, for evaluating preschoolers for special services.

♦ The test is a good screening measure for qualification in early intervention programs like Head Start, Even Start, or Title I.

WEAKNESSES OF THE PLS-3

♦ The areas assessed in some subtests are headed with ambiguous terms such as differentiation of self, temporal ordering, and many others, which are not operationally defined.

♦ The PLS-3 Total Test Score is simply an average of both scales. This presents a problem if there is wide variability between the scales.

DEVELOPMENTAL PROFILE II (DP-II)

GENERAL TEST INFORMATION

Author:	Gerald Alpern, Thomas Boll, and Marsha Shearer
Publisher:	Western Psychological Services
Address of Publisher:	12031 Wilshire Blvd. Los Angeles, CA 90025
Phone Number of Publisher:	310-478-2061 or 800-648-8857
Fax of Publisher:	310-478-7838

Purpose of Test: This test is designed to screen children for developmental delays.

Description of Test: The DP-II includes 186 items, each describing a particular skill. These items are typically answered by the parent or a caregiver who simply indicates whether or not the child has mastered the skill in question.

Type of Test:	Norm-referenced
Administration Time:	20–30 minutes
Type of Administration:	Individual
Who Administers This Test:	Special eduction teacher, psychologist, speech/language therapist
Age/Grade levels:	Birth to 9-1/2 years

Subtest Information: The test consists of five skill areas:

- *Physical*—This area assesses the child's large and small coordination, strength, stamina, flexibility, and sequential motor skills.
- *Self Help*—This area assesses the child's ability to cope independently with the environment, i.e., to eat, dress, work, and take care of self and others.
- *Social*—This area assesses the child on interpersonal abilities, emotional needs, and manner in which the child relates to friends, relatives, and various adults.
- *Academic*—This area assesses the child's intellectual abilities and skills prerequisite to academic achievement.
- *Communication*—This area assesses the child's expressive and receptive communication skills, including written, spoken, and gestural language.

Scoring Information: The test provides scores in the following manners:

- Scaled scores
- Age equivalents

STRENGTHS OF THE DP-II

- The DP-II is easily administered.
- The DP-II is easy to score.
- The test can be used to determine eligibility or special education.

WEAKNESSES OF THE DP-II

At the time of printing, no weaknesses have been found.

METROPOLITAN READINESS TESTS—SIXTH EDITION (MRT-6)

GENERAL TEST INFORMATION

Authors:	Joanne R. Nurss
Publisher:	The Psychological Corporation
Address of Publisher:	555 Academic Court
	San Antonio, TX 78204-2498
Phone Number of Publisher:	800-211-8378
Fax of Publisher:	800-232-1223
TDD of the Publisher:	800-723-1318

Purpose of Test: The test is designed to assess a child's basic and advanced skills that are important in beginning reading and mathematics. This test also helps assess literacy development.

Description of Test: The MRT 6 is the primary assessment tool of the Metropolitan Readiness Assessment Program (MRAP). The MRAP is intended for use in evaluating the general development and prereading skill of students at the prekindergarten, kindergarten, and grade 1 levels of schooling. The test uses a colorful easel format for individualized administration. Each level of the MRT-6 includes a parent-teacher conference report which clearly explains the purpose of the MRT-6, and presents the results in a convenient format to use when conferring with parents.

Type of Test:	Standardized, norm- and criterion-referenced
Administration Time:	Approximately 90 minutes per actual test level and 5 minutes for practice booklet for each level
Type of Administration:	Individual
Who Administers This Test:	Special education teacher, psychologist, speech/language therapist, classroom teacher
Age/Grade Levels:	Ages 4 to 7 years, Pre-K through grade 1

Subtest Information: The MRT 6 Level 1 assesses five areas:

1. Visual Discrimination
2. Beginning Consonants
3. Sound-Letter Correspondence
4. Story Comprehension
5. Quantitative Concepts and Reasoning

Scoring Information: The test provides the following:

- ◆ Standard scores
- ◆ Percentiles
- ◆ Stanines

STRENGTHS OF THE MRT 6

- ◆ The directions provided are clear and well written.
- ◆ The directions and forms for scoring, summarizing, and interpreting completed tests are well written, clear, and user-friendly.
- ◆ There is strong evidence of the test's reliability.
- ◆ The test provides evidence of the internal consistency of the subtests.
- ◆ The test's norms are representative of the United States' population.

WEAKNESSES OF THE MRT 6

- ◆ Due to the updated revision of the test from the fifth edition, no weaknesses have been reported in Buros Mental Measurement Yearbook as of this printing.

BOEHM TEST OF BASIC CONCEPTS—PRESCHOOL VERSION

GENERAL TEST INFORMATION

Author: Ann E. Boehm

Publisher: The Psychological Corporation

Address of Publisher: 555 Academic Court
San Antonio, TX 78204-2498

Phone Number of Publisher: 800-211-8378

Fax of Publisher: 800-232-1223

TDD of the Publisher: 800-723-1318

Purpose of Test: The test is designed to assess children's mastery of the basic concepts that are both fundamental to understanding verbal instruction and essential for early school achievement.

Description of Test: The test consists of 50 concept items placed in two test booklets, Booklet 1 and Booklet 2, to facilitate administration in two sessions to children in grades K, 1, 2, and 3. The test has two alternate forms, C and D. The test questions are read by the examiner and the students are required to mark the correct response directly in the individual test booklet. The test materials include individual student test booklets and the examiner's manual.

Type of Test: Standardized

Administration Time: 0–40 minutes for form C or D, and 15–20 minutes for Applications form

Type of Administration: Group

Who Administers This Test: Special education teacher, psychologist, speech/language therapist, classroom teacher

Age/Grade Levels: Grades K to 3

Subtest Information: The test has no subtests.

Scoring Information: The test provides percentiles.

STRENGTHS OF THE BTBC-R

♦ A section in the manual devoted to score interpretation and to the use of the results instruction is very practical.

♦ Most young children will find this test interesting.

♦ The test has two equivalent forms which allow for the determination of progress with pre- and post-testing.

WEAKNESSES OF THE BTBC-R

♦ The norms of the test are based on a national school population, but only 15 states are reported which might have implications for generalization.

♦ Although the test is a good screening test for language development, better tests are available if the examiner is interested in cognitive development.

BRACKEN BASIC CONCEPT SCALE (BBCS)

GENERAL TEST INFORMATION

Author:	Bruce A. Bracken
Publisher:	The Psychological Corporation
Address of Publisher:	555 Academic Court San Antonio, TX 78204-2498
Phone Number of Publisher:	800-211-8378
Fax of Publisher:	800-232-1223
TDD of the Publisher:	800-723-1318

Purpose of Test: The test is designed to measure children who may be at risk for failure in situations requiring knowledge of basic concepts. Further, the screening portion of the test is used to identify kindergarten and first-grade students whose concept development is below age-level expectations and who would benefit from a more extensive diagnostic assessment.

Description of Test: This test measures 11 diagnostic subtest areas. Items are multiple-choice and the child is shown four monochrome pictures and asked to identify the picture that depicts a particular concept. The test includes an examiner's manual. diagnostic stimulus manual, diagnostic record forms, one Screening Test Form A, and one Screening Test Form B.

Type of Test:	Standardized
Administration Time:	20–40 minutes
Type of Administration:	Group
Who Administers This Test:	Special education teacher, psychologist, speech/language therapist, classroom teacher
Age/Grade Levels:	Age 2.6 to 7.11

Subtest Information: The following lists the subtests and corresponding concepts:

- *Color/Letter Identification*—Children are tested on their knowledge of colors and letters.
- *Numbers/Counting*—Children are required to tell how many items and recognize numbers.
- *Comparisons*—Children are required to compare things.
- *Shapes*—Children are tested regarding their ability to recognize different shapes.
- *Direction/Position*—Children are tested on their ability to distinguish between different directions and positions.
- *Social/Emotional*—This subtest determines children's social and emotional development.
- *Size*—This subtest determines children's ability to differentiate between sizes.
- *Texture/Material*—Children are given objects of different texture and must identify them.
- *Quantity*—Children are tested on their ability to distinguish amounts.
- *Time/Sequence*—Children are given numbers and asked to tell the missing number or the number that comes next.

Scoring Information: The test provides the following:

- Percentile ranks
- Standard scores
- Age equivalents

BRACKEN BASIC CONCEPT SCALE (BBCS)

(continued)

STRENGTHS OF THE BBCS

- One of the major strengths of the BBCS is the detailed and well organized Examiner's Manual.
- The test administration procedures for the BBCS are fairly well planned and coordinated.
- The test is a very comprehensive test of basic concept identification for young children.

WEAKNESSES OF THE BBCS

- The explanation of the standardization sample does not fully elaborate on the minority sample.
- Color-blind children will not perform as well on the color subtests as other children.

THE PRESCHOOL EVALUATION SCALES (PES)

GENERAL TEST INFORMATION

Author:	Stephen B. McCarney
Publisher:	Hawthorne Educational Services
Address of Publisher:	800 Gray Oak Drive Columbia, MO 65201
Phone Number of Publisher:	800-542-1673
Fax of Publisher:	800-442-9509

Purpose of Test: The test is designed to assess a child's behavior related to developmental delays. It is a useful and efficient means of gaining developmental information for preschool screening.

Description of Test: This test is designed as a rating scale completed by the child's parents or child-care provider. The Preschool Evaluation Scale can be completed at the child's home, or while other screening activities are taking place, requiring no additional time on the part of screening or diagnostic personnel. Irregularities in normal development are easily determined in order to provide the most appropriate intervention plan to remediate or otherwise intervene. It consists of a technical manual, rating forms, and a computerized scoring system.

Administration Time:	20–25 Minutes
Type of Administration:	Individual
Who Administers This Test:	Special education teacher, psychologist, occupational therapist
Age/Grade Levels:	Birth to 72 Months

Subtest Information: The subscale areas assessed by this instrument follow:

- Large muscle skill
- Small muscle skill
- Cognitive thinking
- Expressive language
- Social/emotional behavior
- Self-help skills

Scoring Information: The test provides standard scores.

STRENGTHS OF THE PES

- This test is a good screening device for developmental delays for preschool-aged children.
- The test has strong validity and reliability.

WEAKNESSES OF THE PES

- As is true of all rating type scales, the test is subject to interpretation of the individual completing the scale.

DEGANGI-BERK TEST OF SENSORY INTEGRATION (TSI)

GENERAL TEST INFORMATION

Authors:	Ronald A. Berk and Georgia A. De Gangi
Publisher:	Western Psychological Services
Address of Publisher:	12031 Wilshire Blvd. Los Angeles, CA 90025
Phone Number of Publisher:	310-478-2061 or 800-648-8857
Fax of Publisher:	310-478-7838

Purpose of Test: The test is designed to overcome problems in detecting sensory integrative dysfunction in the early years. The basic rationale is that early identification of children with various problems may permit initiation of treatment and thus ameliorate or avoid later academic consequences.

Description of Test: The 36 test items require the child to perform specific tasks or respond to various stimuli. It consists of design sheets, protocol booklets, and a manual. Other test materials (e.g., stopwatch, scooter board, hula hoop) must be supplied by the examiner.

Type of Test:	Norm-referenced
Administration Time:	30 minutes
Type of Administration:	Individual
Who Administers This Test:	Special education teacher, psychologist, occupational therapist
Age/Grade Levels:	Ages 3 to 5

Subtest Information: The test measures the child's ability on three clinically significant subdomains:

- *Postural Control*—This subtest includes antigravity postures necessary for stabilization of the neck, trunk, and upper extremities, and muscle cocontraction of the neck and upper extremities.
- *Bilateral Motor Integration*—This subtest emphasizes bilateral motor coordination and components of laterality including trunk rotation, crossing the midline, rapid unilateral and bilateral hand movements, stability of the upper and lower extremities in bilateral symmetrical postures and disassociation of trunk and arm movements.
- *Reflex Integration*—This subtest includes asymmetrical and symmetrical tonic neck reflexes in the quadruped position and associated reactions of the upper extremities.

These vestibular-based functions are essential to the development of motor skills, visual-spatial and language abilities, hand dominance, and motor planning.

Scoring Information: The therapist simply rates the child's performance on each item using a numerical scale ranging from abnormal to normal development. In addition to a total score, the TSI provides scores for each of the three subdomains measured. Cutoff points allow the examiner to compare the child's performance with that of normal, at-risk, and deficient youngsters.

STRENGTHS OF THE TSI

- The test effectively differentiates normal from developmentally delayed children.
- When used as the basis for screening decisions, the test's total scores demonstrate an 81% accuracy rate.

WEAKNESSES OF THE TSI

- The TSI lacks evidence of reliability.
- The statistics explaining the rationale for certain parts of the test have been criticized.
- The test has been criticized by Buros (10th Edition) as having "an unrepresentative sample."

KINDERGARTEN READINESS TEST (KRT)

GENERAL TEST INFORMATION

Authors:	Sue L. Larson and Gary Vitali
Publisher:	Slosson Educational Publications
Address of Publisher:	P.O. Box 280 East Aurora, NY 14052-0280
Phone Number of Publisher:	888-SLOSSON
Fax of Publisher:	800-655-3840

Purpose of Test: The purpose of this test is to determine the readiness of children to begin kindergarten.

Description of Test: The test assesses five general areas of readiness—awareness of one's environment, reasoning, numerical awareness, fine-motor coordination, and auditory attention span. The test booklet and additional forms are designed to enhance parent conferences or interprofessional presentations by graphically depicting individual strengths, as well as weaknesses, in a concise manner. The KRT consolidates critical areas of various developmental tests into one single form, thereby making identification of school readiness more efficient and valid. The test contains a manual, test booklets, performance grid sheets, a letter to parent, scoring interpretation, and stimulus items.

Type of Test:	Standardized
Administration Time:	15–20 minutes
Type of Administration:	Individual
Who Administers This Test:	Special education teacher, psychologist, speech/language therapist, classroom teacher
Age/Grade Level:	Ages 4 to 6

Scoring Information: The test provides the following:

- Percentiles
- Standard scores

STRENGTHS OF THE KRT

- The test can be readily administered by specialists, teachers, or paraprofessionals.
- The test assesses various key areas proven to be critical for school readiness and consolidates information on one form.
- The test is easy to administer.
- The test is appropriate for preschool, school, and clinical settings.

WEAKNESSES OF THE KRT

- At the time of printing, no review of the KRT was done regarding weaknesses in Buros Mental Measurement Yearbook.

CHILD BEHAVIOR CHECKLIST (CBCL)

GENERAL TEST INFORMATION

Authors:	Thomas H. Achenbach and Craig Edelbrock
Publisher:	University Associates in Psychiatry
Address of Publisher:	1 South Prospect Street Burlington, VT 05401
Phone Number of Publisher:	802-656-4563
Fax of Publisher:	802-656-8747

Purpose of Test: The test is designed to assess the behavioral problems and social competencies of children and adolescents through the use of ratings and reports by different informants.

Description of Test: The test comprises five multiple-item, paper-and-pencil, multiple-choice, and free response inventories that evaluate a child's behavioral problems from four perspectives.

Type of Test:	Norm-referenced
Administration Time:	Varies with age
Type of Administration:	Individual
Who Administers This Test:	Special education teacher, psychologist
Age/Grade Levels:	Ages 4 to 18

Subtest Information: There are three different forms of the CBCL. Each form is answered by a different respondent. Listed below are the three forms:

- *Child Behavior Checklist* (CBCL)—The informants on this scale are the child's parents.
- *Child Behavior Checklist-Teacher Report Form* (CBCL-TRF)—The informants on this scale are the child's teachers.
- *Child Behavior Checklist-Youth Self Report* (CBCL-YSR)—The informant on this scale is the child or adolescent being evaluated.

The CBCL measures numerous behavioral and psychological issues. Listed below are the various scales for each version of the CBCL:

- Social Competence
- Withdrawal
- Somatic complaints
- Anxiety/Depression
- Social problems
- Thought problems
- Attention problems
- Delinquent behavior
- Aggressive behavior
- Academic performance
- Self-destructive/identity problems

Scoring Information: The test provides the following:

- Percentiles
- Standard scores

217

CHILD BEHAVIOR CHECKLIST (CBCL)
(continued)

STRENGTHS OF THE CBCL

- The standardization and technical development of this scale makes it the most well developed, empirically derived behavior rating scale.
- The test is a good indicator for ADHD.
- The test manual is comprehensive and clear.
- The test is very highly recommended by all Buros reviewers.

WEAKNESSES OF THE CBCL

- The language may be difficult for some young children to understand.
- Students should not be classified on the basis of a rating scale.
- Since the test is only a rating scale, final determinations of a child's placement should not be made on the basis of only the scores received on the CBCL.

THE DENVER DEVELOPMENTAL SCREENING TEST—REVISED (DENVER II)

GENERAL TEST INFORMATION

Author:	William K. Frankenburg
Publisher:	Denver Developmental Materials Inc.
Address of Publisher:	P.O. Box 6919 Denver, Colorado 80206-0919
Phone Number of Publisher:	303-355-4729
Fax of Publisher:	303-355-5622

Purpose of Test: The test is designed to evaluate a child's personal, social, fine and gross motor, language, and adaptive abilities as a means of identifying possible problems and screening for further evaluation.

Description of Test: The test is a 105-item "pick and choose" test. The examiner observes what the child does with various items and makes recommendations based on perceived abnormalities.

Type of Test:	Standardized
Administration Time:	10–20 minutes
Type of Administration:	Individual
Who Administers This Test:	Special education teacher, psychologist, speech/language therapist, occupational therapist
Age/Grade Levels:	Birth to 6 years

Subtest Information: The Denver II consists of four assessment sections:

- *Personal-Social Abilities*—assesses the child's ability to get along with others and take care of one's self.
- *Fine Motor Adaptive Abilities*—assesses the child's ability to use hand-eye coordination in such tasks as drawing and picking up objects.
- *Language Abilities*—assesses the child's ability to receive, organize, and express language.
- *Gross Motor Abilities*—assesses the child's ability to use large muscle skills to accomplish certain tasks, e.g., walking, jumping.

Scoring Information: The test provides age-level equivalents.

STRENGTHS OF THE DENVER II

- The test is simple to administer.
- The test is simple to interpret.
- The test is available in Spanish.
- The test has high validity and reliability.

WEAKNESSES OF THE DENVER II

- Examiner ratings of the test behaviors are completely subjective.
- The norming sample only includes children in Colorado, which may affect generalizability.

THE BATTELLE DEVELOPMENTAL INVENTORY (BDI)

GENERAL TEST INFORMATION

Author:	J. Newborg, J.R. Stock, and J. Wnek
Publisher:	The Riverside Publishing Company
Address of Publisher:	8420 Spring Lake Drive Itasca, IL 60143-2079
Phone Number of Publisher:	800-323-9540
Fax of Publisher:	630-467-7192

Purpose of Test: The test is designed for screening, diagnosis, and evaluation of early development.

Description of Test: The BDI is a multiple-item test assessing key developmental skills. Information is obtained through structured interactions with the child in a controlled setting, observation of the child, and interviews with the child's parents, teachers, and caregivers. The test consists of five test-item books, an examiner's manual, scoring booklets, and a VHS overview video tape.

Type of Test:	Standardized
Administration Time:	10 minutes to 2 hours, depending on the age and cognitive ability of the child
Type of Administration:	Individual
Who Administers This Test:	Special education teacher, psychologist, speech/language therapist, occupational therapist
Age/Grade Levels:	Birth to 8 years

Subtest Information: The test consists of five subtests:

- *Personal-Social Domain*—This subtest measures coping skills, self-concept, expressions of feelings, and adult interaction.
- *Adaptive Domain*—This subtest measures attention, eating skills, dressing skills, personal responsibility, and toileting.
- *Motor Domain*—This subtest measures muscle control, body coordination, locomotion, fine muscle skills, and perceptual-motor skills.
- *Communication Domain*—This subtest measures receptive and expressive communication.
- *Cognitive Domain*—This subtest measures memory, reasoning skills, perceptual discrimination, academic skills, and conceptual development.

Scoring Information: The test provides the following:

- ◆ Standard scores
- ◆ Percentile ranks
- ◆ Age equivalents

STRENGTHS OF THE BDI

- ◆ The BDI is a multi-factor assessment measure.
- ◆ The BDI can be administered in the home setting, which may be important when dealing with very young children.
- ◆ The test is very comprehensive.

WEAKNESSES OF THE BDI

- ◆ The scoring procedure may be time-consuming.
- ◆ Learning how to administer this test may require more time due to the five test-item books, screening test, and examiner's manual.
- ◆ Many of the answers to test items for very young children are obtained through parent interviews, which may be problematic with respect to objectivity.

HEARING ASSESSMENT

When people think of someone who is hearing impaired, they often think that the person is "deaf." However, this is not true. Under IDEA, deafness is "a hearing impairment that is so severe that the child is impaired in processing linguistic information through hearing, with or without amplification, that adversely affects a child's educational performance." The following is how IDEA defines hearing impairment: "an impairment in hearing, whether permanent or fluctuating, that adversely affects a child's educational performance but which is not included under the definition of deafness in this section."

When examining the two definitions, it is evident that being deaf means that hearing is disabled to an extent that precludes understanding speech through the ear alone, with or without a hearing aid. Being hearing impaired or hard of hearing makes hearing difficult, but does not preclude the understanding of speech through the ear alone, with or without a hearing aid.

CAUSES OF HEARING IMPAIRMENT

Hearing difficulties need to be identified as early as possible in order to plan an appropriate educational program. Some hearing problems occur from birth while others occur at later stages in a child's development. There are several causes of hearing impairment, such as:

Conductive Hearing Loss—Results from problems with the structures in the outer or middle ear, generally attributed to a blockage in the mechanical conduction of sound. In order to overcome this blockage, the sounds must be amplified. These conditions are usually temporary. The leading causes of this type of hearing loss are:

 ♦ Otitis Media (middle ear infection)

 ♦ Excessive earwax

 ♦ Otosclerosis—formation of a spongy-boney growth around the stirrup which impedes its movement

Sensorineural Hearing Loss—Results from damage to the cochlea or the auditory nerve. This damage is caused by illness and disease, and is not medically or surgically treatable. Causes of this hearing loss include:

 ♦ Viral diseases (i.e., rubella-German measles, meningitis)

 ♦ Rh incompatibility

 ♦ Ototoxic medications (medicines that destroy or damage hair cells in the cochlea, i.e., streptomycin) taken by pregnant mothers or very young children

 ♦ Hereditary factors

 ♦ Exposure to noise

 ♦ Aging

Mixed Hearing Loss—A hearing loss caused by both sensorineural and conductive problems.

Functional Hearing Loss—Those problems which are not organic in origin. Examples include:

 ♦ Psychosomatic causes

 ♦ Hysterical conversion

 ♦ Malingering

 ♦ Emotional or psychological problems

Central Auditory Disorders—These disorders result in no measurable peripheral hearing loss. Children with this disorder have trouble learning and are often considered learning disabled. Causes include:

 ♦ Auditory comprehension problems

 ♦ Auditory discrimination problems

 ♦ Auditory learning difficulties

 ♦ Language development delays

Whatever the cause, a parent or teacher may be the first individual to observe the symptoms of a hearing loss, such as:

 ♦ significant problems in expressive language

 ♦ significant problems in receptive language

 ♦ difficulties with speech development

 ♦ problems in socialization

 ♦ difficulty with alertness or speaking in class

ASSESSMENT MEASURES

When such symptoms are observed, the first step is usually a referral to an audiologist for a screening. There are several assessment measures that are utilized in the possible identification of a hearing loss. They include:

Audiometric Evaluation Measures—These assessment measures are used by audiologists who measure the level of hearing loss through the use of several techniques. These may include:

 • **Pure Tone Audiometric Screening:** Pure tone screening is often referred to as sweep testing and is usually the child's first encounter with a hearing test. This type of testing is common in schools, and presents the child with pure tones over a variety of frequency ranges. The child is then asked to respond if he or she hears a tone, usually by some gesture. If a child is unable to hear sounds at two or more frequencies they are usually referred for further evaluation.

- **Speech Audiometry:** This type of evaluation is used to determine a child's present ability to hear and understand speech through the presentation of words in a variety of loudness levels.

- **Pure Tone Threshold Audiometry:** In this procedure, the child is asked to make a gesture or push a button each time he or she hears a tone. The child is presented with a variety of frequencies through earphones. This type of air conduction test reveals the presence of hearing loss.

  Special Audiometric Tests—These include:

- **Sound field audiometry:** This measure is used with very young children who cannot respond to manual responses or are unable or unwilling to wear headphones. The child is evaluated by observing the intensity levels at which he or she responds to different levels of sounds broadcast through speakers.

- **Evoked response audiometry:** This measure uses an electroencephalograph and a computer, and measures changes in brain wave activity to a variety of sound levels. This measure can be used with infants who are suspected of being deaf.

- **Impedance audiometry:** There are two major impedance audiometry tests. The first, *tympanometry*, measures the functioning level of the eardrum. The second, *stapedial reflex testing*, measures the reflex response of the stapedial muscle to pure tone signals. Since these tests do not require a response on the part of the child, they can be used with very young children.

- **Behavioral play audiometry:** This technique involves placing the child in a series of activities that reward him or her for responding appropriately to tone or speech.

DEGREES OF HEARING IMPAIRMENT

Once the audiologist completes his or her assessment, a determination is made of the level of hearing loss. The chart on the following page offers a comparison of the different levels of hearing loss.

The diagnosis of a hearing loss is the initial step in the treatment and education of the child. Special education teachers need specialized assessment measures to conduct educational screenings and evaluations. These tests for the hearing impaired child are crucial in the educational planning process.

Degree of Hearing Loss	Decibel loss	Resulting Impairment
Slight	27–40dB	Individual has difficulty hearing faint noises or distant conversation. The individual with this slight hearing loss will usually not have difficulties in the regular school setting.
Mild	41–55 dB	This individual may miss as much as 50 percent of classroom conversations. The individual may also exhibit limited vocabulary and speech difficulties.
Moderate	56–70 dB	The individual will only be able to hear loud conversation, and may exhibit defective speech, vocabulary, and language difficulties.
Severe	71–90 dB	Hearing may be limited to a radius of one foot. May be able to discriminate certain environmental sounds, shows defective speech and language ability, and has severe difficulty understanding consonant sounds.
Profound	91 dB or greater	The individual can sense but is unable to understand sounds and tones. Vision becomes the primary sense of communication, and speech and language are likely to deteriorate.

AUDITORY PERCEPTION TEST FOR THE HEARING IMPAIRED (APT/HI)

GENERAL TEST INFORMATION

Authors:	Susan G. Allen and Thomas S. Serwatka
Publisher:	PRO-ED, Inc.
Address of Publisher:	8700 Shoal Creek Boulevard Austin, TX 78758-6897
Phone Number of Publisher:	512-451-3246 or 800-897-3202
Fax of Publisher:	800-FXPROED

Purpose of Test: The test is designed to assess the building-block processes used to decode speech. It allows for specific analysis of the individual's ability to decode phonemes in isolation and in the context of words and sentences.

Description of Test: The APT/HI allows for specific analysis of the student's ability to decode phonemes in isolation and in the context of words and sentences. It consists of a manual, plates, and record forms.

Type of Test:	Criterion-referenced
Administration Time:	30 minutes
Type of Administration:	Individual
Who Administers This Test:	Special education teacher, psychologist, speech/language therapist
Age/Grade Levels:	Ages 5 and over

Scoring Information: The test results are given in a performance profile that enables comparison of an individual's pre- and post-treatment performance to determine the efficacy of treatment and the need for further therapy.

STRENGTHS OF THE APT/HI

- Although designed specifically for the hearing impaired, the test can also be used with children who have other auditory processing deficits.
- The test analyzes auditory decoding skills at the most basic level.

WEAKNESSES OF THE APT/HI

- At the time of printing, no review of this test regarding weaknesses was done in Buros Mental Measurement Yearbook.

CAROLINA PICTURE VOCABULARY TEST FOR DEAF AND HEARING IMPAIRED (CPVT)

GENERAL TEST INFORMATION

Authors:	Thomas L. Layton and David W. Holmes
Publisher:	PRO-ED, Inc.
Address of Publisher:	8700 Shoal Creek Blvd. Austin, TX 78758-6897
Phone Number of Publisher:	512-451-3246 or 800-897-3202
Fax of Publisher:	800-FXPROED

Purpose of Test: The test is designed to measure the receptive sign vocabulary in individuals for whom manual signing is the primary mode of communication.

Description of Test: The test materials consist of a spiral-bound book containing 130 numbered test plates with four pictures per plate, an examiner's manual, and an individual recording form which lists stimulus items, a key for correct responses, and a space for the child's response. The administration of the CPVT requires no special training on the part of the examiner. It is suggested that the examiner be familiar with the deaf and hearing impaired and have some experience with test administration.

Type of Test:	Norm-referenced
Administration Time:	10–30 minutes
Type of Administration:	Individual
Who Administers This Test:	Special education teacher, speech/language therapist, audiologist, and classroom teacher
Age/Grade Levels:	Ages 4 to 11.5

Subtest Information: The test contains no subtests.

Scoring Information: The test provides the following:

♦ Scaled scores

♦ Percentile ranks

♦ Age equivalents

STRENGTHS OF THE CPVT

♦ At the time of printing, no review of this test regarding strengths was done in Buros Mental Measurement Yearbook.

WEAKNESSES OF THE CPVT

♦ At the time of printing, no review of this regarding weaknesses was done in Buros Mental Measurement Yearbook.

HISKEY-NEBRASKA TEST OF LEARNING APTITUDE

GENERAL TEST INFORMATION

Author:	Marshall S. Hiskey
Publisher:	Marshall S. Hiskey
Address of Publisher:	5640 Baldwin Lincoln, NE 68507
Phone Number of Publisher:	601-266-5223
Fax of Publisher:	601-266-5224

Purpose of Test: The test is designed as a nonverbal measure of mental ability that has been found helpful in the intellectual assessment of a variety of children with language impairments and youth.

Description of Test: The test is a performance scale that can be administered entirely via pantomimed instructions and requires no verbal response from the subject. The scale consists of a series of performance tasks that are organized in ascending order of difficulty within subscales.

Type of Test:	Standardized
Administration Time:	Approximately 60 minutes
Type of Administration:	Individual
Who Administers This Test:	Special education teacher, psychologist, speech/language therapist
Age/Grade Levels:	Ages 2 to 18

Subtest Information: The test comprises the following subtests:

- *Memory Colored Objects*—The child is required to perform memory tasks using colored objects.
- *Bead Stringing*—The child is required to put beads on a string.
- *Pictorial Associations*—The child has to decide what various pictures look like.
- *Block Building*—The child is required to build things with blocks.
- *Memory for Digits*—The child is given groups of numbers and asked to repeat them.
- *Completion of Drawings*—The child is required to finish a picture that is not completed.
- *Pictorial Identification*—The child has to say what the picture is that is being shown.
- *Visual Attention Span*—Tests how long a child can focus on an object.
- *Puzzle Blocks*—The child arranges the blocks into a picture that is shown.
- *Pictorial Analogies*—The child compares two pictures and then has to pick a picture that goes with the third picture.

STRENGTHS OF THE HISKEY-NEBRASKA

- ◆ The test is easy to administer.
- ◆ The test results are reported as a learning quotient rather than pure IQ which may be easier for parents to understand.

HISKEY-NEBRASKA TEST OF LEARNING APTITUDE

(continued)

WEAKNESSES OF THE HISKEY-NEBRASKA

♦ The test may be a poor tool for children seven years and over. It can be time-consuming and may be of very little interest to the children.

<u>Note</u>: The Hiskey-Nebraska is currently under revision and was not available at the time of printing.

LEITER-R INTERNATIONAL PERFORMANCE SCALE

GENERAL TEST INFORMATION

Authors:	Russel Graydon Leiter and Grace Arthur
Publisher:	C.H. Stoelting Co.
Address of Publisher:	620 Wheat Lane Wood Dale, IL 60191
Phone Number of Publisher:	630-860-9700
Fax of Publisher:	630-860-9775

Purpose of Test: The test is designed as a totally nonverbal intelligence and cognitive abilities test.

Description of Test: The Leiter-R is completely nonverbal; it does not require the child to read or write any materials. The test does not require a spoken word from the examiner or the child. It is presented in a game-like administration. The test is administered by having the child match the full-color response cards with corresponding illustrations on the easel display.

Type of Test:	Standardized
Administration Time:	30–60 minutes
Type of Administration:	Individual
Who Administers This Test:	Special education teacher, psychologist, speech/language therapist
Age/Grade Levels:	Ages 2 to 17

Subtest Information: The Leiter-R includes 20 subtests, listed below, which are combined to create numerous composites that measure both general intelligence and discrete ability areas. The test consists of two batteries measuring a variety of skills:

1. *Visualization and Reasoning Battery*

   Reasoning skills measured in this battery include:
   - Classification
   - Sequential Order
   - Repeated Patterns
   - Design Analogies

   Visualization skills measured in this battery include:
   - Matching
   - Figure Ground
   - Form Completion
   - Picture Context
   - Paper Folding
   - Figure Rotation

2. *Attention and Memory Battery*

   Memory skills measured in this battery include:
   - Memory Span (Forward)
   - Memory Span (Reversed)

- Spatial Memory
- Visual Coding
- Associative Memory
- Associative Delayed Memory
- Immediate Recognition
- Delayed Recognition

Attention skills measured in this battery include:

- Attention Sustained
- Attention Divided

Scoring Information: The test provides the following:

- IQ scores
- Percentiles
- Grade equivalents
- Age Equivalents

STRENGTHS OF THE LEITER-R

- The scale is a useful instrument, and has made possible the testing of many children who could not be properly evaluated by the WISC-III or Stanford-Binet because of its nonverbal approach.
- The test has a high correlation (.84) with the WISC-III Full Scale IQ.
- The extensive age range measured by the test, ages 2–21, allows for the use of one test throughout a child's school career which enhances comparisons of performance over time.
- Since the test is nonverbal, there is no dominant language bias as found on other IQ tests.

WEAKNESSES OF THE LEITER-R

- Work needs to be done to establish more comprehensive norms.
- A better scoring system may need to be investigated.

RHODE ISLAND TEST OF LANGUAGE STRUCTURE (RITLS)

GENERAL TEST INFORMATION

Authors:	Elizabeth Engen and Trygg Engen
Publisher:	PRO-ED, Inc.
Address of Publisher:	8700 Shoal Creek Boulevard Austin, TX 78758-6897
Phone Number of Publisher:	512-451-3246 or 800-897-3202
Fax of Publisher:	800-FXPROED

Purpose of Test: This test is designed to provide a measure of English language development, and a profile of the child's understanding of language structure.

Description of Test: This test is primarily designed for use with children with hearing impairments. The test measures syntax-response errors for 20 sentence types, both simple and complex. The test utilizes a picture verification task, in which the examiner presents a stimulus sentence and the child chooses the picture from a set of three that matches or represents the sentence. The task, therefore, results in a measure of primary linguistic ability because it does not involve the child's ability to read or write. The test consists of a booklet containing specific directions for test administration, four sample items not to be scored, and 100 test items. The test booklet is arranged so that, when opened, three constrastive pictures face the child and the test sentences face the examiner. Items 1 to 50 consist of simple sentences and items 51 to 100 of complex sentences, each randomly ordered within these categories.

Type of Test:	Criterion-referenced and norm-referenced
Administration Time:	25–35 minutes
Type of Administration:	Individual
Who Administers This Test:	Special education teacher, psychologist, speech/language therapist
Age/Grade Levels:	Hearing-impaired children ages 3 to 20; hearing children ages 3 to 6

Subtest Information: This test measures syntax response errors for 20 sentence types, both simple and complex. The sentence elements tests are:

1. *Relative and Adverbial Clauses*
2. *Subject and Other Complements*
3. *Reversible and Non-reversible Passives*
4. *Datives*
5. *Deletions*
6. *Negations*
7. *Conjunctives*
8. *Embedded Imperatives*

Scoring Information: The test provides the following:

- ♦ Percentiles
- ♦ Age equivalents

STRENGTHS OF RITLS

- ♦ The test includes hearing-impaired individuals as part of the standardized group which adds to the effectiveness of generalizability.

RHODE ISLAND TEST OF LANGUAGE STRUCTURE (RITLS)
(continued)

- The test is useful in areas where level of language development is of concern, e.g., mental retardation, learning disability, and bilingual programs.
- The RITLS is easy to administer, score, and interpret.
- A variety of syntactic structures are included in the test.

WEAKNESSES OF RITLS

- There is absence of reliability and validity information.
- There is an over-reliance on syntax without consideration of the pragmatic aspects of comprehension.
- Omission of morphemes may fail to pick up mildly hearing-impaired children.
- There is a lack of a complete test subject description.
- There is a limited number of minority individuals in the sample.
- There is an absence of a method of error analysis that misses valuable data interpretation.

SCREENING INSTRUMENT FOR TARGETING EDUCATIONAL RISK (SIFTER)

GENERAL TEST INFORMATION

Author:	Karen Anderson
Publisher:	PRO-ED, Inc.
Address of Publisher:	8700 Shoal Creek Blvd. Austin, TX 78758-6897
Phone Number of Publisher:	512-451-3246 or 800-897-3202
Fax of Publisher:	800-FXPROED

Purpose of Test: The test intends to provide a method by which children with hearing problems, either known or suspected, who are mainstreamed can be educationally screened.

Description of Test: The test takes the form of a 15-item questionnaire about the classroom performance of children who are hearing impaired and mainstreamed in regular classes.

Type of Test:	Rating scale
Administration Time:	Untimed
Type of Administration:	Individual
Who Administers This Test:	Special education teacher, psychologist, speech/language therapist
Age/Grade Levels:	Elementary-school age

Subtest Information: The subtests are listed below:

- *Academics*
- *Attention*
- *Communication*
- *Class participation*
- *School behavior*

Scoring Information: The teacher rates the students in each of the above areas using a rating scale.

STRENGTHS OF THE SIFTER

- The content of individual items in the questionnaire was well evaluated.

WEAKNESSES OF THE SIFTER

- The weakness of this test is its poor inter-scorer reliability, which may completely undermine its norm-referenced use.

TEST OF EARLY READING ABILITY-2—DEAF OR HARD OF HEARING
(TERA-2—D/HH)

GENERAL TEST INFORMATION

Authors:	D. Kim Reid, Wayne P. Jiresko, Donald D. Hammill, and Susan Wiltshire
Publisher:	PRO-ED, Inc.
Address of Publisher:	8700 Shoal Creek Blvd. Austin, TX 78758-6897
Phone Number of Publisher:	512-451-3246 or 800-897-3202
Fax of Publisher:	800-FXPROED

Purpose of Test: The test is designed to measure the ability of children with moderate to profound hearing loss to attribute meaning to printed symbols, their knowledge of the alphabet and its functions, and their knowledge of the conventions of print.

Description of Test: The test isolates key components of early print experiences and assesses children's relative competence in deriving meaning from these print symbols. The test includes a sheet which allows the examiner to picture the student's "Instructional Target Zone." By examining the student's item performance in the three components of early reading, the examiner can identify the types of concepts that might be profitably taught.

Type of Test:	Norm-referenced
Administration Time:	15–30 minutes
Type of Administration:	Individual
Who Administers This Test:	Special education teacher, psychologist, speech/language therapist
Age/Grade Level:	Ages 3 to 10

Subtest Information: Three aspects of early reading behavior are specifically addressed:

- *Constructing meaning from print*—Here the construction of meaning encompasses a child's ability to read frequently encountered signs, logos, and words; relate words to one another; and understand the contextual nature of written discourse.

- *Knowledge of the alphabet*—This aspect is defined as letter and word decoding (either orally or through sign).

- *Understanding print conventions*—This aspect evaluates the child's awareness of text orientation and organization (i.e., book handling, the spatial orientation of print on a page, and ability to uncover textual or print errors).

Scoring Information: The test provides the following:

- Standard scores
- Percentiles
- Normal curve equivalents

STRENGTHS OF THE TERA-2-D/HH

- The authors provide a comprehensive and informative manual.
- The student record form is complete and easy to follow.

TEST OF EARLY READING ABILITY-2—DEAF OR HARD OF HEARING
(TERA-2—D/HH)
(continued)

♦ According to the manual, the test is the only individually administered test of reading designed for students with sensory hearing loss.

♦ According to the manual, it is the only test normed on deaf and hard of hearing children that is recommended for those younger than 8 years old.

WEAKNESSES OF THE TERA-2-D/HH

♦ Some of the test materials may be dull and uninteresting for younger children.

♦ There is little reliability information on preschool-aged groups. Standard deviations were not offered in the manual on the standardization sample's mean raw score performance on the test. This is most damaging to its use as a measure of early reading skill because of its affect on generalizability.

♦ The lack of reliability and validity information raises serious questions regarding the measure's capacity to provide more than a gross and limited overview of deaf and hard-of-hearing children's recognition of print.

OCCUPATIONAL AND PHYSICAL THERAPY ASSESSMENT

Physical and occupational therapies are important components of the special education process. Many school districts now have occupational and physical therapists as part of their staff. These therapists may help students individually or in small groups or as consultants. These two services are related therapies but specific in their function. *Occupational therapy* focuses mainly on fine motor/upper body functions, whereas *physical therapy* concentrates on lower body/gross motor difficulties. The services are provided for students with disabilities who exhibit a range of difficulties such as learning disabilities (e.g., fine and gross motor problems or perceptual problems), developmental delays (e.g., mental retardation, vision or hearing impairment), respiratory problems (e.g., cystic fibrosis, asthma), neuromuscular problems (e.g., muscular dystrophy, cerebral palsy), musculoskeletal problems (e.g., arthritis, orthopedic problems, postural deviations), traumatic accidents (e.g., amputations, brain injuries, burns). In addition to providing therapy for such students, physical and occupational therapists provide many other services including evaluations, screenings, consultations, education, and training.

EVALUATIONS

Occupational and physical therapy evaluations may be referred to the CSE by any number of school or medical professionals. Parents may also ask for a referral for occupational and physical therapy services for their child. In any case, parental written consent is required for an evaluation.

As with other evaluations, those of occupational and physical therapists need to be individualized, well documented, and specific. The physical and occupational therapists play a significant role in regards to the service provided to the student; the more thorough their documentation, the more appropriate the services will be. The evaluation will serve as a blueprint for the development of an IEP should one be necessary. The evaluation will identify the child's current level of performance as well as his or her deficient areas of development in the physical realm. It will also suggest what he or she needs in order to achieve the next higher level of function. Parents need to be aware that the evaluation process is subjective and varies from district to district. In some districts if a child can walk into a classroom, he or she is not provided with physical therapy. In some districts where a child can hold a pencil, he or she is not provided with occupational therapy, while in other districts such services are provided for only marginal problems.

ASSESSMENT AREAS

In general, both occupational therapy and physical therapy assess the following:

◆ range of motion

◆ sensory integration

◆ activities for daily living

- physical and mental development
- muscular control
- need for and uses of adaptive equipment

Certain assessments are unique to physical therapy:

- posture
- gait
- endurance
- personal independence
- joint abnormalities
- wheelchair management
- transportation needs
- architectural barriers
- prosthetic and orthotic equipment checks

Other assessments are unique to occupational therapy:

- neuromuscular functioning
- sensory processing
- manual dexterity
- leisure time abilities
- physical facilities
- prevocational skills
- oral motor and feeding problems

THE THERAPIST'S MANY ROLES

Therapists should meet with all of the professionals involved with a particular child as well as the child's parents to fully explain the nature of the disability, to train them to work with the child in the areas of dysfunction, and to provide assistive devices or environmental aids that will help the child function in the least restrictive environment. The therapists should also model remedial techniques that can be duplicated by the parents and by other teaching professionals. Parents should be reminded that many of the school activities suggested by occupational and physical therapists can be duplicated in the home. Many of the exercises are really activities for daily living such as hopping, jumping, buttoning, etc.

Occupational and physical therapists serve important roles as consultants. Some examples of their services follow:

- referring families to appropriate sources for assistance
- helping families order adaptive or prosthetic equipment

- coordinating with physical education programs

- instructing families regarding methods used in physical therapy

- formulating long-range developmental plans for children's education

- training school professionals with special equipment

- helping families and children learn how to deal with architectural barriers

The following is a list of problems requiring occupational therapy:

- perceptual problems (eye-hand coordination)

- sensory problems (sensitive to sound, sensitive to visual changes, sensitive to odors, overly sensitive to touch)

- gross motor difficulties (trouble with balance, coordination, moving)

- fine motor problems (difficulty with coordination, handwriting, using scissors)

- hardship with daily living activities (cannot dress, feed, or care for self)

- organizational problems (difficulties with memory, time, spatial concepts)

- attention span difficulties (difficulties focusing on task, short attention span)

- interpersonal problems (difficulty with environmental and school-related social situations)

The following is a list of the kinds of evaluations an occupational therapist can conduct:

- Vision

- Abnormal movement patterns

- Range of motion

- Skeletal and joint conditions

- Behavior

- Skin and soft tissue

- Fine motor

- Perceptual

- Gross motor

- Balance and equilibrium

- Activities for daily living

- Equipment analysis

Occupational therapists may act as liaisons between the CSE, the teaching staff, medical professionals, outside agencies, and parents. Many pupils in need of occupational therapy have severe medical conditions. These conditions often require supervision of a family doctor. The occupational therapist should help with the coordination between the school physician and the family doctor. Consequently, the occupational therapist may play an important role in the special education process.

Several tests already described in other chapters are also frequently used by occupational therapists during their evaluation. These include:

- Bruininks-Oseretsky Test of Motor Proficiency (page 149)

- Degangi-Berk Test of Sensory Integration (TSI) (page 215)

- The Denver Developmental Screening Test—Revised (Denver II) (page 219)

- McCarthy Scales of Children's Abilities (MSCA) (page 59)

- Motor Free Visual Perception Test—Revised (page 141)

MILANI-COMPARETTI MOTOR DEVELOPMENT TEST

GENERAL TEST INFORMATION

Authors:	Wayne Stuberg, Pam Dehne, Jim Miedaner, and Penni White
Publisher:	Meyer Rehabilitation Institute
Address of Publisher:	University of Nebraska Medical Center 600 South 42nd St. Box 985450 Omaha, NE 68198
Phone Number of Publisher:	402-559-6430
Fax of Publisher:	402-559-5737

Purpose of Test: The test is designed to provide the clinician with a synopsis of the child's motor development by systematically examining the integration of primitive reflexes and the emergence of volitional movement against gravity.

Description of Test: The test consists of 27 motor behaviors that are evaluated in two categories: evoked responses and spontaneous behaviors.

Administration Time:	10–15 minutes
Type of Administration:	Individual
Who Administers This Test:	Special education teacher, psychologist, occupational therapist
Age/Grade Levels:	1–16 months

Subtest Information: There are a total of 27 motor behaviors involved with two subtests.

- *Evoked Responses*—These include equilibrium reactions (tilting), protective extension reaction (parachute), righting reaction, and primitive reflexes.

- *Spontaneous Behaviors*—These include postural control and active movements such as sitting, crawling, and walking. Twenty-seven scores include: Body Lying Supine, Hand Grasp, Foot Grasp, Supine Equilibrium, Body Pulled Up From Supine, Sitting Posture, Sitting Equilibrium, Sideways Parachute, Backward Parachute, Body Held Vertical, Head Righting, Downward Parachute, Standing, Standing Equilibrium, Locomotion, Landau Response, Forward Parachute, Body Lying Prone, Prone Equilibrium, All Fours, All Fours Equilibrium, Symmetric Tonic Neck Reflex, Body Denotative, Standing Up From Supine, Body Rotative, Asymmetrical Tonic Neck Reflex, Moro Reflex.

STRENGTHS OF THE MILANI-COMPARETTI

- One of the major strengths of this instrument is that it incorporates both quantitative and qualitative judgments about motor performance.
- The test manual provides good interrater and test reliability.
- The test is quick to administer.

WEAKNESSES OF THE MILANI-COMPARETTI

- There are norming sample limitations in the population used for standardization.
- There is a lack of validity data.

MILLER ASSESSMENT FOR PRESCHOOLERS (MAP)

GENERAL TEST INFORMATION

Author:	Lucy Jane Miller
Publisher:	The Psychological Corporation
Address of Publisher:	555 Academic Court San Antonio, TX 78204-2498
Phone Number of Publisher:	800-211-8378
Fax of Publisher:	800-232-1223
TDD of the Publisher:	800-723-1318

Purpose of Test: This test is designed to identify children who exhibit moderate preacademic problems.

Description of Test: The MAP is a short but comprehensive preschool assessment instrument that evaluates children for mild to moderate developmental delays. Items are objective and easy to administer, providing the examiner with a broad overview of the child's developmental status with respect to that of other children of the same age. The test includes an examiner's manual, item score sheets, and all materials needed for administration.

Type of Test:	Standardized, norm-referenced
Administration Time:	20–30 minutes
Type of Administration:	Individual
Who Administers This Test:	Special education teacher, psychologist, occupational therapist
Age/Grade Levels:	Ages 2.9 to 5.8

Subtest Information: The test consists of five performance areas:

- *Foundations Index*—assesses abilities involving basic motor tasks and the awareness of sensations, both of which are fundamental for the development of complex skills.
- *Coordination Index*—assesses complex gross, fine, and oral motor abilities.
- *Verbal Index*—assesses memory, sequencing, comprehension, association, and expression in a verbal context.
- *Nonverbal Index*—assesses memory, sequencing, visualization, and the performance of mental manipulations not requiring spoken language.
- *Complex Tasks Index*—assesses sensorimotor abilities in conjunction with cognitive abilities.

Scoring Information: The test provides:

- Percentile ranks
- Standard scores

STRENGTHS OF THE MAP

- A strong feature of the MAP is the detailed information presented in the manual for the administration of each of the five indexes.
- It is a short, carefully developed and well standardized test.
- The test is quick to score.

WEAKNESSES OF THE MAP

- The cost of the MAP is moderately high.
- It is unable to do predictive validity studies because children in the standardization sample have not reached school age.

QUICK NEUROLOGICAL SCREENING TEST (QNST)

GENERAL TEST INFORMATION

Authors:	Margaret Motti, Harold M. Steling, Norma V. Spalding, and C. Slade Crawfold
Publisher:	Academic Therapy Publications
Address of Publisher:	20 Commercial Blvd. Novato, CA 94949-6191
Phone Number of Publisher:	415-883-3314 or 800-422-7249
Fax of Publisher:	415-883-3720

Purpose of Test: The test is designed to assess neurological integration as it relates to learning. It is used for the early screening of learning disabilities.

Description of Test: The QNST is a screening test that assesses 15 areas of neurological integration. It requires the examinee to perform a series of motor tasks adapted from neurological pediatric examinations, and from neuropsychological and developmental scales. Each of the 15 areas tested involves a motor task similar to those observed in neurological pediatric examinations. The test includes recording forms, examiner's manual, reproduction sheets, remedial guidelines, and an administration and scoring flipcard.

Type of Test:	Criterion-referenced
Administration Time:	Untimed
Type of Administration:	Individual
Who Administers This Test:	Special education teacher, psychologist, occupational therapist
Age/Grade Levels:	Ages 5–18

Subtest Information: The areas of neurological integration measured by the QNST include:

- Motor development
- Fine/gross motor control
- Motor planning and sequencing and rhythm
- Visual/spatial perception
- Spatial organization
- Balance/vestibular function
- Attentional disorders

Scoring Information: Since this test is subjectively scored, scoring patterns are used to suggest possible avenues of further diagnostic assessment.

STRENGTHS OF THE QNST

- The test is useful as a supplement for the pediatric neurological examination.
- The test is exceptionally good in identifying subjects with abnormal neurological patterns.

WEAKNESSES OF THE QNST

- The term *learning disabilities* is never defined by the authors even though they propose the test as an LD screener.
- The test is scored subjectively.
- No direct measure of scorer reliability exists for the test.

SENSORY INTEGRATION AND PRAXIS TEST (SIPT)

GENERAL TEST INFORMATION

Author:	Jean Ayres
Publisher:	Western Psychological Services
Address of the Publisher:	12031 Wilshire Blvd. Los Angeles, CA 90025
Phone Number of Publisher:	310-478-2061 or 800-648-8857
Fax of Publisher:	310-478-7838

Purpose of Test: The test is designed to measure the sensory integration processes that underlie learning and behavior.

Description of Test: By showing how children organize and respond to sensory input, the SIPT helps pinpoint specific organic problems associated with learning disabilities, emotional disorders, and minimal brain dysfunction. The test measures visual, tactile, and kinesthetic perception as well as motor performance.

Type of Test:	Norm-referenced
Administration Time:	The entire battery can be administered in two hours
Type of Administration:	Individual
Who Administers This Test:	Special education teacher, psychologist, occupational therapist
Age/Grade Levels:	Ages 4 to 9

Subtest Information: The SIPT measures visual, tactile, and kinesthetic perception as well as motor performance. It is composed of 17 brief tests:

1. *Space Visualization*—This subtest requires visual space perception and, in the more advanced items, mental manipulation of objects in space.

2. *Figure Ground Perception*—This subtest requires the child to separate a foreground figure from a rival background.

3. *Standing and Walking Balance*—This subtest evaluates the ability to balance on one or both feet, with eyes open and closed.

4. *Design Copying*—This subtest requires the child to reproduce designs on paper.

5. *Postural Praxis*—This subtest requires the child to assume each of 17 different postures while it is being demonstrated by the examiner, and to hold each posture for 7 seconds.

6. *Bilateral Motor Coordination*—The student is required to imitate rhythmic patterns of movement initiated by the examiner.

7. *Praxis on Verbal Command*—In this subtest the examiner verbally requests the child to assume each of 24 different unusual positions, and each position is scored for accuracy and time.

8. *Constructional Praxis*—This subtest assesses practic skill in relating objects to each other in an orderly arrangement or systematic assembly through building with blocks.

9. *Postrotary nystagmus*—This subtest requires the child to sit on a nystagmus board which the examiner rotates by hand. After rotation, the board is stopped abruptly, and the child looks ahead while the examiner observes and records nystagmus duration with a stopwatch.

10. *Motor Accuracy*—This subtest requires the child to draw a red line over a heavy curved black line.

11. ***Sequencing Praxis***—This subtest assesses the child's ability to execute a series of planned hand or finger movements demonstrated by the examiner.

12. ***Oral Praxis***—This subtest requires the child to imitate the examiner's movements of the tongue, teeth, lips, cheeks, or jaw.

13. ***Manual Form Perception***—This subtest requires the child to identify, by pointing, the visual counterparts of various geometric forms held and manipulated one at a time in the hand.

14. ***Kinesthesia***—This subtest requires the child to move his or her fingers from one location to another location.

15. ***Finger Identification***—This subtest requires the child to point to or touch the finger previously touched by the examiner.

16. ***Graphesthesia***—This subtest requires the child to duplicate a design that was traced on the back of the child's hand by the examiner.

17. ***Localization of Tactile Stimuli***—This subtest requires the child to place his or her finger on the spot on the child's hand or arm that was previously touched by the examiner.

Scoring Information: All SIPT tests are computer scored, using WPS Test Report. Any combination of the 17 tests can be scored; the entire battery need not be administered. Scores are presented in the following manners:

- Percentiles
- Standard scores

STRENGTHS OF THE SIPT

- This test is a helpful clinical tool.
- Any of the individual tests can be administered separately and therefore one does not need to administer the entire battery.
- The computerized scoring provides a detailed report explaining the SIPT results.

WEAKNESSES OF THE SIPT

- SIPT administration and interpretation requires professional training.
- A training program may be necessary to administer, score the test, and interpret the results.

PURDUE PERCEPTUAL MOTOR SURVEY (PPM)

GENERAL TEST INFORMATION

Authors:	Eugene G. Roach and Newell C. Kephart
Publisher:	The Psychological Corporation
Address of Publisher:	555 Academic Court San Antonio, TX 78204-2498
Phone Number of Publisher:	800-211-8378
Fax of Publisher:	800-232-1223
TDD of the Publisher:	800-723-1318

Purpose of Test: The test is designed to identify those children lacking perceptual-motor abilities necessary for acquiring academic success.

Description of Test: This is not a test, but a series of tasks designed to provide the examiner with a structure for observing a student's motor skills. In order for the examiner to ensure the child's optimum performance levels, each subtest allows the examiner four possible levels of administration: unstructured instruction (general verbal directions), verbal directions (more explicit verbal directions), demonstration (task demonstrated by evaluator), or guided movements (child is physically guided through task).

Type of Test:	Criterion-referenced
Administration Time:	30–40 minutes
Type of Administration:	Individual
Who Administers This Test:	Special education teacher, psychologist, occupational therapist
Age/Grade Levels:	Preschool to Grade 8

Subtest Information: There are five skill areas measured, composing a total of eleven subtests:

BALANCE AND POSTURE—This skill area includes:

1. *Walking Board:* This subtest measures the child's ability to walk and balance him- or herself on a narrow walking board, forward, backward, and sideways.

2. *Jumping:* This subtest measures the child's ability to jump and hop on each foot and both feet.

BODY IMAGE AND DIFFERENTIATION—This skill area includes:

3. *Identification of Body Parts:* This subtest measures the child's ability to recognize and point to different body parts.

4. *Imitation of Movement:* This subtest measures the child's ability to transfer visually presented information by the examiner into motor acts.

5. *Obstacle Course:* This subtest measures the child's spatial orientation through a series of obstacle course maneuvers, e.g., duck under a broom handle.

6. *Kraus-Weber Test of Physical Fitness:* This subtest is a measure of the child's physical strength and muscular fitness.

7. *Angels in the Snow:* This subtest measures the child's ability to perform a series of tasks involving specific limbs individually and in pairs.

PERCEPTUAL MOTOR MATCH—This skill area includes:

8. *Chalkboard:* This subtest measures the child's ability with visual-motor coordination tasks and directionality.

PURDUE PERCEPTUAL MOTOR SURVEY (PPM)

(continued)

9. *Rhythmic Writing:* This subtest measures the child's ability to reproduce a series of continuous writing themes on a chalkboard.

OCULAR CONTROL—This includes:

10. *Ocular Pursuits:* This subtest measures a child's visual tracking skills.

FORM PERCEPTION—This skill area includes:

11. *Developmental Drawings:* This subtest measures a child's ability to copy geometric forms to assess his or her visual-motor coordination.

Scoring Information: No objective scores are obtained but a profile is determined. The examiner notes the level of structure that the child requires for each task and other observations on the record form. Each task-item is then rated on a four-point scale following the guidelines in the examiner's manual.

STRENGTHS OF THE PPM

- The PPM is explicitly based on a well developed perceptual motor theory described by Kephart (1960) in his book *The Slow Learner in the Classroom*.
- Provides a good basis for assessing gross and fine motor tasks.
- The manual is clearly written.
- The test is easy to score.

WEAKNESS OF THE PPM

- On several subtests the equipment must be gathered from around the school, which may hinder the administration of certain subtests (e.g., walking board, small pillow).
- The abilities tested sometimes overlap, resulting in redundancy.
- The test requires a skilled examiner.
- Many abilities tested are unrelated to academic success, and are not well assessed by the survey.

BILINGUAL ASSESSMENT

Under federal law, all children have the right to tests which are free of cultural bias. Furthermore, all tests must be conducted in the child's native language and reports must be written in the parent's language. Given these mandates under the federal law, it is evident that educators must be very aware of a child's native language. Consequently, it is critical that assessments done on children who are bilingual be done in a manner that is in compliance with all federal laws. Educators need to be aware of variables associated with the assessment of bilingual children since the number of bilingual children with suspected disabilities is increasing.

The majority of tests used for assessment in special education are based on standards of the English speaking culture. Given this fact, the use of these instruments on students who are bilingual may not be appropriate under the federal law. Consequently, special educators must devise a way to assess children whose primary language may not be English. This is commonly referred to as dynamic assessment whereby information is obtained through interviews, observations, and other methods not simply based on objective criteria based on national norms. "Professionals must attend carefully to the overall picture of a child's background and performance," states Harry (1992), and adds that "assessment cannot be complete without an understanding of whether prior instruction has been adequate and appropriate" (p. 87). To this end, Ortiz (1986) recommends that such students first undergo the prereferral process mentioned earlier. Many schools are moving toward requiring a prereferral process before any individualized evaluation is done. The purpose of the prereferral process is "to determine if appropriate and sufficient approaches have been attempted" (Wallace, Larsen, & Elksnin, 1992, p. 467). This allows the school to adjust instruction or make other classroom modifications and see if these changes address the problem being noted.

According to Waterman (1994), from her article "Assessing Children for the Presence of a Disability" (published by the National Information Center for Children and Youth with Disabilities), the prereferral process includes:

♦ direct observation of the student in the regular classroom

♦ analyzing how the student behaves and interacts verbally in different settings

♦ reviewing the methods of instruction that are used in the regular classroom

It is also important to interview people who are familiar with the student, for these individuals can provide a wealth of information about his or her interests, adaptive behavior, how he or she processes information and approaches learning, language ability, and (in the case of students who are not native speakers of English) language dominance. Interviewers should be aware, however, that the differing culture and/or language of those being interviewed can seriously affect the nature and interpretation of information gathered. Some understanding of how individuals within that culture view disability, the educational system, and authority figures will be helpful in designing, conducting, and interpreting a culturally sensitive interview. It may be particularly useful to gather information from the home environment, which will help the assessment team develop an understanding of the student within his or her own culture. To facilitate this, parents need to communicate openly with the school and share their insight into their child's behaviors, attitudes, successes, and needs, and, when appropriate, information about the minority culture. Before conducting any formal testing of a student who is a non-native speaker of English, it is vital to determine the student's preferred language and to conduct a comprehensive language assessment in both English and the native language.

Dominant language

Examiners need to be aware that it is highly inappropriate to evaluate students in English when that is not their dominant language (unless the purpose of testing is to assess the student's English language proficiency). Translating tests from English is not an acceptable practice either; the IDEA states that tests and other evaluation materials must be provided and administered in the child's primary language or mode of communication unless it is clearly not feasible to do so [34 CFR Section 300.532(a)(1)]. If possible, the evaluator in any testing situation or interview should be familiar to the child and speak the child's language. When tests or evaluation materials are not available in the student's native language, examiners may find it necessary to use English-language instruments. Because this is a practice fraught with the possibility of misinterpretation, examiners need to be cautious in how they administer the test and interpret results.

Alterations may need to be made to the standardized procedures used to administer tests for bilingual students. These can include paraphrasing instructions, providing a demonstration of how test tasks are to be performed, reading test items to the student rather than having him or her read them, allowing the student to respond verbally rather than in writing, or allowing the student to use a dictionary (Wallace, Larsen, & Elksnin, 1992, p. 471). However, if any such alterations are made, it is important to recognize that standardization has been broken, limiting the usefulness and applicability of test norms. Results should be cautiously interpreted, and all alterations made to the testing procedures should be fully detailed in the report describing the student's test performance. As mentioned earlier, it is also essential that other assessment approaches be an integral part of collecting information about the student.

Ascher (1990), in her article "Assessing Bilingual Students," addesses options commonly used in testing limited English speakers: nonverbal tests, translated tests, interpreters, and tests that are norm-referenced in the primary language. Following is a brief description of each of these options:

1. *Nonverbal tests* are the most common procedure used with bilingual students. Unfortunately, nonverbal measures of intelligence predict less reliably than verbal measures, and, despite appearances, may even be hypersensitive to language background.

2. *Translated tests* are always different tests, unknown and unfair. While it is not difficult to translate a test, it is extremely difficult, if not impossible, to translate psychometric properties from one language to another. A word in English is simply not the same word in terms of difficulty in Spanish, Hmong, Russian, or Chinese.

3. Both *trained and untrained interpreters* are widely used in assessment. However, this practice remains risky. The research on interpreters is negligible. Although a number of commercial models exist for training and using interpreters, there is no empirical validation of their suggested procedures.

4. Many *testing specialists* have become sensitive to the problems of testing bilingual individuals. However, because standardized tests in any language remain biased in favor of persons for whom that language is native, low test scores received by bilinguals often are interpreted as evidence of deficits or even disorders. This creates difficulties with every kind of assessment, from tests for English language proficiency—used most often to place students in bilingual classes—to intelligence tests—the prime source of information for special education placement.

REFERRAL OF CULTURALLY AND LINGUISTICALLY DIVERSE STUDENTS

The materials and procedures required for a referral of culturally and linguistically diverse children to the CSE may involve more than the normal packet of materials. The evaluation team needs to:

♦ Identify the reason for the referral and include any test results in both languages as appropriate.

♦ Include any records or reports upon which the referral is based.

♦ Attach a home language survey indicating the home language(s).

♦ Specify the level of language proficiency.

♦ Describe the extent to which the LEP student has received native language instruction and/or ESL services prior to the referral.

♦ Describe experiential and/or enrichment services for students from diverse cultural and experiential backgrounds.

♦ Describe the school's efforts to involve parents prior to referral.

♦ Describe the amount of time and extent of services in an academic program for students who have had little or no formal schooling.

♦ Identify length of residency of the referred student in the United States and prior school experience in the native country and in an English language school system.

♦ Describe all attempts to remediate the pupil's performance prior to referral, including any supplemental aids or support services provided for this purpose.

In conclusion, it is necessary for those entering into or currently involved in the field of special education to be aware of the growing number of students designated as limited English proficient. Federal law mandates that minority students have rights for protection when being assessed. Consequently, knowledge of various tests, their limitations, and controversies surrounding the biases of bilingual assessment is imperative.

ESL LITERACY SCALE (ESL)

GENERAL TEST INFORMATION

Author:	Michael Roddy
Publisher:	Academic Therapy Publications
Address of Publisher:	20 Commercial Blvd. Novato, CA 94949-6191
Phone Number of Publisher:	415-883-3314 or 800-422-7249
Fax of Publisher:	415-883-3720

Purpose of Test: The test was designed with the purpose of identifying the appropriate starting level for ESL(English as a Second Language) and literacy instruction with adolescent to adult learners.

Description of Test: This test is a quick informal assessment developed over a five-year period with adult school students of many different backgrounds, including Hispanic, Asian, Middle Eastern, and European. The test includes testing booklets, administration and instruction card, and a scoring template.

Type of Test:	Informal assessment
Administration Time:	15–20 minutes
Type of Administration:	Individual or group
Who Administers This Test:	Special education teacher, psychologist, speech/language therapist
Age/Grade Levels:	Ages 16 to Adult

Subtest Information: Subtests include the following areas:

- *Listening Comprehension*
- *Grammar*
- *Life Skills*
- *Reading Comprehension*
- *Composition*

Scoring Information: The test results are charted on a profile showing which level ESL classes (beginning, intermediate, or advanced) will best suit each student.

STRENGTHS OF THE ESL

- The test is easy to administer.
- The test is easy to score.
- The test is normed on many different ethnic backgrounds, including Hispanic, Asian, Middle Eastern, and European.

WEAKNESSES OF THE ESL

- The test should only be used as a screening device because of the lack of standardized information required for the determination of suspected disabilities.
- Group administration may prevent the examiner from effectively observing individual test-taking behaviors (e.g., impulsivity, avoidance). These behaviors may have significant negative effects on the test results.

LANGUAGE PROFICIENCY TEST (LPT)

GENERAL TEST INFORMATION

Authors:	Joan Gerard & Gloria Weinstock
Publisher:	Academic Therapy Publications
Address of Publisher:	20 Commercial Blvd. Novato, CA 94949-6191
Phone Number of Publisher:	415-883-3314 or 800-422-7249
Fax of Publisher:	415-883-3720

Purpose of Test: The test is designed to assess oral/aural, reading, and writing skills used with students whose English speaking, reading, or writing skills are preventing them from succeeding in the academic or vocational environment.

Description of Test: The test assesses a wide range of English language ability and uses materials that are suitable for older students. The test covers nine areas of language functioning, including an optional translation section with passages in Spanish, German, French, Tagalog, and Japanese. The test includes an examiner's manual and student test booklets.

Type of Test:	Criterion-referenced
Administration Time:	90 minutes
Type of Administration:	Individual or group
Who Administers This Test:	Special education teacher, psychologist, speech/language therapist
Age/Grade Levels:	Grades 9 and over

Subtest Information:

- *Aural/Oral Commands Test*—consists of commands, short answers, and comprehension questions.
- *Reading Test*—consists of vocabulary and comprehension.
- *Writing Test*—consists of grammar, sentence response, paragraph response, and translation.

Scoring Information: The test provides:

- Percentile ranks
- Levels of English competency

STRENGTHS OF THE LPT

- The test is very appropriate for identifying competency levels of ESL students.
- The test is very appropriate for discerning the specific language deficiencies of ESL students.
- The test assesses a wide range of English language abilities.
- The test uses materials that are not insulting to older students.

WEAKNESSES OF THE LPT

- The test should only be used as a screening device in determining the need for a more thorough evaluation.
- Group administration may limit direct student observation of behaviors, e.g., avoidance, resistance, impulsivity, which may affect results.

MATRIX ANALOGIES TEST—EXPANDED FORM (MAT-EXPANDED FORM)

GENERAL TEST INFORMATION

Author:	Jack A. Naglieri
Publisher:	The Psychological Corporation
Address of Publisher:	555 Academic Court San Antonio, TX 78204-2498
Phone Number of Publisher:	800-211-8378
Fax of Publisher:	800-232-1223
TDD of the Publisher:	800-723-1318

Purpose of Test: The test was designed to measure nonverbal reasoning ability.

Description of Test: The test is especially appropriate for assessing the abilities of children with learning disabilities, mental retardation, hearing or language impairments, physical disabilities, ability to speak in more than one language, and ability to perform at the gifted level. The test items present a visual stimulus with a missing element or sequence. The student selects the option that best completes the stimulus; variables include size, shape, color, and direction. The matrix design of the stimulus items requires minimal verbal comprehension and no verbal response. Directions are brief and can be communicated nonverbally if necessary. The test includes an examiner's manual, stimulus manual, and answer sheets.

Type of Test:	Norm-referenced
Administration Time:	Short Form, 25–30 minutes; Expanded Form, 20–25 minutes
Type of Administration:	Individual
Who Administers This Test:	Special education teacher, psychologist, speech/language therapist
Age/Grade Levels:	Ages 5.0 to 17.11

Subtest Information: The following describes the test's four subtests:

- *Pattern Completion*—In this subtest the student is asked to accurately complete the pattern shown to him or her.

- *Reasoning by Analogy*—Here the student is asked to determine how changes in two or more variables converge to result in a new figure.

- *Serial Reasoning*—In this subtest the student is asked to discover the order in which items appear throughout a matrix.

- *Spatial Visualization*—Here the student is asked to imagine how a figure would look when two or more components are combined.

Scoring Information: The test provides scores in the following manners:

- Overall standard scores with a mean of 100 and standard deviation of 15
- Item-group standard score with a mean of 10 and standard deviation of 3
- Percentile ranks
- Age equivalents

STRENGTHS OF THE MAT-EXPANDED FORM

- The MAT offers U.S. norms.
- Signs of bias for women and blacks are minimal or nonexistent.

MATRIX ANALOGIES TEST—EXPANDED FORM (MAT-EXPANDED FORM)

(continued)

♦ The test format is designed to reduce color blindness effects.

♦ The test has high internal consistency reliability.

WEAKNESSES OF THE MAT-EXPANDED FORM

♦ The test does not distinguish well in the upper-age ranges among students of superior ability or in the lower age ranges among students of low average ability.

SCREENING TEST OF SPANISH GRAMMAR

GENERAL TEST INFORMATION

Author:	Allen S. Toronto
Publisher of the Test:	Northwestern University Press
Address of the Publisher:	625 Colfax St., Evanston, Illinois. 60201
Phone Number of Publisher:	847-491-5313
Fax of Publisher:	847-491-8150

Purpose of Test: The test is designed to be used as a syntax screening device that identifies Spanish-speaking children who do not demonstrate native syntactic proficiency commensurate with their age.

Description of Test: The test is organized in two parts—receptive and expressive language. In the receptive section, the subject has to point to one of the four pictures that best corresponds to the sentence uttered by the examiner. In the expressive section, an examiner utters two sentences that relate to one of the four pictures on a page. The subject then has to repeat the one sentence that best corresponds to the picture indicated by the examiner. There are two test sentences for each page of four pictures.

Type of Test:	Standardized
Administration Time:	15–25 minutes
Type of Administration:	Individual
Who Administers This Test:	Special education teacher, psychologist, speech/language therapist
Age/Grade Levels:	Spanish-speaking children, ages 3-6

Scoring Information: The scores are presented in the following manners:

- ◆ Percentiles
- ◆ Scaled scores

STRENGTHS OF THE SCREENING TEST OF SPANISH GRAMMAR

- ◆ This test helps to meet the needs of an educational community lacking in Spanish-speaking faculty and material resources in this language.
- ◆ The test helps to point out children with comprehension and identification problems.

WEAKNESSES OF SCREENING TEST OF SPANISH GRAMMAR

- ◆ Some of the test's visual stimuli are ambiguous or misleading.
- ◆ The test's reliability and validity have not yet been adequately established.

SYSTEM OF MULTICULTURAL PLURALISTIC ASSESSMENT (SOMPA)

GENERAL TEST INFORMATION

Authors:	Jane R. Mercer and June F. Lewis
Publisher:	The Psychological Corporation
Address of Publisher:	555 Academic Court San Antonio, TX 78204-2498
Phone Number of Publisher:	800-211-8378
Fax of Publisher:	800-232-1223
TDD of the Publisher:	800-723-1318

Purpose of Test: This test is designed as a comprehensive system for assessing the level at which children function in cognitive abilities, perceptual motor abilities, and adaptive behavior.

Description of Test: The SOMPA is an assemblage of assessment devices designed for preschool and early age children. This test is used and developed for use with culturally different English-speaking children, particularly for determining these children's needs for educational programs for the mentally retarded and gifted.

The SOMPA consists of two major components: The *Parent Interview* is conducted in the home and the *Student Assessment* conducted in school. The test provides nine different measures that estimate the child's learning potential by considering sociocultural and health factors. The test includes a parent interview manual, parent interview record forms, scoring keys, student assessment manual, student assessment record forms, profile folders, and technical manual.

Type of Test:	Norm-referenced
Administration Time:	Student Assessment—60 minutes; Parent Interview—20 minutes
Type of Administration:	Individual
Who Administers This Test:	Special education teacher, psychologist, speech/language therapist
Age/Grade Levels:	Ages 5–11

Subtest Information: The SOMPA is composed of nine instruments divided into two major components:

1. *Student Assessment Instruments*—This component of the test is administered in the schools and utilizes the following information:

   - Physical Dexterity Tasks
   - Bender Visual Motor Gestalt Test results
   - Weight by Height
   - Visual Acuity
   - Auditory Acuity
   - WISC-III or WPPSI-R Test results

2. *Parent Interview Instruments*—This component of the test is administered in either English or Spanish in the home to the child's primary care provider. It comprises two sociocultural scales:

   - Adaptive Behavior Inventory for Children
   - Health History Inventories

Scoring Information: The test provides the following:

- Scaled scores
- Percentile scores

SYSTEM OF MULTICULTURAL PLURALISTIC ASSESSMENT (SOMPA)

(continued)

STRENGTHS OF THE SOMPA

♦ Because of its global approach to assessment, the SOMPA is one of the best current adaptive behavior measures for children ages 5 to 11 years old.

♦ The test's materials, interview forms, and manuals are clear and easy to follow.

WEAKNESSES OF THE SOMPA

♦ According to McLoughlin and Lewis (1990, p. 206), "the SOMPA has been heavily criticized for its lack of national norms, failure to include school performance tasks, validity, and failure to provide guidelines for use of the battery in educational decisions."

Section 9

IDENTIFICATION OF POSSIBLE HIGH–RISK CHILDREN

The first stage of the diagnostic process for children with suspected disabilities occurs prior to evaluation—namely, identification of possible high-risk children or children with suspected disabilities. A high-risk child or a child with suspected disabilities is defined as a child who exhibits one or more of the following symptoms for more than six months:

♦ Serious inconsistencies in intellectual, emotional, academic, or social performance

♦ Inconsistency between ability and achievement, ability and classroom performance, or ability and expected performance

♦ Impairment in one or more life functions, i.e., socialization, academic performance, adaptive behavior

SYMPTOMS VS. PROBLEMS

It is very important that parents and educators recognize the difference between symptoms of problems and actual problems. Many times, parents, teachers, and professionals mistakenly try to correct a child's symptoms, e.g., stubbornness, procrastination, daydreaming, thinking that the symptoms might be the problem. However, when a serious problem exists within a child, the problem creates tension that is released as symptomatic behavior. Symptoms reduce the tension created by a conflict or a problem, but treating the symptom will not alleviate the problem.

Symptoms work like signals to allow us the opportunity to realize that a serious problem exists. Negative symptomatic behavior results from serious conflicts or problems. Positive symptomatic behavior results when a child is free from serious conflicts or problems. Therefore, it is crucial that educators and parents understand both types of symptoms and what they represent so that they can deal with a potential problem as soon as possible.

How Serious Problems Affect a Child's Behavior and Ability to Learn

If a child is experiencing many conflicts, problems, insecurities, etc., there will be an increase in the number, types, and degree of negative symptoms exhibited by the child. All conflicts require energy; therefore, the greater the frequency, duration, and intensity of the

257

symptoms, the greater the energy drain on the child. The energy required to deal with these conflicts must come from somewhere, and it tends to come from constructive processes such as concentration, memory, and attention. Since these constructive processes—so necessary for success in school—become threatened, the child will begin to suffer.

Everyone has a certain amount of psychic energy to use in dealing with the everyday stresses of life. In normal development there is a certain amount of stress but, because of an absence of major conflicts that would tend to drain energy, the individual has more than enough energy to keep things in perspective.

POSITIVE BEHAVIORS

The division of energy and the generally positive symptoms that result when a child is relatively "conflict free" may take on a certain pattern. As a result, the child will exhibit behaviors that include good concentration, responsibility with school work, consistency, age-appropriate attention span, flexibility, appropriate memory, high frustration tolerance, appropriate peer interaction, organization, and an appropriate ability to focus on tasks. Parents will notice these behaviors at home when the child does homework, and educators will notice it at school. Not every child who is conflict free will exhibit these symptoms all the time, but the child's habits and behaviors will be predominately positive and constructive.

The child will also exhibit positive behavior patterns at home. These will generally include normal strivings for parental approval, resiliency, willingness to reason, willingness to try, exercising appropriate judgment, and responding normally to discipline. These patterns may vary to some degree during adolescence and still be within "normal" limits.

A relatively "conflict-free" child will usually have little difficulty falling asleep. While he or she may have problems waking up, as many of us do, it will not interfere in his or her ability to get to school. Socially, the child will generally maintain social interactions, show a willingness to try new social experiences, and treat his/her peers appropriately.

NEGATIVE BEHAVIORS

When a child is troubled by serious conflicts, his or her available energy must be "pulled" to deal with the conflicts, like white blood cells to an infection. Therefore, the child has less energy available to keep things in perspective. In this case the resulting symptoms and behaviors take on a different look.

Educators and/or parents who suspect that a child is experiencing some difficulty because he or she exhibits negative behaviors should not hesitate to contact the school psychologist or a local therapist for a consultation. Following are examples of some of the causes of serious problems which might result in negative symptomatic behavior:

Intellectual Reasons

◆ Limited intelligence; slow learner

◆ Retardation

Social Reasons

◆ Peer pressure

◆ Peer rejection

Emotional Reasons

- Consistent school failure

- Traumatic emotional development

- Separation or divorce of parents

- High parental expectations

- Sibling performance

- Health-related problems

- Change in environment as a result of moving

- Abuse

- Dysfunctional family situation

- Parental loss of job

- Death in the family

Academic Reasons

- Learning disabilities

- Poor academic skills

- Style of teacher incompatible with style of student

- Language difficulties

- Falling behind in school because of an imbalance in other areas, i.e., too social

Negative behavior patterns such as those listed above will be evident in many areas of the child's life. For instance, at school the child may be unable to focus on task, may procrastinate, daydream, be disorganized, reject help, be irresponsible, inflexible, selectively forgetful, and may project reasons for problems on everyone and everything else. At home the child may be oversensitive, forgetful, reclusive, unreasonable, overactive, stubborn, untruthful, exaggerative, and may express somatic complaints such as stomachaches, and headaches. The child's sleeping patterns may change. He or she may have great difficulty falling asleep, since tension interferes with relaxation, and may even begin to sleepwalk or show other signs of restless sleep. The child may resist getting up in the morning which may result in lateness or absence. More frequent nightmares may also be a signal of some unresolved inner conflicts. Furthermore, the child may withdraw socially—constantly finding fault with peers, be unwilling to try new social experiences, expressing social fears or beliefs that no one likes him or her, and so on.

It is important to remember that such symptoms will often occur as a result of a deeper undefined problem. Once the problem is identified and resolved, and once the tension is alleviated, the negative symptomatic behavior will dissipate. If caught early, many such issues can be resolved in a relatively quick period of time. However, if the underlying problem is not identified for many months or years, the treatment period will be longer.

Therapy can be a long-term process, especially if a child's problems have been around for a long period of time. However, a child's therapeutic progress makes itself evident by the reduction of the negative symptomatic behavior patterns. As a child begins to verbalize the issues and find better ways of coping, the tension diminishes. And as the tension is reduced, the need for negative symptomatic behaviors also diminishes.

School Symptoms Exhibited by High-Risk Students

A high-risk student is usually one who is experiencing severe emotional, social, environmental, or academic stress. As a result of this intense turmoil, the student exhibits many symptoms in a dynamic attempt to alleviate the anxiety. These symptoms can show up in many different behavior patterns. Some of the more common ones exhibited by elementary or secondary students while in school are listed below:

- A history of adequate or high first-quarter grades followed by a downward trend leading to failures in the final quarter

- A history of excessive absences

- A history of excessive lateness

- Frequent difficulty separating from a parent at the start of the school day. (While this can be normal behavior in very young children, it becomes a more serious symptom after age 6 or 7.)

- High achievement scores and high school abilities indexes coupled with a history of low academic performance

- Consistent failure in two or more quarters of at least two subjects

- Wandering the halls after school with no direction or purpose

- A history of constant blaming of others for a lack of performance, handing in work, failures, or cutting

- A history of feeling powerless to confront his or her problems

- Recent stress–related experiences, e.g., divorce or separation of parents, death of a parent, or parent's loss of employment

- A history of constant visits to the nurse

- Social withdrawal from peers with an emphasis on developing relationships with adults

Typical descriptions of the child showing symptomatic behavior that may be indicative of more serious concerns, include those listed below. The troubled child . . .

- is impulsive
- frequently hands in incomplete work
- gives many excuses for inappropriate behavior
- constantly blames others for problems
- panics easily
- is highly distractible

- lies constantly
- is awkward
- is fearful of adults
- is fearful of new situations
- is verbally hesitant
- is hypoactive

- has a short attention span
- is overactive
- is physical with others
- is intrusive
- is unable to focus on task
- procrastinates
- turns his or her head while listening
- is disorganized
- is inflexible
- is irresponsible
- exercises poor judgment
- is in denial
- is a daydreamer
- is unwilling to venture a guess
- is unwilling to reason
- demonstrates social withdrawal
- is constantly self-critical
- bullies other children
- needs constant reassurance
- is a poor reader

- is hyperactive
- fears criticism
- rarely takes chances
- is moody
- defies authority
- is anxious
- is not able to generalize
- is insecure
- has trouble starting work
- tires easily
- is controlling
- is overly critical
- is forgetful
- is painfully shy
- is overly social
- is a slow starter
- is argumentative
- destroys property
- is inconsistent
- is a poor speller

HOW TO DETERMINE THE SEVERITY OF A CHILD'S PROBLEM

While many of the symptoms listed above may indicate a problem, the *frequency, intensity,* and *duration* of the symptoms are crucial in determining a pattern of high risk. The more often symptoms occur, the longer they last, and the more intense their form, the greater the chance that the child is experiencing a serious problem. The more immediately parents and educators respond to such problems, the greater their chances of success with the child.

AVOIDANCE BEHAVIOR PATTERNS

Some of the first signs that a child experiencing problems with learning are *avoidance behaviors.* These are techniques used by children to avoid what they perceive as a failure-provoking or an ego-deflating situation. Children will often exhibit these symptoms at home and at school to avoid loss of parental approval, peer humiliation, or failure. They are avoiding:

♦ showing their parents they are not capable

♦ dealing with possible parental anger and frustration

♦ coming face to face with their own inadequacy

♦ dealing with peer pressure and possible ridicule.

Some of the more common avoidance behaviors are discussed in detail below:

Selective forgetting—If a child knows the batting averages of all baseball players, the words of most songs on the radio, the times of most TV shows, but habitually "forgets" to bring home his or her math book, then the child is exhibiting selective forgetting. The selectivity of the forgetfulness usually centers around areas of learning that the child may find frustrating.

Forgetting to write down assignments day after day—This symptom may continue even after repeated requests or threats. The child exhibiting this symptom is most likely trying to avoid a perceived-failure experience.

Taking hours to complete homework—In this avoidance pattern the child seems to labor or procrastinate over school work. Frequent trips to the kitchen for food, to the bathroom, to get a drink, and/or to sharpen a pencil delay the possibility of what the child perceives as a failure experience. This symptom also occurs if a child is under tension and having difficulty concentrating for long periods of time. He or she will tend to "burn out" quickly and daydream the time away.

Finishing homework very quickly—The child exhibiting this symptom is trying to get the ego-threatening situation (homework) over as quickly as possible. The child makes every attempt to "rush" through the assignments with little if any care or patience. Getting it over as quickly as possible almost makes it seem as if it never existed.

Not being able to get started with homework—When a child's anxiety level is very high, it is very difficult to "start the engine." He or she may spend a great deal of time getting ready for homework by arranging books, getting the paper out, opening the textbooks, and so on. Once again, the child is trying to avoid the task that he or she finds threatening.

Frequently bringing home unfinished classwork—A child can exhibit this symptom for several reasons. *One reason* could be that the child has a low energy level and therefore has difficulty dealing with tasks involving sustained concentration. The *second reason* could be that the child is dependent upon parental assistance with homework. If the child's parents constantly sit next to the child when he or she is doing homework, the child becomes conditioned to their assistance and feels helpless without it. Since the child misses such support in the classroom, the child procrastinates when doing classwork so that he or she can bring it home and complete it with parental assistance. The *third reason* could be the child's need for attention. Bringing home unfinished classwork may necessitate a parent's sitting with him or her to complete the work. The child may see the parent as a "captive audience" and thus stop working or complain that he or she "can't do the work" if the parent tries to leave. This situation prolongs the period of attention the child receives from his or her parents; however, these situations usually become more tense and negative as the hours progress and the parent's patience wavers.

Consistently leaving long-term assignments until the last minute—Avoidance of school-related tasks, especially long-term ones, is a frequent symptom of children with low energy levels. The behavior is analogous to avoiding paying a big bill when one has very little money. Another way one can avoid paying a bill is to forget that the bill exists. Similarly, children who are anxious about being able to complete an assignment successfully try "magical thinking"; in other words, they wish the assignment out of existence or believe that it will magically be finished without any participation on their part.

Complaining of headaches, stomachaches, etc., before or after school—A child's very high tension levels over an extended period of time may result in somatic (bodily) complaints. These complaints, while real to the child, may indicate his or her avoidance of an uncomfortable or ego-deflating situation. The physical discomfort or ailment becomes the excuse for not performing well or not performing at all.

Exhibiting "spotlight" behaviors—"Spotlight" behaviors are behaviors that focus attention on the child—calling out, laughing out loud, getting up out of seat, and/or annoying other children. When a child "spotlights," it is usually a release of tension. Some children use these behaviors to alleviate the tension of academic inadequacy and may even hope to get into trouble to leave the room. In this way, they will not have to deal with possible academic failure. Another reason for "spotlight " behaviors is the need on the part of the child to be in control. However, the more controlling a child is, the more out of control that child may feel. The final reason for "spotlight" behaviors is to gain the teacher's attention. Thus, the child is determining when he or she gets attention, not the teacher. It is better for the teacher to spontaneously and randomly pay attention to such a child when he or she is not expecting it. In this way, the teacher (or the parent) can reduce the child's impulsive need to seek attention.

Section 10

UNDERSTANDING A STUDENT'S BEHAVIOR DURING TESTING

There are many behaviors that should be watched for when a student undergoes testing and that should be noted in reports about the student. Some of these behaviors include the student's adjustment to the testing situation, reaction to test items, verbalizations during testing, if any, and general approach to the test.

It is important that evaluators carefully consider any peculiarities exhibited by a student during evaluation. Almost any peculiarity can be seen as either a symptom or a problem. For example, a student who hesitates for long periods before answering may hesitate as a symptom of a difficulty processing information or as a symptom of low self-esteem. However, the hesitation itself becomes a problem during evaluation because it slows the student down considerably and therefore limits strong performance. Evaluations must consider what peculiarities reveal as well as the impact they have on student performance.

ADJUSTMENT TO THE TESTING SITUATION

Children's adjustment to the testing situation can vary greatly. The significance of any adjustment period is not necessarily the student's initial reactions but the duration of the period of maladjustment. Children are usually initially nervous and uptight, but relax as time goes on with reassurances from the examiner. However, children who maintain a high level of discomfort throughout the sessions may be harboring more serious problems.

Elements of the testing environment itself should be considered as possible distracters for the student being tested. Noise, poor lighting, the presence of antagonistic peers, even an intimidating examiner can adversely impact a student during testing. It is the evaluator's responsibility to limit such variables and to consider the special needs of each student.

Examiners should be aware of any overt signs of tension (observable behaviors indicative of underlying tension) exhibited by a child that may affect the outcome of the test results, such as constant leg motion, little or no eye contact with the examiner, and/or consistent finger or pencil tapping. Any oppositional behaviors (behaviors that test the limits and guidelines of the examiner) should also be noted, such as singing or making noises while being tested, keeping a jacket on, and/or covering most of his or her face with a hat. If this type of tension is extreme, the examiner may want to note in the report the effects of such factors on performance and alert the reader to the possibility that the results may be minimal indicators of ability.

Reaction Time

The speed with which a child answers questions on a test can indicate several things. The child who impulsively answers incorrectly without thinking may be a child with high levels of anxiety that interfere with his or her ability to concentrate before responding. On the other hand, the child who blocks or delays may be one who is afraid of reaction or criticism and thus uses these techniques to ward off what he or she perceives will be an ego-deflating situation.

Nature of Responses

The types of response a child gives during an evaluation may indicate certain difficulties. For example, a child who constantly asks to have questions repeated may have hearing difficulties. (Hearing and vision acuity should be determined prior to a testing situation.) Or, the child who asks to have questions repeated may be having problems processing information and may need more time to understand what is being asked.

If a child is overtly negative or self-defeating in his or her responses (e.g., "I'm so stupid," "I'll never get any right"), the child is probably exhibiting his or her very low level of self-esteem or is hiding a learning problem.

Verbalizations

A student's verbal interaction with the examiner during an evaluation can be very telling. Some children with high levels of anxiety may try to vent their tension through constant verbalizations. Of course, the tension can interfere with their ability to think clearly and to focus on task, and the verbalizing can also disrupt hearing and thought processes.

Examiners should also be aware that verbal hesitations may indicate other problems: immature speech patterns, expressive language problems, poor self-esteem, or lack of understanding of the question due to limited intellectual capacity.

Organizational Approach Used During Testing

A child who sizes up a situation and systematically approaches short- and long-term tasks using trial and error may be a child with excellent internal organization, the ability to concentrate and delay, and low levels of tension and anxiety. However, some children with emotional problems may also perform well on short-term tasks because they see these tasks as a challenge and can organize themselves to perform well over a relatively short period of time. Their particular problems in organization and consistency may come when they are asked to perform this way over an extended period of time. Some children become less organized under the stress of a time constraint. The child's organizational and performance style when dealing with a task under time restrictions is one factor considered in the investigation of his or her overall learning style.

Children with chaotic internal organization may appear to know what they are doing, but the overall outcome of the task indicates a great deal of energy input with very low production. They essentially "spin their wheels," and the energy output is a cover for not knowing what to do. Children with attention deficit/hyperactive disorder may also exhibit a confused sense of organization. However, there are other factors in addition to attentional ones that go into the diagnosis of this disorder.

Adaptability

The ability of a student to adapt or shift from one task to another without difficulty is a very important factor in determining learning style and may be one predictor of the student's successful completion of a task. A student's ability to shift from one task to another without expending a great deal of energy allows him or her more available resources for the next task. A student who is rigid and does not adapt well uses much of his or her available energy to switch tasks, thereby reducing the chances of success on the new task.

The ability to sustain interest may also be a direct result of available energy. A child who loses interest quickly may be immature, overwhelmed, or preoccupied. Some of these reactions may be normal for young children. However, as the child gets older, such reactions may be symptomatic of other factors like learning problems, emotional issues, or limited intellectual capacity.

Attitude

The attitude that a child demonstrates toward a testing situation may be reflective of his or her attitude within the classroom. A child who is oppositional or uncooperative may be a child who needs to feel in control of the situation. The more controlling a child is, the more out of control he or she actually feels. Control is aimed at securing predictability so that the child can deal with a situation even though his or her energy levels may be lowered by conflict and tension. Children under tension do not adapt well and are easily thrown by new situations or people, and thus by controlling a situation or a person they know what to expect. On the other hand, the child who tries hard to succeed may do so for several reasons (e.g., parental approval or personal satisfaction). He or she may enjoy success and find the tasks normally challenging. Generally this type of child is not thrown by a mistake and can easily move to the next task without difficulty.

In conclusion, all behavior is essentially a message, and the way a child reacts to being tested can be a clue to learning style or problem areas. If the evaluator can attend to a child's behavior by being aware of significant signs, he or she may come to a better understanding of the child's needs and may learn even more about the child than the test results will tell.

Section 11

THE PARENTS' ROLE IN THE ASSESSMENT PROCESS

While designing, conducting, interpreting, and paying for the assessment are the school system's responsibilities, parents have an important part to play before, during, and after the evaluation. One of the purposes of this section is to provide parents with suggestions for the range of ways in which they might involve themselves in the assessment of their child. The extent to which parents involve themselves, however, is a personal decision and will vary from family to family.

EVALUATION OPTIONS, RESPONSIBILITIES, AND EXPECTATIONS

Waterman (1994) lists parental options, responsibilities, and expectations *prior to evaluation*:

♦ Parents may initiate the evaluation process by requesting that the school system evaluate their child for the presence of a disability and the need for special education.

♦ Parents must be notified by the school, and give their consent, before any initial evaluation of the child may be conducted.

♦ Parents may wish to talk with the person responsible for conducting the evaluation to find out what the evaluation will involve.

♦ Parents may find it very useful to become informed about assessment issues in general and any specific issues relevant to their child (e.g., assessment of minority children, use of specific tests or assessment techniques with a specific disability).

♦ Parents should advocate for a comprehensive evaluation of their child—one that investigates all skill areas apparently affected by the suspected disability and that uses multiple means of collecting information (e.g., observations, interviews, alternative approaches).

♦ Parents may suggest specific questions they would like to see addressed through the evaluation.

♦ Parents should inform the school of any accommodations the child will need (e.g., conducting interviews/testing in the child's native language, adapting testing environment to child's specific physical and other needs).

269

♦ Parents should inform the school if they themselves need an interpreter or other accommodations during any of their discussions with the school.

♦ Parents may prepare their child for the evaluation process, explaining what will happen and, where necessary, reducing the child's anxiety. It may help the child to know that he or she will not be receiving a "grade" on the tests he or she will be taking.

The following is a list of parental options, responsibilities, and expectations *during evaluation*:

♦ Parents need to share with the school their insights into the child's background (developmental, medical, and academic) and past and present school performance.

♦ Parents may wish to share with the school any prior school records, reports, tests, or evaluation information available on their child.

♦ Parents may need to share information about cultural differences that can illuminate the educational team's understanding of the student (see Section Four).

♦ Parents need to make every effort to attend interviews the school may set up with them and provide information about their child.

The following is a list of parental options, responsibilities, and expectations *after evaluation*:

♦ Parents need to carefully consider the results that emerge from their child's evaluation, in light of their own observation and knowledge of the child. Do the results make sense in terms of the behaviors, skills, needs, and attitudes they have observed in their child? Are there gaps, inconsistencies, or unexpected findings in the results that parents feel are important to address, if a comprehensive picture of the student's strengths and needs is to be developed?

♦ Parents may share their insights and concerns about the evaluation results with the school and suggest areas where additional information may be needed. Schools may or may not act upon parents' suggestions, and parents have certain recourses under law should they feel strongly about pursuing the matter.

♦ Parents should participate fully in the development of their child's Individualized Education Program (IEP), using information from the evaluation.

PARENT INTAKES AND INTERVIEWS

There may be times when a member of the assessment team is called upon to gather pertinent information from a parent or parents. This may involve interviewing the parent to obtain a complete social history or description of the family life situation. In some cases, this part of the assessment process may not be possible to obtain because of a number of variables, such as parents' work restrictions, inability to obtain coverage for younger siblings, resistance, or apathy.

In many schools, the psychologist or social worker will normally meet with the parent to gather this information. However, it is important that each member of the assessment team understand the process in case he or she is asked to do the interview. When the interview is arranged, there are several things to consider before the meeting:

♦ Evaluators should help the parent feel comfortable and at ease by setting up a receptive environment. If possible, meetings should be held in a pleasant setting, around a table rather than a desk. All effort to extend cordiality and ease tension should be made, such as offering simple refreshments or encouraging parents to take notes so they feel more in control of information about their child.

♦ Evaluators should never view parents as adversaries even if they are angry or hostile. Any anger or hostility that the parents may exhibit could be a defense mechanism because they may not be aware of what the evaluator will be asking or because they may have experienced negative school meetings over the years. Since this may be an opportunity for parents to "vent," evaluators should listen to their concerns, and strive to understand their concerns without being defensive.

♦ Evaluators should inform parents every step of the way as to the purpose of meetings and the steps involved in the referral process. Parents need to be reassured that no recommendation will be made without their input and permission.

♦ Evaluators should inform parents of the purpose of any testing that the child will undergo. Parents need to be reassured that the evaluation is looking for a way to help the child.

♦ Evaluators need to let parents know that if the testing reveals a significant discrepancy between ability and achievement, then the case needs to be reviewed by the CSE. This is an important piece of information to convey to the parents since it involves their rights to due process (discussed later in this chapter).

♦ Evaluators should review the testing release form with the parents and explain each test and its purpose. The more information the parents have, the less fearful they will be. Parents need to be made aware that their signature on the form requires that the testing be completed within thirty days.

♦ Evaluators need to reassure parents about the confidentiality of information gathered about their child. They should know which individuals on the team will be seeing the information and the purpose for their review of the facts. Evaluators should also make every effort to make parents feel free to call with any questions or concerns they may have.

PARENTAL CONSENT FOR EVALUATION

During the assesment process, another purpose of a parent interview is to secure parental consent for testing their child, procured through their signing a release form such as the one presented on page 272.

PARENTAL RIGHTS DURING THE EVALUATION PHASE

If a child has a disability, he or she has certain rights protected by law. Both the parents and the child have the right to challenge any recommendation made by the school. This type of challenge encourages schools to work with parents and ensure that the child receives an appropriate education in the least restrictive environment.

Should a disagreement arise regarding the process or the outcome, there are formal and informal procedures available to parents for recourse, including, but not limited to an impartial hearing provided by the school district. Under the Individuals with Disabilities Education Act (IDEA), parents are afforded many rights to protect their children during

---

PARENT CONSENT FOR EVALUATION

To the Parent/Guardian of: _____

Birth Date _____

School _____ Grade _____

We would like to inform you that your child_____ is being referred for individual testing which will help us in his/her educational planning. You have had the opportunity to discuss the need for this testing with the school principal/designee. Consequently, you should be aware that referral was made for the following reasons:

_____

Testing results will help us to determine your child's educational needs and to plan his or her most appropriate program. The evaluation procedures and/or tests may include the following:

Intelligence: _____

Communication/Language/Speech: _____

Physical: _____

Behavior/Emotional: _____

Academic: _____

Vocational: _____

Other: _____

The evaluation will be conducted by a multidisciplinary team who will share the results of the evaluation with you at a future meeting. Both this meeting and a Committee on Special Education (CSE) meeting will be held within 30 school days of receipt of this notice. It is necessary that the School District CSE have your written permission to evaluate your child.

☐ I grant permission for the evaluation(s) mentioned above.

☐ I do not grant permission for the evaluation(s) mentioned above.

Parent's Signature _____ Date _____

Administrator/Designee _____ Date _____

---

the assessment process. The following are examples of certain rights guaranteed to parents during the evaluation phase of the assessment process:

1. The parent should receive a notice regarding the evaluation and their due process rights. The parent must consent to the evaluation.

2. The parent may give consent for evaluation or withhold consent, or request a conference regarding an initial evaluation.

3. It is the parents' guarantee that more than one evaluation should be involved in assessing their child's suspected disability.

4. Evaluations should be administered in the child's dominant language.

5. The child will undergo a complete evaluation within 30 school days from the time of the parent's consent.

6. The parent will be provided a list of resources where independent evaluations can be obtained.

7. If the parents' dominant language is other than English, all information provided to the parent must be in the dominant language.

8. The child must be observed in his or her classroom by someone other than his or her classroom teacher.

9. The parent should be given a description of the proposed evaluation and its intended purpose prior to testing.

10. The parents are entitled to receive information on their child's areas of educational need.

11. Parents should have the opportunity to provide information to assist in the completion of the evaluation.

12. Under the Freedom of Information Act, parents have the right to review their child's records and make copies at a reasonable cost at any time.

How to Report Test Results to Parents

An important skill for special education teachers to acquire is the ability to report test results to other professionals and to parents in a nonthreatening and informed way. Professionals and parents should come away from a meeting with a special education teacher understanding the causes of a child's difficulties, the child's specific areas of strength and weakness, and practical means of helping the child. They should not leave a conference feeling "bombarded" with jargon and statistics, and understanding very little of what just took place.

When setting up an appointment with a parent, the evaluator should never begin an explanation of the results over the phone, even if the parent requests a "quick" idea of how his or her child performed. If the parent does request this, the evaluator should gently say that information is better explained and understood in person. If the parent still seems anxious, then every effort should be made to meet as soon as possible. It is important to see the parents in conference so that areas in which they seem confused or uncomfortable can be explained thoroughly. Face-to-face contact humanizes the conference and allows the parent to feel more comforted if necessary. The following steps will lead to a satisfying and informative conference:

♦ Evaluators should do everything possible to hold conferences in a receptive environment.

♦ The evaluator should refresh the parent's memory about the reasons for the evaluation and the symptoms that brought the child to the attention of the team. He or she should also familiarize the parent once again with the test battery, explain why it was used, and decribe the specific types of information gathered from the tests.

♦ The evaluator needs to emphasize and review the child's strengths with the parent no matter how few they may be. Any other information that may help set the tone for a positive conference and parental acceptance of problem areas should also be presented early in the conference.

♦ The evaluator should make every effort to have the child's evaluation report typed and ready to hand to the parent. When reports are sent home after the conference and the parent reads it without a professional present, it is understandable for the parent to be frustrated by unanswered questions. If the evaluation report is not yet ready, the evaluator should at least provide a typed outline of the scores for the parent to review.

♦ The evaluator should explain any statistical terms, e.g., percentiles, stanines, and mental ages, in simple terms. It is a good idea to define these on the same sheet with the scores so that the parent has a key when he or she reviews the scores and/or reads the report later on.

♦ The evaluator should offer the parent a pad and pen so he or she can write down information, terms, or notes from the meeting. The parent should also be made to feel free to call with any questions or concerns he or she may have after the meeting.

♦ Evaluators should consider the nature of upcoming conferences and be certain to allow sufficient time for each. The parent should leave each conference in a natural manner, not feeling rushed.

♦ The evaluator should take time to explain to parents the differences between symptoms and problems. This explanation can go a long way in alleviating a parent's frustration with what is frequently a complex and difficult situation.

♦ It is helpful for the parent to hear from the evaluator how the problems or deficiencies revealed by the evaluation were contributing to the child's symptoms in the classroom and at home. It is reassuring for the parent to know that what he or she was seeing were only symptoms, even though they may have been quite intense, that the problems have been identified, and that recommendations are available. The parent should be offered as much realistic hope as possible.

♦ The evaluator should be as practical and specific as possible when offering suggestions on how the parent can help at home. He or she should offer the parent printed handouts with step-by-step procedures for any recommendation made. The parents should never be given general recommendations that require interpretation.

♦ If a child's case is going to be reviewed by the CSE, the evaluator should take some time to alleviate parental fears by explaining the process. The evaluator should indicate that his or her report is part of the packet that will be presented to the CSE and that the parent is entitled to a copy of all materials. Some school districts charge for copies, so the evaluator should indicate that fact if it is a policy.

Once again, the evaluator should reassure the parent about the confidentiality of the information gathered about the child, and indicate the individuals on the team who will be seeing the information and the purpose for their review of these facts. Parents should also be assured that the evaluator is unable to distribute the information without permission from the parent in the form of a signed release.

WRITING AND DEVELOPING AN INDIVIDUALIZED EDUCATION PROGRAM

The Individualized Education Program (IEP) is a legally binding contract of services provided by a school district for children classified as having a disability. Only children who are classified by the Committee on Special Education (CSE) receive an IEP. While certain information is required by each state to be included in this document, there is no specific form that a school district must follow. An IEP should contain seven basic sections like the following:

I. GENERAL IDENTIFYING DATA

Under this section the school district provides information on a variety of different areas pertaining to a child's background. The information for this section is taken from the background history form. This section may include:

Name:

Address:

Phone:

Date of Birth:

Parents' Names:

Dominant Language of Child:

Dominant Language Spoken at Home:

Date Child Entered Program: This is only filled in for previously classified students and basically informs the reader about when the child first started receiving special education services.

II. CURRENT PLACEMENT DATA

This part of the IEP contains all the necessary information pertaining to the current educational placement of the child. This information is usually taken from evaluation reports, prior IEPs (if child has already been classified), school records, and so on.

Classification: This is filled in only if the child is presently classified.

Grade: Current grade

Current Placement: Regular class if an initial review by the CSE is required, or special education setting if the child has already been classified. Examples that may appear in this section include, but are not limited to, self-contained, residential facility, inclusionary program, or hospital setting.

Class Size Ratio: This is filled in for previously classified students only. For example, ratios may be reported in the following manners:

♦ 15:1:1—This type of program requires a maximum student population of 15, one teacher and one assistant.

♦ 8:1:2—This type of program requires a maximum student population of 8, one teacher and two assistants.

It should be understood that there can be any combination of student: teacher: assistant ratio. The general rule is that the smaller the student population in the ratio, the more restrictive the program.

Length of Program: 10– or 12–month program. A 12–month program is usually designed for more severely disabled children or children who may lose the skills they have acquired over the course of the school year.

School: Current school

Teacher: This refers to the child's current mainstream teacher if the case is an initial evaluation, a guidance counselor if he or she is a secondary-level student, or a designated member of the special education staff, sometimes referred to as the contact teacher, if the child is already classified.

Diploma: This will be either a local diploma or an IEP diploma, which can be given to classified students who may not meet the school requirements for graduation, but have accomplished all the objectives on their IEP.

Transportation: This is filled in if the child is presently receiving special transportation arrangements.

Physical Education: Current class type (i.e., regular if in the mainstream *or* adaptive if the child is classified as disabled) and recommendation that appears on IEP.

Annual Review Date: This usually occurs in the spring of the school year.

Triennial Review Date: This usually takes place three years from the date of the last full evaluation.

III. TESTING INFORMATION

This section reviews the various results of the assessment process. Scores derived from the test measures are listed with percentiles, grade equivalents, and/or standard scores. This information provides the reasoning for the basis of a suspected disability and for the determination of future goals. An example of this section is shown below:

Test	Test Area	Score Type	Percentile	Range
WISC-III	Intelligence	VIQ (110)	75	High Average
WISC-III	Intelligence	PIQ (85)	16	Low Average
WISC-III	Intelligence	FSIQ (100)	50	Average
K-TEA	Achievement	Reading	33	Below GE
K-TEA	Achievement	Math	24	Below GE
K-TEA	Achievement	Spelling	15	Below GE
K-TEA	Achievement	Comprehension	26	Below GE
DTLA	Perceptual	Auditory Processing	50	Average
DTLA	Perceptual	Visual Processing	23	Below Average
Beery VMI	Perceptual	Visual/Motor Integration		Below Average

Note: GE in the above table refers to grade expectancy.

IV. RECOMMENDATIONS BY THE CSE

Under this section, the recommendations of the CSE meeting are recorded which indicate the proposed plan of placement and services for the student until the annual review *or* until another CSE meeting is called to reevaluate the IEP (normally done by the school or parent if a change or addition to an IEP is requested). Usually, no changes to the document or plan can take place without a full meeting of the CSE. This is a very important section of the IEP since it indicates to the reader the plan for special educational services for the coming year. Information contained in this section might include the following:

Classification: The child must fit the criteria for one of the state-defined classification categories, and the disability must significantly impede his or her ability to learn. The classification categories may include the following:

1. **Autism**—A *developmental disability* significantly affecting verbal and nonverbal communication and social interaction, generally evident before age three, that adversely affects educational performance.

2. **Deafness**—A hearing impairment which is so severe that a child is impaired in processing *linguistic* information through hearing, with or without amplification, which adversely affects educational performance.

3. **Deaf-Blindness**—Simultaneous hearing and visual impairments, the combination of which causes such severe communication and other developmental and educational problems that a child cannot be accommodated in special education programs solely for children with deafness or children with blindness.

4. **Hearing Impairment**—A hearing impairment, whether permanent or fluctuating, which adversely affects a child's educational performance but which is not included under the definition of "deafness."

5. **Mentally Disabled**—Significantly subaverage general intellectual functioning existing concurrently with deficits in adaptive behavior and manifested during the developmental period, which adversely affects a child's educational performance.

6. **Multiple Disabilities**—Simultaneous impairments (such as mental retardation/blindness, mental retardation/orthopedic impairment, etc.), the combination of which causes such severe educational problems that the child cannot be accommodated in a special education program solely for one of the impairments. The term does not include children with deaf-blindness.

7. **Orthopedic Impairment**—A severe orthopedic impairment which adversely affects a child's educational performance. The term includes impairments caused by a *congenital anomaly* (e.g., clubfoot, absence of some member, etc.), impairments caused by disease (e.g. poliomyelitis, bone tuberculosis, etc.), and impairments from other causes (e.g., cerebral palsy, amputations, and fractures or burns which cause *contractures*).

8. **Other Health Impairment**—Having limited strength, vitality, or alertness, due to chronic or acute health problems such as a heart condition, tuberculosis, rheumatic fever, nephritis, asthma, sickle cell anemia, hemophilia, epilepsy, lead poisoning, leukemia, or diabetes, which adversely affects a child's educational performance. According to the Office of Special Education and Rehabilitative Services' clarification statement of September 16, 1991, eligible children with ADD may also be classified under "other health impairment."

9. **Serious Emotional Disability**—A condition exhibiting one or more of the following characteristics over a long period of time and to a marked degree, which adversely affects educational performance: (a) an inability to learn which cannot be explained by intellectual, sensory, or health factors; (b) an inability to build or maintain satisfactory interpersonal relationships with peers and teachers; (c) inappropriate types of behavior or feelings under normal circumstances; (d) a general pervasive mood of unhappiness or depression; or (e) a tendency to develop physical symptoms or fears associated with personal or school problems. The term includes children who have schizophrenia. The term does not include children who are socially maladjusted, unless it is determined that they have a serious emotional disturbance.

10. **Specific Learning Disability**—A disorder in one or more of the basic psychological processes involved in understanding or in using language, spoken or written, which may manifest itself in an imperfect ability to listen, think, speak, read, write, spell, or to do mathematical calculations. The term includes such conditions as perceptual disabilities, brain injury, minimal brain dysfunction, *dyslexia*, and *developmental aphasia*. The term does not include children who have learning problems which are primarily the result of visual, hearing, or motor disabilities, of mental retardation, of emotional disturbance, or of environmental, cultural, or economic disadvantage.

11. **Speech or Language Impairment**—A communication disorder such as stuttering, impaired articulation, a language impairment, or a voice impairment, which adversely affects a child's educational performance.

12. **Traumatic Brain Injury**—An injury to the brain caused by an external physical force, resulting in total or partial functional disability or psychosocial maladjustment, or both, which adversely affects educational performance. The term does not include brain injuries that are congenital or degenerative, or brain injuries induced by birth trauma.

13. **Visual Impairment, Including Blindness**—A visual impairment which, even with correction, adversely affects a child's educational performance. The term includes both children with partial sight and those with blindness.

Grade: Projected grade for the coming year.

Placement: This depends upon the child's least restrictive educational (LRE) setting. The CSE has a series of options but usually works from the least restrictive setting possible before attempting a more restrictive setting. In order, these include:

- Regular class placement with few or no supportive services
- Regular class placement with consulting teacher assistance
- Regular class placement with itinerant specialist assistance
- Regular class placement with resource room assistance
- Special class placement with part time in regular class
- Full-time special class
- Special day school
- Residential school
- Homebound instruction
- Hospital or institution

There are ten educational settings listed. The least restrictive setting is at the top and the most restrictive is at the bottom. Children should only be placed in a more restrictive environment if it is to their educational advantage. However, they should be moved to a less restrictive setting as soon as they are capable of being educated in that environment. It is also noted that the more restrictive environment will have fewer children, and these will have more severe disabilities. Finally, it must always be remembered that the LRE is unique for each individual child. For example, a child with serious clinical depression may be placed in a hospital setting as the LRE.

Class Size Ratio: This recommendation by the CSE will indicate the maximum student population allowed, the number of teachers required, and the number of assistant teachers or aides required.

Length of Program: Some special education programs maintain a 10–month calendar. Programs for more seriously disabled students may be yearlong.

School: The student's projected school for the coming year.

Teacher: This identifies the child's special education contact teacher assigned for the coming year. When a child has several special education teachers as in a departmentalized special education high school program, one teacher is assigned as the contact teacher. On the elementary and secondary levels it can also be the resource room teacher, if the child is assigned there, or the child's self-contained special education teacher if this more restrictive program is used.

Program Initiation Date: Indicates when the special education services will begin.

Transportation Needs: Indicates whether or not the child has special transportation needs as with a severely physically disabled child who may require door-to-door service with a special bus to allow easy access and departure.

Physical Education: Indicates whether the child is being recommended for regular physical education or adaptive physical education. Adaptive Physical Education is a specially designed program of developmental activities, games, sports, and rhythms suited to the interests, capacities, and limitations of pupils with disabilities who may not safely or successfully engage in unrestricted participation in the activities of the regular physical education program.

Related Services: This section indicates other services the child will be receiving that support the academic special education process. Also noted in this section would be the number of sessions per week, minutes per session, maximum group size, start date and end date. Related services may include:

- **In-school individual counseling**—When this service is recommended on an IEP, it usually means that the child would benefit from a more intimate therapeutic situation with emphasis on control, insight, cause-and-effect awareness, special attention, and developing a trusting relationship with an authority figure. While some children only need individual counseling, others might move from individual to group to try out the insights and experiences learned from the individual experience.

- **In-school group counseling**—When this service is recommended on an IEP, it means that the child would benefit from a group situation that emphasizes interpersonal relations, social skills, cooperative play and interaction, interdependence, social delay of gratification, peer feedback, and social connections. The group usually meets once or twice a week and many times may be combined with individual in-school counseling.

- **Resource room**—This service is recommended when the CSE feels that the child would benefit from extra academic assistance depending upon the recommendations of the diagnostic evaluation, IEP recommendation, and teacher observation. This assistance might involve remediation, compensation, or survival skills depending upon the age and grade of the child. Most children will be recommended for a minimum of three hours per week (divided as needed) to a maximum of fifty percent of the child's school day.

- **Speech/language therapy**—This service is recommended when the CSE feels that the child's poor performance is directly related to disabilities in language or speech development. The emphasis with this service might include remediation in expressive or receptive language, articulation, voice disorders, fluency disorders, and so on. These services may be administered in small group or individual settings. This recommendation can also be made in conjunction with some other service, such as resource room, if indicated.

- **Physical therapy and occupational therapy**—This recommendation is usually made by the CSE when the child is suffering from some physical or motor impairment. Physical therapists usually provide exercise therapy and special devices to improve the total physical functioning and strength of a disabled student. Generally occupational therapists will focus more on fine motor skills such as hand control, using the mouth to chew, and any other factor involved in daily living skills.

- **Art therapy**—This recommendation, while not as common as some other services, is usually recommended when the CSE feels that the production of art in its various forms would have beneficial qualities for exceptional students. Major factors involved in this recommendation include the opportunity for the disabled child to express creativity, to improve fine motor skills, and to develop appropriate leisure-time activities.

- **Adaptive physical education**—This service is usually recommended when the CSE feels that the disabled child's general physical development is impaired or delayed. When these programs are instituted, they tend to have a therapeutic orientation. The teachers utilized for this service must have special training in the use of specialized equipment to improve muscle development and coordination.

- **Music Therapy**—This recommendation may be made by the CSE when they feel that music can be used to prompt the development of various functional behaviors for disabled students, such as motivation and improvement of speech, language, and communication skills through singing.

Mainstreamed Courses: A listing must be included on the IEP if the child's disability allows for his or her participation in any mainstreamed class.

Special Classes: This indicates the types of special education classes the child will have in the coming year.

V. GOALS AND OBJECTIVES

This section of the IEP usually contains two separate parts. The <u>first</u> deals with general social, physical, academic, and management goals (SPAM goals) that relate to the environment and specific conditions under which the child will be learning or learns best. Examples of these are as follows:

Social Development: This includes the degree and quality of the pupil's relationships with peers and adults, feelings about self, and social adjustment to school and community environments.

Physical Development: This includes the degree or quality of the pupil's motor and sensory development, health and vitality, and physical skills or limitations that pertain to the learning process.

Academic Development: This includes the levels of knowledge and development in subject and skill areas, including activities of daily living, intellectual functioning, adaptive behavior, expected rate of progress in acquiring skills and information, and learning style.

Management Needs: This includes the nature and degree to which environmental modifications and human material resources are required to enable the pupil to benefit from instruction.

Each of the above categories is normally divided into mild, moderate, and severe goals from which the IEP coordinator chooses, based on the assessment results. Examples of goals that may be found in each area include, but are not limited to, the following:

Social Goals—mild problem

- Acts appropriately to criticism from peers.

- Has some difficulty working cooperatively with peers.

- Is prone to distraction and off-task behaviors.

Physical Goals—severe problem

- Requires medication because of a medical problem.

- Requires a wheelchair.

- Has a hearing impairment which affects learning.

Academic—moderate problem

- Works best with a structured goal-oriented approach.

- Will benefit from a phonetic approach to reading.

- Will require taped materials.

Management Needs—severe problem

- Must learn to function in a group situation.

- Cannot be mainstreamed in nonacademic courses because of severe academic problems that interfere with ability to learn.

- Requires small class placement because of behavior.

The second part of goals and objectives deals with the student's remedial academic goals and objectives as determined through the evaluation and the diagnosis of the student's strengths and weaknesses. The basis for this area comes from the evaluation and the diagnosis of strengths and weaknesses. Also included in this section may be specific content area goals—e.g., science, social studies, math, English, if the child is in a special education setting for these subjects.

When determining an objective, mastery levels need to be considered. A mastery level is a predetermined level of competency determined by a teacher or evaluator as indicating a clear understanding of a particular skill. This is the evaluator's or teacher's way of validating a child's movement to the next objective.

Setting the mastery levels too low will increase the possibilities of luck or chance influencing success, while setting them too high may set the child up for constant frustration and failure because of careless mistakes or minute errors. Examples of the types of mastery levels are shown below:

- **ratio-based mastery level**—Thomas will be able to . . . 8 out of every 10 attempts.

- **percent-based mastery level**—Jane will be able to . . . 75% of the time.

- **time-based mastery level**—Ben will be able to . . . 12 responses within a 10–minute period.

There may be times when one general statement of mastery level can apply to all the objectives, i.e., "All objectives will be completed with 80% accuracy."

In an initial review, content area goals included on a child's IEP are normally determined by the results of the assessment. If the child is already classified, then new content area goals are developed at the annual review. These goals are based on the special education teacher's experience with that child, and in consultation with other staff members working with the child over the course of the school year. Some examples of content area goals are:

Mathematics—numeration

♦ Will identify the number of objects in a set up to ten.

♦ Will identify the math symbols such as +, −, =, and ×.

Mathematics—computation

♦ Will understand the concept of a savings account.

♦ Will apply calculations involving percentage.

Language Arts—grammar

♦ Will define common and proper nouns.

♦ Will understand that an action word is called a verb.

Language Arts—writing competency

♦ Will be able to write a persuasive composition.

♦ Will be able to write a business letter correctly.

Perceptual Skills—auditory perceptual skills

♦ Will identify from choices the picture of the object that produces a particular sound.

♦ Will identify and state the different sounds the child hears in a room.

Perceptual Skills—visual perceptual skills

♦ Will match pictures of geometric forms.

♦ Will recognize and name familiar objects.

The entire list of these goals can usually be obtained from the Director of Pupil Personnel Services in the district. Normally, this list, along with the list of content area goals, is provided to all special education teachers involved in IEP development.

VI. EVALUATION PROCEDURES

IEPs include measures or techniques that will be used to evaluate the success levels for each objective. These techniques or measures are used to determine the mastery levels applied to each objective. They also indicate whether or not the child has accomplished the objective and is competent enough to move to the next objective. There are many available evaluation procedures for the teacher to use. These include, but are not limited to:

♦ Student assignments and projects

♦ Informal conferences between student and teacher

- Student self evaluation
- Textbook tests and quizzes
- Standardized tests
- Review of quarterly report cards
- Discussions with classroom teachers
- Parent-teacher conferences
- Record of Attendance
- Stanford Diagnostic Test
- Teacher-made tests
- Teacher evaluation
- Homework assignments
- Criterion-referenced Tests

VII. TESTING AND CLASSROOM MODIFICATIONS

Testing modifications take into account the individual needs of a child having a disability. These modifications attempt to provide a student with a disability equal opportunity to participate in classroom and standardized testing situations. These modifications, which must appear in the student's IEP, provide the opportunity to demonstrate a mastery of skills without being unfairly restricted by the presence of his or her disability.

Students who have been identified as having a disability by the Committee on Special Education normally receive testing modifications on their IEP. Testing modifications are determined by the CSE for students identified as having a disability. The Committee takes into account several variables when making this determination:

- The individual needs of the child as determined by evaluation, observation, background history, and other pertinent information presented at the CSE meeting.
- The necessity for modification in light of the student's past academic and test performance without modifications.
- The student's potential benefit from the modification.

Testing Modifications That Change Manner of Presentation

Modifications that alter a student's manner of presentation constitute the largest category of modifications that may appear on a student's IEP. These are separated into several categories and each contains several options.

FLEXIBLE SCHEDULING—This modification is usually applied for students who, due to physical disabilities such as motor or visual impairments, have problems in the rate at which they process information. Examples of such modifications include:

- extended time
- administration of a test in several sessions during the course of the day

♦ administration of a test in several sessions over several days

FLEXIBLE SETTING—This modification allows students with disabilities to take a test in a setting other than a regular classroom. This may become necessary in cases where a child has health impairments and may be unable to leave home or the hospital, or where a child's disability interferes with his or her remaining on task or where a child is easily distracted, or where a student requires special lighting or acoustics or a specially equipped room. Examples of such modifications include:

♦ individual administration of a test in a separate location

♦ small group administration of a test in a separate location

♦ provisions for special lighting

♦ provisions for special acoustics

♦ provisions for adaptive or special furniture

♦ administration of a test in a location with minimal distractions

REVISED TEST FORMAT—This modification is utilized by students whose disability may interfere with their ability to take a test using the standard test format, e.g., students with visual or perceptual disabilities who may not be able to read regular size print. Examples of such modifications include:

♦ use of a large print edition

♦ increased spacing between test items

♦ reduction in the number of test items per page

♦ use of a Braille edition of the test

♦ increased size of answer bubbles on test answer forms

♦ rearrangement of multiple-choice items so that the answer bubble is right next to each choice

REVISED TEST DIRECTIONS—This modification allows students with certain disabilities a greater chance of understanding directions and thereby successfully completing a test. Examples of such modifications include:

♦ reading directions to the child

♦ rereading the directions to the child or allowing the child to reread the directions

♦ simplifying the language and the directions

♦ providing the child with additional examples

USE OF AIDS—Some students with disabilities, such as those who are hearing impaired, require the use of aids in order to interpret test items. Examples of such modifications include:

♦ auditory amplification devices

♦ visual magnification devices

- an auditory tape of the questions
- masks or markers to maintain the student's place on a page
- reading questions to the student
- signing questions to the student

Testing Modifications That Change the Manner of Response

Another kind of testing modification used to assist students involves various alterations in the ways that students respond to test items. Some response modifications are described below:

USE OF AIDS—These modifications allow a student with a disability to record his or her answers to examination questions in unconventional ways. Examples of such modifications include:

- the student's use of a tape recorder
- the student's use of a typewriter
- the student's use of a communication device
- the student's use of a word processor
- the student's use of an amanuensis (secretary)

REVISED FORMAT—Some students with disabilities may be unable to record their responses to test questions on conventional answer forms. As a result, they may require changes in the test format. Examples of such modifications include:

- recording answers directly in the test booklet
- increasing the spacing between questions or problems
- increasing the size of the answer blocks
- providing cues (stop sign, arrows) directly on the answer form

Testing Modifications That Change the Process Used to Derive a Response

USE OF AIDS—Some students who may possess the innate ability to process mathematical information, for example, may have a disability that prohibits them from using paper and pencil to solve computations. Others may not be able to memorize arithmetic facts but can solve difficult word problems. When such problems occur, the following modifications can be made:

- allowing for use of a calculator
- allowing for use of an abacus
- allowing for use of arithmetic tables

CLASSROOM REMEDIATION TECHNIQUES

With the trend in special education moving towards inclusionary programs within school districts, many classroom teachers will be called upon to educate students with disabilities in the regular classroom setting. As a result, these teachers will turn to special educators for guidance, recommendations, and strategies. An evaluation of a child is only as good as the recommendations made by the evaluator in an attempt to improve the child's situation. The disabilities presented in this section are by no means exhaustive, but are representative of what a teacher may encounter either in a regular classroom setting, an inclusionary program, or a self-contained class.

WORKING WITH THE CHILD WHO IS LEARNING DISABLED

From time to time, most classroom teachers will come in contact with a child who has been diagnosed as learning disabled. When this occurs, the teacher may be concerned with his or her lack of understanding of how to help this child succeed in the classroom. Many times, the teacher may not have resources for the student available or individuals at hand who can offer practical suggestions and techniques.

There is no doubt that most teachers, given the right assistance and training, would be more than competent to become actively involved with this student's education. However, without these factors, many teachers feel inadequate and hesitant to make adjustments for fear that they may not do what is best for the child. The following information offers general instructional techniques that the teacher should find helpful for students with particular problems. Not all techniques work with all students, but the teacher should try as many of them as possible in order to create a better learning environment for children with special needs.

Learning Materials and Assignments

♦ Give shorter but more frequent assignments, shorten the length of the assignments to ensure the student's sense of success and the teacher's contact with the student, and increase the frequency of assignments to provide more chances of success. This can be accomplished by, for example, breaking assignments down to smaller units. Allow the child to do five problems at a time, or five sentences, so that he or she can feel success and receive immediate feedback.

♦ Copy chapters of textbooks so that the child can use a highlighter pen to underline important facts.

♦ Correct the student's work as soon as possible to allow for immediate gratification and feedback.

♦ Allow the student several alternative methods for both obtaining and reporting information—tapes, interviews, and so on.

♦ Hold frequent, even if short, conferences with the student to allow him or her to ask questions, to find sources of confusion, to feel a sense of connection, and to avoid isolation which often occurs if the work is too difficult.

Learning Space and Time

♦ Make sure that the child's desk is free of all unnecessary and potentially distracting materials. Permit the child to work in a quiet corner or a study carrel when requested or necessary. This technique should not be used all the time since isolation may have negative consequences, but used in moderation it is appropriate for a student who may be less distracted by working under these conditions.

♦ When beginning a relationship with a child, the teacher may want to place the child close to himself or herself for more immediate feedback and supervision.

♦ The teacher should make every effort to separate the student from students who may be distracting.

♦ Alternate quiet and active time for the student to maintain a level of interest and motivation.

♦ Make up and maintain a work contract for the student with specific assignments so that the child has a structured idea of his or her responsibilities.

♦ Keep work periods short and gradually lengthen them as the student begins to experience success.

♦ Try to place the student near a peer helper who can help him or her with understanding assignments, reading important directions, practicing drills, summarizing important textbook passages, and working on long-range assignments.

Presentation and Evaluation

Some students learn better by seeing (visual learners), some by listening (auditory learners), some by feeling (tactile learners), and some by a combination of approaches. Adjustments should be made by the teacher to determine the best functional system of learning for the child with learning disabilities. This will vary from child to child and is usually included in the child's evaluation.

If the child is primarily an auditory learner, offer adjustments in the mode of presentation by use of the following techniques:

♦ Give verbal as well as written directions to assignments.

♦ Place assignment directions on tape so that the student can replay them when necessary.

♦ Give the student oral rather than written tests.

♦ Have the student drill on important information by reciting information into the recorder and having the student play it back.

♦ Have the student drill aloud to himself or herself or to other students.

♦ Have the child close his or her eyes to try to hear and visualize words or information.

If the child is primarily a <u>visual learner</u>, offer adjustment in the mode of presentation by:

♦ Have the student use flash cards printed in bold, bright colors.

♦ Let the student close his or her eyes to try to visualize words or information.

♦ Provide visual clues on chalkboard for all verbal directions.

♦ Encourage the student to write notes and memos to himself or herself concerning important words, concepts, and ideas.

WORKING WITH THE CHILD WHO IS EMOTIONALLY DISABLED

Since the behavior of children who are emotionally disabled can vary from withdrawal, in the case of depression, to aggressive tendencies, in the case of a conduct disorder, teachers need to be aware of techniques that can be utilized in a variety of situations. However, certain pervasive behaviors should be targeted as priorities when dealing with emotionally disabled children in the classroom:

♦ Poor attendance and frequent tardiness

♦ Challenges to authority

♦ Inappropriate verbalizations and outbursts

♦ Incomplete classwork

♦ Difficulty remaining seated

♦ Troubled social relationships

♦ Difficulty following directions and paying attention

While many or all of these behaviors may be exhibited by the child, the teacher should try to focus on one pattern at a time. Patience, fairness, willingness to confront inappropriate behaviors, a sense of conviction in maintaining boundaries, and a sense of fair play in establishing consequences are all required by the teacher in these situations.

Problems of Attendance and Tardiness

♦ Reward the child in some way for being on time—extra free time, a token (if a token economy is being used), a positive note home, a verbal compliment, and so on.

♦ Work with the parent on rewarding on-time behavior.

♦ Plan a special class or individual activity in the morning so that the student is particularly motivated to be prompt.

- Use a chart to project a pattern of punctuality and lateness for the child. This will reduce the child's level of denial and may make him or her more aware of his or her behavior.

- Encourage and assist the child to start a club in his or her area of greatest interest and make his or her participation contingent upon a positive pattern of attendance.

- Use a point system for on-time attendance. These points may later be turned in for class privileges.

- If the child walks to school, set up a buddy system to encourage on-time behavior.

- Set up a nightly contract for the child listing all the things he or she needs to do to make the morning easier to manage. Have the parent sign it, and reward the child when he or she brings it in.

Problems of Challenges to Authority, Inappropriate Verbalizations, and Outbursts

- Arrange a time-out area in the classroom to use when the child's behavior is disruptive. The amount of time the child spends in a time-out area is not as significant as your being in control of it. Therefore, make the time-out period something you can control.

- Structure a time when the child is allowed to speak to the teacher freely without an audience around. In this way, the child will have an opportunity to speak his or her concerns rather than act them out, and the teacher will be able to deflect any confrontations to that specific time.

- Approach the child as often as possible and ask if there is anything bothering him or her that he or she would like to speak about. Offering the child the opportunity to be vocal, even if he or she refuses, may reduce the child's need for "spotlight" behaviors in front of the class.

- Offer an emotional vocabulary so that the child is more able to identify, label, and communicate his or her feelings. Consequently, the child is likely to express emotions verbally rather than behaviorally. Providing the student with the proper labels may also reduce his or her frustration that would normally be exhibited through impulsive or inappropriate behavior.

- Move the student away from those who might annoy or distract him or her.

- Preempt the child's behavior by waiting outside before class and telling him or her in private what you expect during class. Also, make the child aware of the rewards and consequences of actions.

- Offer other behavioral response options and indicate that any inappropriateness is the student's decision. Making the child aware that behavior is his or her responsibility helps the child to realize that not doing something inappropriate is also in his or her control.

- Establish clear classroom rules stating rewards and consequences.

- Praise the student when appropriate for complying with rules and carrying out directions without verbal resistance.

Problems of Incomplete Classwork

♦ Work out a contract with the child where he or she can determine the rewards for completing assignments.

♦ Give frequent, shorter assignments.

♦ Do not force the child to write if handwriting is beyond correction as in the case of a high school student or a student with severe problems in graphomotor functioning. Allow the child to use a word processor or typewriter.

♦ Correct assignments as soon as possible and hand them back so as to offer immediate gratification.

♦ Reward the student for handing in neat, completed, and timely assignments.

♦ Help the student become organized by allowing him or her to keep very little in his or her desk, by encouraging the use of a bound book for writing rather than looseleaf pages, and by providing large folders for the child to keep work in, etc.

♦ Be very specific on what you mean by "neat," "organized," and so on.

Problems Remaining Seated

♦ Try to determine the child's pattern of getting up out of his or her seat. Once this is determined you can arrange to have him or her run an errand, come up to your desk, and so on when the child is unusually unsettled. In this way the teacher is channeling the child's tension and remaining in control.

♦ Use an external control like an egg-timer to help the child control his or her behavior.

♦ Praise other students or hand out rewards to the other students when they remain in their seats and follow the rules.

♦ Give the child a written copy of those rules that, when followed, will result in reward or positive feedback. Also give the child a list of the behaviors that are acceptable and their consequences.

♦ The teacher's close proximity to the child will assist him or her in staying in his or her seat. Seat the child close to your desk or stand near the child during a lesson.

Problems with Social Relationships

♦ Provide the child with a "toolbox" of responses and options for typical social situations.

♦ Speak with the school psychologist about including the child in a group for children with social skill issues.

♦ Arrange for a peer to guide the child through social situations during private time. The child may be more willing to model peer behavior than the teacher's advice.

♦ Expose the child to small group activity with only one child. Slowly increase the size of the group as the child becomes more comfortable.

♦ Expose the child to goal-oriented projects where students must work together to accomplish a task. At first limit this to the student and one other child, then slowly increase the size of the group and the magnitude of the task as the child becomes more comfortable.

♦ Have the child and a responsible peer organize team activities or group projects. Some children rise to the occasion when placed in a leadership role.

♦ Praise the student as often as possible when he or she is not exhibiting aggressive or inappropriate social behavior.

Problems Following Directions and Paying Attention

♦ Use a cue before giving the child directions or important information so that the child knows to concentrate.

♦ Give one direction at a time, and make it as simple as possible.

♦ Have the child chart his or her own patterns of behavior in relation to attention and direction.

♦ Your close physical proximity may assist the child in focusing on your directions.

♦ Praise the student when he or she follows directions or pays attention. However, for those students who have a hard time accepting praise, especially in front of a group, do this in private.

♦ Provide the student with optional work areas that may have few distractions.

♦ During the lesson, randomly question the child and try to have him or her participate as often as possible to increase his or her interest in the lesson.

♦ Make sure the materials being presented are compatible with the child's learning levels so as to avoid frustration, which can cause inattention.

♦ Use a variety of visual and auditory techniques—overhead projector, tape recorder, computer—to enhance the lesson and stimulate the child's attention.

WORKING WITH THE CHILD WHO IS MILDLY MENTALLY DISABLED

Students who are mildly mentally disabled have an easier time learning new material when teachers employ a variety of techniques and adaptations. The development of certain behaviors should be priorities when dealing with these children in the classroom. While many areas are in need of attention (e.g., academics, work habits, career awareness), the teacher should try to focus on one area at a time. Patience, fairness, nurturance, humor, and conviction in maintaining boundaries are all required by the teacher in this situation.

General Academics

♦ Design practice activities in any basic skill that may relate to the child's daily life problems.

♦ Provide materials that are commensurate with the child's skill levels.

♦ Provide activities that will reinforce independent work. If the activity is too hard, the child may become too dependent on teacher supervision.

Reading

- ◆ Provide activities that focus on reading for information and leisure.

- ◆ Provide activities that require the child to become more aware of his or her environment. For example, having the child list the names of all food stores in the community or all hospitals and so on will increase the child's familiarity with the surroundings, or having the child collect and compare food labels will increase the child's familiarity with something in the immediate environment.

- ◆ Develop activities that will allow the child to become familiar with menus, bus and train schedules, movie and television timetables, job advertisements, and directories. Asking a child to find classmates' phone listings, for example, is an excellent activity that exercises many real-life skills.

Handwriting/Spelling

- ◆ Have the child make a list of things to do for the day.

- ◆ Have the child run a messenger service in the classroom so that he or she can write the messages and deliver them from one student to another.

- ◆ Provide activities for an older child that incorporate daily writing skills necessary for independence, such as filling out social security forms, employment forms, bank account applications, and so on.

Math

- ◆ Have the child make up a budget or savings plan for his or her allowance.

- ◆ Encourage the child to cook in school or at home, with adult supervision, so that he or she can become more familiar with measurements.

- ◆ Have the child record the daily temperature.

- ◆ Involve the child in measuring the height of classmates.

- ◆ Have older children apply for a loan or credit card or keep a balanced checkbook.

- ◆ Require the child to use a daily planning book.

- ◆ Provide activities that teach the child how to comparison-shop.

- ◆ Provide the child with a make-believe amount of money and a toy catalog and have him or her purchase items and fill out the forms.

Helping the Child Improve General Work Habits

This particular area is composed of many skill areas that are necessary to allow the child success in the regular classroom. They include:

WORK COMPLETION

- ◆ Have reward activities contingent upon the successful completion of work.

- ◆ Have the child maintain a performance chart on the number of tasks completed each day.

◆ Evaluate the length and level of an assignment to make sure it is within the ability level of the child.

◆ Give shorter but more frequent assignments.

◆ Build a foundation of success by providing a series of assignments that the child is likely to complete successfully. In this way the child can gain a sense of confidence.

ATTENDANCE AND PUNCTUALITY

◆ Communicate to the child the importance of being on time to class.

◆ Let the child know your expectations in clear terms concerning attendance and punctuality.

◆ Have the child maintain a record of attendance and on-time behavior.

◆ Develop a make-believe time clock that the child has to punch in on when he or she enters the classroom.

◆ Encourage a student's punctuality by scheduling a favorite activity in the morning.

◆ Have the child sign a contract with you establishing the consequences and rewards of on-time behavior.

WORKING WITH OTHERS

◆ Provide the child with small-group activities that are geared to his or her ability level.

◆ Utilize peer tutors for the child so that he or she can establish relationships.

◆ Have the child participate in many group activities that require sorting, pasting, addressing, folding, simple assembly, and so on.

◆ Provide the child with some simple job that requires the other students to go to him or her. For example, place the child in charge of attendance and have him or her check off the other children when they report in.

◆ Help the child start a hobby, and then start a hobby club involving other students.

◆ Have the child be part of a team that takes care of the class pets or some other class activity. Calling it a team will make the child feel more connected.

WORKING WITH THE CHILD WHO HAS TOURETTE'S SYNDROME

Many students who have Tourette's Syndrome face social and academic pressures in school associated with their tics, vocal reactions, and associated learning difficulties. The teacher's response to the child and his or her dificulties can make a critical difference in the child's ability to succeed. Following are some classroom suggestions:

◆ Remember that the child's motor or vocal tics are occurring involuntarily, so do not respond with anger or annoyance. Instead, try to be a role model for the other students as to how to react to the Tourette symptoms.

♦ Provide the child with opportunities for short breaks out of the classroom to relieve stress.

♦ Try to find a private place somewhere in the school where the child can "let out" the tics; some students try to supress the tics for a period of time, and this causes buildup of tension in the child.

♦ Allow the student to take tests in a private room so that the student does not waste energy supressing the tics as this may interfere with the child's ability to concentrate.

♦ Work with the student's classmates to help them understand the tics and, therefore, to reduce ridicule and teasing. To this end, secure materials (e.g., audiovisuals and pamphlets) to provide information for your pupils and colleagues.

♦ If the student's tics are particularly disruptive, avoid having the child recite in front of the class. Instead, have the student tape record oral reports.

♦ Keep in mind that students with Tourette's Syndrome often have visual motor difficulties. Consequently, modify the student's written assignments by reducing the number of exercises and by limiting the amount the student has to copy.

♦ Allow the student to dictate writing assignments to his or her parents so that the writing process itself does not inhibit the student's ability to form concepts.

♦ Allow the student to write answers directly on a test paper or booklet rather than having to black in scoring sheets.

♦ Allow the child untimed tests to reduce stress.

♦ Allow another child to take notes for the student so that they can listen to the lecture without the added stress of copying notes.

♦ Try not to penalize the student for spelling errors, since loss of concentration and focus are common.

♦ Try to use a multisensory approach whenever possible, since this may increase the child's ability to retain information.

WORKING WITH THE CHILD WHO HAS ADD/ADHD

Classroom teachers of children with ADD/ADHD can adjust certain factors to accommodate the individual needs of these children. Some examples include:

Social Interaction

♦ Identify appropriate social behavior for the child by pointing it out in others and reinforce when the student exhibits it.

♦ Sit with the child and establish a social contract that clearly outlines what goals the child would like to accomplish. Be sure to delineate the behaviors required to attain these goals.

♦ Use verbal and written praise whenever possible. Clear and immediate praise gives the child the feedback necessary to understand and assess his or her own behavior.

♦ Expose the child to small group interactions at first. Placing the child in large groups may be detrimental. The groups endeavors should be goal-oriented and interdependent so that they can accomplish some simple task and feel success as a unit.

♦ Use peer interaction and cooperative learning as frequently as possible so the student is not required to sit for long periods of time.

♦ Try to identify strengths in the child that can be publicly announced or praised. In this way the other students will develop a more positive perception of the child.

♦ Role-play social situations in private with the child and emphasize the use of specific skills. In this way the child can develop a "toolbox" of skills that can be applied at a later time.

Organization Skills

♦ Prepare a copy of the homework assignments and hand it to the child at the end of the day. This will alleviate a great deal of stress on the part of the child, especially if he or she is disorganized and frequently forgets to copy the homework. The goal here is to create a comfortable and successful environment. In this case, having the child accomplish the homework is more important than the difficulty encountered in copying the assignment.

♦ Ask the parent to organize the child at home too, by developing a checklist so that the child's clothes, books, assignments, and so on are ready for the next morning. The stress and disorganization of the morning should be avoided at all costs so as to increase the child's sense of security about going to school.

♦ Avoid multiple directions or assignments. Allow the child to finish one assignment or direction at a time before going on to the next.

♦ Reinforce word processing and computer skills—typing, spell checking—and use of the computer in general. The computer can be very motivating, and its end product—a typed report—will increase the child's self-esteem.

♦ Children with organizational problems will usually maintain very disorganized notes, notebooks, desks, and lockers. Try to make a weekly task of having the child organize these areas. Making it part of their contract and routine will also make them feel better about themselves and their ability to be in control.

Attention Problems

♦ If necessary, you may want to have the child finish all assignments in school. There may be times when the child is so inattentive that sending homework home may result in more stress, especially given parental interaction.

♦ Always allow the child extra time for completing assignments. Sometimes the time constraints set up by teachers may be appropriate for students without difficulties but may not reflect the time required by children with ADD/ADHD.

♦ Try to give shorter but more frequent assignments. Remember, confidence grows with repeated successful experiences, and the child will have a greater chance of success with shorter assignments.

♦ If the child has problems listening and taking notes, have a "buddy" take notes that can be copied.

♦ Stand in close proximity to the student while lecturing.

Impulsiveness

♦ Be realistic about your expectations concerning the child's behavior. Choose your guidelines wisely. Try to ignore minor incidents and focus on the more intrusive or inappropriate ones.

♦ Shape appropriate behavior by reinforcing the child's positive responses or actions immediately; on the other hand, do not hesitate to set up specific consequences for inappropriate actions. In this way the child will have to work at being more consciously aware of his or her behavior.

♦ Schedule periods of time when the child can leave his or her seat for some activity (e.g., collecting homework, getting some material for you from the closet, and so on); this will help the child release energy in acceptable ways.

♦ Assign a monitoring "buddy" to offer the child feedback and hints about appropriate and inappropriate behaviors. This may be especially helpful during recess and lunch.

♦ Try to preempt the child's behavior especially when there is a change in classroom activity. Inform the child of the change about five minutes before the change, and offer him or her your expectations of what will be appropriate behavior during this change.

Academic Skill Areas

♦ Allow the child to use graph paper while doing math. In this way the child will have a structured paper on which to place numbers. Use very large graph paper so that the child has little difficulty placing one number in each box. This will help keep the child organized and focused.

♦ Allow the child to use a calculator or basic math tables when doing his or her assignments. The goal here is for the successful accomplishment of the assignment. If the child becomes frustrated because he or she can't recall the facts, the child may give up. Use of such aids can taper off as the child's confidence builds.

♦ Allow the child to use means other than paper and pencil for recording and presenting information—tape recorders and videos, visual aids and recordings.

♦ Do not have the student use bubble sheets for recording test responses. Allow the child to answer directly in the booklet or on the paper. Reducing the amount of movement during academic tasks is beneficial for these children since they have difficulty refocusing.

♦ Use manipulative materials as often as possible to maintain high levels of interest.

♦ Have the child listen to books on tape and have the parent tape record text chapters so that the child can then read and listen at the same time.

♦ Isolate math problems so that the child only sees one at a time. This can be accomplished by cutting out a square on a piece of paper that the child can move from problem to problem. When the student does this, all the other problems will be covered and the child will be able to focus on a single problem.

♦ Allow older children to have a sheet with any formulas they need already printed. Asking them to memorize may reduce their ability to accomplish the task. The less they have to worry about, the more they may be able to finish.

♦ Determine what your goal is when presenting an assignment to the child. Then pave all the roads for the child. For example, if your goal is to see if the child can find the circumference of a circle, provide him or her with the formulas, definitions, and examples. These materials will reduce the child's frustration and confusion and will increase his or her chances of success.

♦ Have the child do just a few exercises at a time. Then give him or her immediate feedback. Numerous successful tasks can only add to the child's confidence levels. This will also prevent the child from progressing too far with making the same error.

♦ Use unison reading when the child reads aloud. This means that you and the child have the same book and read out loud together. The added sensory feedback and pacing will keep the child more focused.

♦ Try to use interactive CD reading programs if possible. The multisensory stimulation will keep the child focused. However, make sure the program does not require the child to do too many tasks at one time.

Emotional Expression

♦ Be aware of the child's limitations in terms of attention and frustration. Knowing when an ADD/ADHD child is about to lose focus can prevent his or her inappropriate behavior and feelings of failure. Do not be afraid to discusss this with the child so that both of you can identify the factors that lead to frustration.

♦ Offer the child an emotional vocabulary. Tension and frustration come out either verbally or behaviorally. Having the proper labels enhances a child's ablity to communicate feelings and to reduce tension verbally rather than behaviorally.

♦ Teach students the concept of healthy anger. Offer them the rules of healthy anger: deal with the situation as immediately as possible, deal directly with the person who made you angry, and never use the word "you" when conveying feelings of anger—use "I," "me," "we," and "us" instead.

♦ Try to empower the child by focusing on all the parts of the child's life over which he or she has control. Children with ADD/ADHD frequently feel out of control and helpless. This feeling can lead to depression and victimization. Empowering them with simple jobs, simple hobbies, choices of food, clothing, room arrangement, and so on will offer them some control over their environment and may help them to balance their feelings of powerlessness.

Section 14

APPENDICES

APPENDIX A—NAMES AND ADDRESSES OF TEST PUBLISHERS

Academic Therapy Publications
20 Commercial Blvd.
Novato, CA 94949-6191
Phone: 415-883-3314 or 800-422-7249
Fax: 415-883-3720

American Guidance Service
4201 Woodland Rd.
Circle Pines, MN 55014-1796
Phone: 612-786-4343 or 800-328-2560
Fax: 612-786-9077

The American Orthopsychiatric Association Inc.
19 W. 44th Street
Suite 1616
New York, NY 10036
Phone: 212-564-5930
Fax: 212-564-5930

C.H. Stoelting Co.
620 Wheat Lane
Wood Dale, Illinois 60191
Phone: 630-860-9700
Fax: 630-860-9775

Consulting Pychologists Press (Davis Black Publications)
P.O. Box 10096
3803 East Bayshore Rd.
Palo Alto, CA 94303

Phone: 415-969-8901
Fax: 415-969-8608

C.P.S. Incorporated
P.O. Box 83
Larchmont, NY 10538
Phone: 914-833-1633
Fax: 914-833-1633

CTB MacMillan/McGraw-Hill
Del Monte Research Park
Garden Road
Monterey, CA 93940
Phone: 800-538-9547
Fax: 800-282-0266

Curriculum Associates, Inc.
5 Esquire Road, N.
Billerica, MA 01862-2589
Phone: 800-225 0248
Fax: 800-366-1158

Denver Developmental Materials Inc.
P.O. Box 6919
Denver, Colorado 80206-0919
Phone: 303-335-4729

Educators Publishing Service, Inc.
31 Smith Place
Cambridge, MA 02138
Phone: 800-225-5750
Fax: 617-547-0412

Harvard University Press
79 Garden Street
Cambridge, MA 02138
Phone: 617-495-2600
Fax: 617-495-5898

Hawthorne Educational Services
800 Gray Oak Drive
Columbia, MO 65201
Phone: 800-542-1673
Fax: 800-442-9509

Jastak Associates Wide Range Inc.
Jastak Associates/Wide Range Inc.
P.O. Box 3410
Wilmington, DE 19804-0250
Phone: 800-221-9728
Fax: 302-652-1644

Learning Concepts
2501 North Lamar
Austin, Texas 78705

Marshall S. Hiskey
5640 Baldwin
Lincoln, Neb. 68507
Phone: 402-466-6145

Meyer Rehabilitation Institute
  University of Nebraska Medical Center
600 South 42nd St.
Box 985450
Omaha, NE 68198
Phone: 402-559-4000
Fax: 402-559-4987

Modern Curriculum Press
320 W. 200 South
Suite 100 B
Salt Lake City, UT 84101
Phone: 801-533-9503
Fax: 801-533-9506

Multi-Health Systems Incorporated
908-Niagra Falls Blvd.
N. Tonawanza, NY 14120-2060
Phone: 800-456-3003
Fax: 416-424-1736

Northwestern University Press
625 Colfax St.
Evanston, lllinois 60201
Phone: 847-491-5313
Fax: 847-491-8150

PRO-ED, Inc.
8700 Shoal Creek Blvd.

Austin, TX 78757-6897
Phone: 512-451-3246 or 800-897-3202
Fax: 800-FXPROED

Psychological and Educational Publications
P.O. Box 520
Hydesville, CA 95547-0520
Phone: 800-523-5775
Fax: 800-447-0907

The Psychological Corporation
555 Academic Court
San Antonio, TX 78204-2498
Phone: 800-211-8378
Fax: 800-232-1223
TDD: 800-723-1318

Psychologists and Educators Incorporated
P.O. Box 513
Chesterfield, MO 63006
Phone: 314-576-9127
Fax: 314-878-3090

The Riverside Publishing Company
8420 Spring Lake Drive
Itasca, Illinois 60143-2079
Phone: 800-323-9540
Fax: 630-467-7192

Slosson Educational Publications
P.O. Box 280
East Aurora, NY 14052-0280
Phone: 888-SLOSSON
Fax: 800-655-3840

Teachers College Press
1234 Amsterdam Ave.
New York, NY 10027
Phone: 212-678-3929
Fax: 212-678-4149

University Associates in Psychiatry
1 South Prospect Street
Burlington, VT 05401
Phone: 802-656-4563

University of Illinois Press
54 East Gregory Drive
Champaign, Illinois 61820
Phone: 217-333-0950
Fax of Publisher: 217-244-8082

Western Psychological Services
12031 Wilshire Blvd.
Los Angeles, CA 90025
Phone: 310-478-2061 or 800-648-8857
Fax: 310-478-7838

APPENDIX B—TEST REFERENCE GUIDE BY CATEGORY

MEASURES OF INTELLECTUAL ABILITY

- Columbia Mental Maturity Scale (CMMS), *page 58*
- Comprehensive Test of Nonverbal Intelligence (CTONI), *page 63*
- Kaufman Assessment Battery for Children (K-ABC): Mental Processing Scales, *page 55*
- Kaufman Brief Intelligence Test (K-BIT), *page 57*
- McCarthy Scales of Children's Abilities (MSCA), *page 59*
- Otis-Lennon School Ability Test (OLSAT), *page 66*
- Slosson Intelligence Test—Revised (SIT-R), *page 62*
- Stanford Binet Intelligence Scale—Fourth Edition (SB:FE), *page 52*
- Test of Nonverbal Intelligence—Third Edition (TONI-3), *page 65*
- Wechsler Scales of Intelligence, *page 32*

READING ASSESSMENT MEASURES

- Decoding Skills Test (DST), *page 88*
- Durrell Analysis of Reading Difficulty (DARD), *page 77*
- Gates-MacGinitie Silent Reading Tests—Third Edition, *page 73*
- Gates-McKillop-Horowitz Reading Diagnostic Test, *page 79*
- Gilmore Oral Reading Test, *page 81*
- Gray Oral Reading Test—3 (GORT-3), *page 75*
- Nelson-Denny Reading Test (NDRT), *page 90*
- Slosson Oral Reading Test—Revised (SORT-R), *page 82*
- Spache Diagnostic Reading Scales (DRS), *page 83*
- Test of Reading Comprehension—Third Edition (TORC-3), *page 86*
- Woodcock Reading Mastery Tests—Revised (WRMT-R), *page 84*

ARITHMETIC ASSESSMENT MEASURES

- Enright Diagnostic Inventory of Basic Arithmetic Skills (Enright), *page 117*

SPELLING ASSESSMENT MEASURES

HANDWRITING ASSESSMENT MEASURES

COMPREHENSIVE ACHIEVEMENT MEASURES

TESTS THAT SPECIFICALLY MEASURE AREAS OF VISUAL PECEPTION

♦ Marianne Frostig Developmental Test of Visual Perception (DTVP), *page 139*

♦ Motor Free Perceptual Test—Revised (MVPT-R), *page 141*

TESTS THAT SPECIFICALLY MEASURE AREAS OF AUDITORY PERCEPTION

♦ Goldman-Fristoe-Woodcock Test of Auditory Discrimination (GFW), *page 144*

♦ Lindamood Auditory Conceptualization Test (LACT), *page 145*

♦ Test of Auditory Perceptual Skills—Revised (TAPS-R), *page 146*

♦ Wepman Test of Auditory Discrimination—Second Edition (ADT-2), *page 147*

COMPREHENSIVE MEASURES OF PERCEPTUAL ABILITIES

♦ Bruininks-Oseretsky Test of Motor Proficiency, *page 149*

♦ Detroit Tests of Learning Aptitudes—Third Edition (DTLA-3), *page 151*

♦ Illinois Test of Psycholinguistic Abilities (ITPA), *page 154*

♦ Slingerland Screening Tests for Identifying Children with Specific Language Disability, *page 161*

♦ Test of Gross Motor Development (TGMD), *page 160*

♦ Woodcock-Johnson Psycheducational Battery—Revised (WJ-R), *page 156*

EXPRESSIVE AND RECEPTIVE LANGUAGE MEASURES

♦ Boehm Test of Basic Concepts—Revised (BTBC-R), *page 170*

♦ Comprehensive Receptive and Expressive Vocabulary Test (CREVT), *page 171*

♦ Goldman-Fristoe Test of Articulation, *page 172*

♦ Goldman-Fristoe-Woodcock Test of Auditory Discrimination (GFW), *page 144*

♦ Kaufman Survey of Early Academic and Language Skills (K-SEALS), *page 173*

♦ Peabody Picture Vocabulary Test-III (PPVT-III), *page 168*

♦ Test for Auditory Comprehension of Language—Revised (TACL-R), *page 169*

♦ Test of Adolescent and Adult Language—Third Edition (TOAL-3), *page 174*

♦ Test of Early Language Development—Second Edition (TELD-2), *page 176*

♦ Test of Language Development—Intermediate 2 (TOLD-I:2), *page 179*

♦ Test of Language Development—Primary 2 (TOLD-P:2), *page 177*

Psychological Measures

- Attention Deficit Disorders Evaluation Scale—Revised (ADDES), *page 194*
- Children's Apperception Test (CAT), *page 185*
- Conners' Parent and Teacher Rating Scales (CPRS/CTRS), *page 191*
- Draw-A-Person: Screening Procedure for Emotional Disturbance (DAP:SPED), *page 187*
- Goodenough-Harris Drawing Test (GHDT), *page 186*
- Kinetic-House-Tree-Person Drawings (K-H-T-P), *page 193*
- The Politte Sentence Completion Test (PSCT), *page 189*
- Rorschach Psychodiagnostic Test, *page 188*
- Thematic Apperception Test for Children and Adults (TAT), *page 190*

Social Maturity and Adaptive Behavior Scales

- AAMR Adaptive Behavior Scale—School (ABS-S:2), *page 197*
- AAMR Adaptive Behavior Scale—Residential and Community—2 (ABS-RC-2), *page 196*
- Developmental Assessment for the Severely Handicapped (DASH), *page 200*
- Light's Retention Scale (LRS), *page 202*
- The Adaptive Behavior Evaluation Scale—Revised (ABES-R), *page 199*
- Vineland Adaptive Behavior Scale (VABS), *page 201*

Early Childhood Assessment Measures

- The Battelle Developmental Inventory (BDI), *page 220*
- Bayley Scales of Infant Development—Second Edition (BSID-II), *page 205*
- Boehm Test of Basic Concepts—Preschool Version, *page 211*
- Bracken Basic Concept Scale (BBCS), *page 212*
- Child Behavior Checklist (CBCL), *page 217*
- Degangi-Berk Test of Sensory Integration (TSI), *page 215*
- The Denver Developmental Screening Test—Revised (Denver II), *page 219*
- Developmental Profile II (DP-II), *page 209*
- Kindergarten Readiness Test (KRT), *page 216*
- Metropolitan Readiness Tests—Sixth Edition (MRT-6), *page 210*
- Preschool Language Scale—3 (PLS-3), *page 207*
- The Preschool Evaluation Scales (PES), *page 214*

TESTS FOR THE HEARING IMPAIRED

ASSESSMENT MEASURES USED BY OCCUPATIONAL THERAPISTS

BILINGUAL ASSESSMENT INSTRUMENTS

≡ APPENDIX C—TEST REFERENCE GUIDE BY NAME ≡

Appendix D—Who Administers the Test

Measures of Intellectual Ability—Normally administered by the Psychologist

- Columbia Mental Maturity Scale (CMMS)
- Comprehensive Test of Nonverbal Intelligence (CTONI)
- Kaufman Assessment Battery for Children (K-ABC): Mental Processing Scales
- Kaufman Brief Intelligence Test (K-BIT)
- McCarthy Scales of Children's Abilities (MSCA)
- Otis-Lennon School Ability Test (OLSAT)
- Slosson Intelligence Test—Revised (SIT-R)
- Stanford Binet Intelligence Test
- Test of Nonverbal Intelligence—Third Edition (TONI-3)
- Wechsler Scales of Intelligence

Reading Assessment Measures—Normally administered by the special education teacher, psychologist, classroom teacher

- Decoding Skills Test (DST)
- Durrell Analysis of Reading Difficulty (DARD)
- Gates-MacGinitie Silent Reading Test—Third Edition
- Gates-McKillop-Horowitz Reading Diagnostic Tests
- Gilmore Oral Reading Test
- Gray Oral Reading Test—3 (GORT-3)
- Nelson-Denny Reading Test (NDRT)
- Slosson Oral Reading Test—Revised (SORT-R)
- Spache Diagnostic Reading Scales (DRS)
- Test of Reading Comprehension—Third Edition (TORC-3)
- Woodcock Reading Mastery Test—Revised (WRMT-R)

Arithmetic Assessment Measures—Normally administered by the special education teacher, psychologist, classroom teacher

- Enright Diagnostic Inventory of Basic Arithmetic Skills (Enright)
- Key Math Diagnostic Arithmetic Test—Revised (Key Math-R)
- The Steenburgen Diagnostic-Prescriptive Math Program and Quick Math Screening Test (Steenburgen)
- Test of Early Mathematics Ability—2 (TEMA-2)
- Test of Mathematical Abilities—2 (TOMA-2)

Spelling Assessment Measures—Normally administered by the special education teacher, psychologist, classroom teacher

- Diagnostic Word Patterns
- Test of Written Spelling—3 (TWS-3)

Handwriting Assessment Measures—Normally administered by the special education teacher, psychologist, speech and language therapist, classroom teacher

- Denver Handwriting Analysis(DHA)—**and occupational therapist**
- The Picture Story Language Test (PSLT)
- Test of Early Written Language—2 (TEWL-2)
- Test of Written Language—2 (TOWL-2)
- Test of Written Language—3 (TOWL-3)
- Written Language Assessment (WLA)

Comprehensive Achievement Measures—Normally administered by the special education teacher, psychologist, classroom teacher

- Brigance Diagnostic Inventory of Basic Skills
- Kaufman Test of Educational Achievement (KTEA)
- Norris Educational Achievement Test (NEAT)
- Peabody Individual Achievement Test—Revised (PIAT-R)
- Test of Academic Achievement Skills—Reading, Arithmetic, Spelling, and Listening (TAAS-RASLC)
- Wechsler Individual Achievement Test (WIAT)
- Wide Range Achievement Test—3 (WRAT-3)

Tests That Specifically Measure Areas of Visual Peception—Normally administered by the special education teacher, psychologist

- Developmental Test of Visual Motor Integration—Fourth Edition
- Bender Visual Motor Gestalt Test (BVMGT)
- Marianne Frostig Developmental Test of Visual Perception (DTVP)
- Motor Free Perceptual Test—Revised (MVPT-R)

Tests That Specifically Measure Areas of Auditory Perception—Normally administered by the special education teacher, psychologist, classroom teacher, speech/language therapist

- Goldman-Fristoe-Woodcock Test of Auditory Discrimination (GFW)
- Lindamood Auditory Conceptualization Test (LACT)
- Tests of Auditory Perceptual Skills—Revised (TAPS-R)
- Wepman Test of Auditory Discrimination—2 (ADT-2)

Comprehensive Measures of Perceptual Abilities—Normally administered by the special education teacher, psychologist, classroom teacher, speech/language therapist, or occupational therapist

- Bruininks-Oseretsky Test of Motor Proficiency
- Detroit Tests of Learning Aptitudes—Third Edition (DTLA-3)

♦ Illinois Test of Psycholinguistic Abilities (ITPA)
♦ Slingerland Screening Tests for Identifying Children with Specific Language Disability
♦ Test of Gross Motor Development (TGMD)
♦ Woodcock-Johnson Psycheducational Battery—Revised(WJ-R)

Expressive and Receptive Language Measures—Normally administered by the speech and language therapist, special education teacher, psychologist

♦ Boehm Test of Basic Concepts—Revised (BTBC-R)
♦ Comprehensive Receptive and Expressive Vocabulary Test (CREVT)
♦ Goldman-Fristoe Test of Articulation
♦ Goldman-Fristoe-Woodcock Test of Auditory Discrimination (G-F-WTAD)
♦ Kaufman Survey of Early Academic and Language Skills (K-SEALS)
♦ Peabody Picture Vocabulary Test—III (PPVT-III)
♦ Test for Auditory Comprehension of Language—Revised (TACL-R)
♦ Test of Adolescent and Adult Language—Third Edition (TOAL-3)
♦ Test of Early Language Development—Second Edition (TELD-2)
♦ Test of Language Development—Intermediate (TOLD-I:2)
♦ Test of Language Development—Primary-2 (TOLD-P:2)

Psychological Measures—Normally administered by the psychologist

♦ Attention Deficit Disorders Evaluation Scale—Revised (ADDES)
♦ Children's Apperception Test (CAT)
♦ Conners' Parent and Teacher Rating Scales (CRS)—**and classroom teacher and parent**
♦ Draw-A-Person: Screening Procedure for Emotional Disturbance (DAP:SPED)
♦ Goodenough-Harris Drawing Test (GHDT)—**and special education teacher**
♦ Kinetic-House-Tree-Person Drawings (K-H-T-P)
♦ The Politte Sentence Completion Test (PSCT)
♦ Rorschach Psychodiagnostic Test
♦ Thematic Apperception Test for Children and Adults (TAT)

Social Maturity and Adaptive Behavior Scales—Normally administered by the psychologist

♦ AAMR Adaptive Behavior Scale—School(ABS-S:2)
♦ AAMR Adaptive Behavior Scales—Residential and Community—2 (ABS-RC-2)
♦ Developmental Assessment for the Severely Handicapped (DASH)
♦ Light's Retention Scale (LRS)
♦ The Adaptive Behavior Evaluation Scale—Revised (ABES-R)
♦ Vineland Adaptive Behavior Scale (VABS)

Early Childhood Assessment Measures—Normally administered by the special education teacher, psychologist, speech and language therapist

♦ The Battelle Developmental Inventory (BDI)

- Bayley Scales of Infant Development—Second Edition (BSID-II)-Ages 1–42 months—**psychologist only**
- Boehm Test of Basic Concepts—Preschool Version-K–Grade 2
- Bracken Basic Concept Scale(BBCS)-Ages 2.6–8
- Child Behavior Checklist (CBCL)
- Degangi-Berk Test of Sensory Integration (TSI)—**occupational and physical therapists only**
- Developmental Profile II (DP-II)
- The Denver Developmental Screening Test—Revised (Denver II)—**and occupational therapist**
- Kindergarten Readiness Test (KRT)
- Metropolitan Readiness Tests—Sixth Edition (MRT-6)-PreK–Grade 1
- Preschool Language Scale—3 (PLS-3)-Birth–6
- The Preschool Evaluation Scales (PES)-Birth–72 months

Tests for the Hearing Impaired—Normally administered by the speech and language therapist

- Auditory Perception Test for the Hearing Impaired (APT/HI)-Ages 5 and up
- Carolina Picture Vocabulary Test for Deaf and Hearing Impaired (CPVT)-Ages 4–11.5
- Hiskey-Nebraska Test of Learning Aptitude-Ages 3–18
- Leiter-R International Performance Scale-Ages 2–17
- Rhode Island Test of Language Structure (RITLS)-Ages 3–20
- Screening Instrument for Targeting Educational Risk (SIFTER)-for children with identified hearing loss
- Test of Early Reading Ability—2 Deaf or Hard of Hearing (TERA-2—D/HH)-Primary grades

Assessment Measures Used by Occupational Therapists—Normally administered by the occupational therapists

- Milani-Comparetti Motor Development Test
- Miller Assessment for Preschoolers (MAP)
- Quick Neurological Screening Test (QNST)
- Sensory Integration and Praxis Test (SIPT)
- Purdue Perceptual-Motor Survey (PPMS)

Bilingual Assessment Instruments—Normally administered by the special education teacher, speech and language therapist, psychologist

- ESL/Literacy Scale (ELS)
- Language Proficiency Test (LPT)
- Matrix Analogies Test—Expanded Form (MAT-Expanded Form)
- Screening Test of Spanish Grammar
- System of Multicultural Pluralistic Assessment (SOMPA)

Appendix E—Terminology & Definitions

Test and Measurement

Achievement Test—An objective examination that measures educationally relevant skills or knowledge about such subjects as reading, spelling, or mathematics.

Age Equivalents—A very general score that is used to compare the performance of children at the same age with one another. It is the estimated age level that corresponds to a given score.

Age Norms—Values representing typical or average performance of people in age groups.

Average—A statistic that indicates the central tendency or most typical score of a group of scores. Most often average refers to the sum of a set of scores divided by the number of scores in the set.

Battery—A group of carefully selected tests that are administered to a given population, the results of which are of value individually, in combination, and totally.

Ceiling—The upper limit of ability that can be measured by a particular test.

Composite Scores—A combination of subtest scores averaged out to give one score reflecting a total score in a specific area.

Concurrent Validity—Determined by comparing test performance and some criterion data that are available at the time of testing.

Content Validity—Indicates whether the test covers a sufficiently representative sample of the behavior domain being considered for study.

Correlation—Describes a relationship between variables.

Criterion-Referenced Test—A measurement of achievement of specific criteria or skills in terms of absolute levels of mastery. The focus is on performance of an individual as measured against a standard or criteria rather than against performance of others who take the same test, as with norm-referenced tests.

Deciles—May be used to divide the scale of measurement into 10 larger units. The first decile is the same as the 10th percentile, and so on.

Diagnostic Test—An intensive, in-depth evaluation process with a relatively detailed and narrow coverage of a specific area. The purpose of this test is to determine the specific learning needs of individual students and to be able to meet those needs through regular or remedial classroom instruction.

Domain-Referenced Test—A test in which performance is measured against a well-defined set of tasks or body of knowledge (domain). Domain-referenced tests are a specific set of criterion-referenced tests and have a similar purpose.

Equivalent Form Reliability—Refers to the use of two equivalent or parallel forms of the test and the correlation between the two sets of scores obtained.

Grade Equivalent—A very general score that is used to compare the performance of children in the same grade with one another. It is the estimated grade level that corresponds to a given score.

Informal Test—A nonstandardized test that is designed to give an approximate index of an individual's level of ability or learning style; often teacher-constructed.

Interval scale—At this level there are equal intervals, or distances, between each number and the next higher or lower number, but no known zero point.

Inventory—A catalog or list for assessing the absence or presence of certain attitudes, interests, behaviors, or other items regarded as relevant to a given purpose.

Item—An individual question or exercise in a test or evaluative instrument.

Item Analysis—Refers to the analysis of individual items on a test, i.e., level of difficulty.

Mean—The arithmetic average and most commonly used measure of central tendency.

Median—The point which has the same number of scores above and below it in the distribution.

Mode—The score among a set of scores that occurs most often.

Nominal scale—The lowest, or simplest, level of measurement characterized by the use of numbers to classify or identify.

Norm—Performance standard that is established by a reference group and that describes average or typical performance. Usually norms are determined by testing a representative group and then calculating the group's test performance.

Normal Curve—A theoretical representation of the manner in which an infinite number of scores will vary by chance. Also referred to as the bell-shaped curve.

Normal Curve Equivalent—Standard scores with a mean of 50 and a standard deviation of approximately 21.

Norm-Referenced Test—An objective test that is standardized on a group of individuals whose performance is evaluated in relation to the performance of others; contrasted with criterion-referenced test.

Objective Percent Correct—The percent of the items measuring a single objective that a student answers correctly.

Ordinal Scale—Used to rank according to some characteristic that must be measured but cannot be measured accurately in a manner to indicate the exact amount of difference between those in different ranks.

Percentile Rank—The percent of people in the norming sample whose scores were below a given score. For example, a score at the 63rd percentile means that approximately 26% of the students scored higher and 62% scored lower.

Percent Score—The percent of items that are answered correctly.

Performance Test—Designed to evaluate general intelligence or aptitudes. Consists primarily of motor items or perceptual items because verbal abilities play a minimal role.

Predictive Validity—Involves testing the effectiveness of a test against future performance in the areas measured by the test.

Published Test—A test that is publicly available because it has been copyrighted and published commercially.

Quartiles—May be used to divide the scale of measurement into 4 larger units. The first quartile is the same as the 25th percentile.

Range—The numerical difference between the high and low scores.

Rating Scales—Subjective assessments made on predetermined criteria in the form of a scale. Rating scales include numerical scales or descriptive scales. Forced choice rating scales require that the rater determine whether an individual demonstrates more of one trait than another.

Ratio Scale—This is the highest level of measurement. This scale has a zero point but is otherwise like an interval scale.

Raw Score—The number of items that are answered correctly.

Reliability—The extent to which a test is dependable, stable, and consistent when administered to the same individuals on different occasions. Technically, this is a statistical term that defines the extent to which errors of measurement are absent from a measurement instrument.

Sampling—A relatively small sample of a much larger population whose results will hopefully resemble those of the larger population.

Screening—A fast, efficient measurement for a large population to identify individuals who may deviate in a specified area, such as the incidence of maladjustment or readiness for academic work.

Semi-Interquartile Range—Refers to one-half the range of the middle 50% of the scores.

Specimen Set—A sample set of testing materials that are available from a commercial test publisher. May include a complete individual test without multiple copies or a copy of the basic test and administration procedures.

Split-half Reliability—Involves the division of a test into two comparable halves and the correlation between the two halves is determined.

Standard Deviation—Indicates variation within a total set of scores.

Standard Error of Measurement—Indicates the extent to which chance errors may cause variations in the scores that might be obtained by an individual if the test were administered an infinite number of times. The smaller the standard error, the more desirable the test.

Standardized Test—A form of measurement that has been normed against a specific population. Standardization is obtained by administering the test to a given population and then calculating means, standard deviations, standardized scores, and percentiles. Equivalent scores are then produced for comparisons of an individual score to the norm group's performance.

Standard Score—A score that is expressed as a deviation from a population mean.

Stanine—A weighted scale divided into 9 equal segments which represent 9 levels of performance on any specific testing instrument. The mean is 5 with a standard deviation of 2.

Statistical Significance—Refers to the significance of the results in predicting how a population feels or how it will act.

Test-retest Reliability—Refers to the readministration of the same test and the degree of correlation between the scores.

Validity—The extent to which a test measures what it was intended to measure. Validity indicates the degree of accuracy of either predictions or inferences based upon a test score.

SPECIAL EDUCATION

Ability Grouping—The grouping of children based on their achievement in an area of study.

Accelerated Learning—An educational process that allows students to progress through the curriculum at an increased pace.

Achievement—The level of a child's accomplishment on a test of knowledge or skill.

Adaptive Behavior—Refers to an individual's social competence and ability to cope with the demands of the environment.

Adaptive Physical Education—A modified program of instruction implemented to meet the needs of special students.

Advocate—An individual, either a parent or professional, who attempts to establish or improve services for exceptional children.

Age Norms—Standards based on the average performance of individuals in different age groups.

Agnosia—Refers to the child's inability to recognize objects and their meaning, usually resulting from damage to the brain.

Amplification Device—Any device that increases the volume of sound.

Anecdotal Record—A procedure for recording and analyzing observations of a child's behavior; an objective, narrative description.

Annual Goals—Yearly activities or achievements to be completed or attained by the disabled child that are documented on the Individual Educational Plan.

Aphasia—The inability to acquire meaningful spoken language by the age of three, usually resulting from damage to disease of the brain.

Articulation—The production of distinct language sounds by the vocal chords.

At Risk—Usually refers to infants or children with a high potential for experiencing future medical or learning problems.

Attention Deficit Disorder (ADD)—Same as Attention Deficit Hyperactive Disorder (ADHD), but without the hyperactivity.

Attention Deficit Hyperactive Disorder (ADHD)—A psychiatric classification used to describe individuals who exhibit poor attention, distractibility, impulsivity, and hyperactivity.

Baseline Measure—The level or frequency of behavior prior to the implementation of an instructional procedure that will later be evaluated.

Behavior Modification—The techniques used to change behavior by applying principles of reinforcement learning.

Bilingual—The ability to speak two languages.

Career Education—Instruction that focuses on the application of skills and content area information necessary to cope with the problems of daily life, independent living, and vocational areas of interest.

Categorical Resource Room—An auxiliary pull-out program which offers supportive services to exceptional children with the same disability.

Cognition—The understanding of information.

Consultant Teacher—A supportive service for disabled children in which the services are provided by a specialist in the classroom.

Criterion-Referenced Tests—Tests in which the child is evaluated on his/her own performance to a set of criteria and not in comparison to others.

Declassification—The process in which a disabled child is no longer considered in need of special education services. This requires a meeting of the CSE and can be requested by the parent, school, or child if over the age of 18.

Deficit—A level of performance that is less than expected for a child.

Desensitization—A technique used in reinforcement theory in which there is a weakening of a response, usually an emotional response.

Diagnosis—Refers to the specific disorder/s identified as a result of some evaluation.

Distractibility—Refers to difficulty in maintaining attention.

Due Process—Refers to the legal steps and processes outlined in educational law that protects the rights of disabled children.

Dyscalculia—A serious learning disability in which the child has an inability to calculate, apply, solve, or identify mathematical functions.

Dysfluency—Difficulty in the production of fluent speech as in the example of stuttering.

Dysgraphia—A serious learning disability in which the child has an inability or loss of ability to write.

Dyslexia—A severe type of learning disability in which a child's ability to read is greatly impaired.

Dysorthographia—A serious learning disability that affects a child's ability to spell.

Enrichment—Providing a child with extra and more sophisticated learning experiences than those normally presented in the curriculum.

Exceptional Children—Children whose school performance shows significant discrepancy between ability and achievement and as a result require special instruction, assistance, and/or equipment.

Etiology—The cause of a problem.

Free Appropriate Public Education (FAPE)—Used in PL94-142 to mean special education and related services that are provided at public expense and conform to the state requirements and conform to the individual's IEP.

Group Home—A residential living arrangement for handicapped adults, especially the mentally retarded along with several nonhandicapped supervisors.

Habilitation—An educational approach used with exceptional children which is directed toward the development of the necessary skills required for successful adulthood.

Homebound Instruction—A special education service in which teaching is provided by a specially trained instructor to students unable to attend school. A parent or guardian must always be present at the time of instruction. In some cases, the instruction may take place on a neutral site and not in the home or school.

Hyperactivity—Behavior which is characterized by excessive motor activity or restlessness.

Impulsivity—Non–goal-oriented activity that is exhibited by individuals who lack careful thought and reflection prior to a behavior.

Individualized Educational Program—A written educational program that outlines a disabled child's current levels of performance, related services, educational goals, and modifications. This plan is developed by a team including the child's parent(s), teacher(s), and supportive staff.

Inclusion—Returning disabled children to their home school so that they may be educated with non-handicapped children in the same classroom.

Interdisciplinary Team—The collective efforts of individuals from a variety of disciplines in assessing the needs of a child.

Intervention—Preventive, remedial, compensatory, or survival services made on behalf of a disabled individual.

Itinerant Teacher—A teacher hired by a school district to help in the education of a disabled child. The teacher is employed by an outside agency and may be responsible for several children in several districts.

Learning Disability—Refers to children with average or above average potential intelligence who are experiencing a severe discrepancy between their ability and achievement.

Least Restrictive Environment—Applies to the educational setting of exceptional children and the education of handicapped children with non-handicapped children whenever realistic and possible. It is the least restrictive setting in which the disabled child can function without difficulty.

Mainstreaming—The practice of educating exceptional children in the regular classroom.

Mental Age—The level of intellectual functioning based on the average for children of the same chronological age. When dealing with severely disabled children, the mental age may be more reflective of levels of ability than the chronological age.

Mental Disability—Refers to a disability in which the individual's intellectual level is measured within the subaverage range and there are marked impairments in social competence.

Native Language—The primary language used by an individual.

Non-Categorical Resource Room—A resource room in regular school that provides services to children with all types of classified disabilities. The children with these disabilities are able to be maintained in a regular classroom.

Norm-Referenced Tests—Tests used to compare a child's performance to the performance of others on the same measure.

Occupational Therapist—A professional who programs and/or delivers instructional activities and materials to assist disabled children and adults to participate in useful daily activities.

Paraprofessionals—A trained assistant or parent who works with a classroom teacher in the education process.

Physical Therapist—A professional trained to assist and help disabled individuals maintain and develop muscular and orthopedic capability and to make correct and useful movements.

PINS Petition—A PINS petition stands for "Person in Need of Supervision" and is a family court referral. This referral can be made by either the school or the parent and is usually made when a child under the age of 16 is out of control in terms of attendance, behavior, or some socially inappropriate or destructive pattern.

Positive Reinforcement—Any stimulus or event which occurs after a behavior has been exhibited that affects the possibility of that behavior occurring in the future.

Pupil Personnel Team—A group of professionals from the same school who meet on a regular basis to discuss children's problems and offer suggestions or a direction for resolution.

Pupils with Special Educational Needs (PSEN)—Students defined as having math and reading achievement lower than the 23rd percentile and requiring remediation. These students are not considered disabled but are entitled to assistance to elevate their academic levels.

Pupils with Handicapping Conditions (PHC)—Refers to any child classified as disabled by the Committee on Special Education.

Related Services—Services provided to disabled children to assist in their ability to learn and function in the least restrictive environment. Such services may include in-school counseling, speech and language services, and so on.

Remediation—An educational program designed to teach children to overcome some deficit or disability through education and training.

Resource Room—An auxiliary service provided to disabled children for part of the school day. It is intended to service children's special needs so that they can be maintained within the least restrictive educational setting.

Screening—The process of examining groups of children in hopes of identifying potential high-risk children.

Section 504—Refers to Section 504 of the Rehabilitation Act of 1973 in which guarantees are provided for the civil rights of disabled children and adults. It also applies to the provision of services for children whose disability is not severe enough to warrant classification but who could benefit from supportive services and classroom modifications.

Self-Contained Class—A special classroom for exceptional children usually located within a regular school building.

Sheltered Workshops—A transitional or long-term work environment for disabled individuals who cannot, or who are preparing for, work in a regular setting. Within this setting the individual can learn to perform meaningful, productive tasks and receive payment.

Surrogate Parent—A person other than the child's natural parent who has legal responsibility for the child's care and welfare.

Total Communication—The approach to the education of deaf students which combines oral speech, sign language, and finger spelling.

Token Economy—A system of reinforcing various behaviors through the delivery of tokens. These tokens can be in the form of stars, points, candy, chips, and so on.

Underachiever—A term generally used in reference to a child's lack of academic achievement in school. However, it is importat that the school identify the underlying causes of such underachievement since it may be a symptom of a more serious problem.

Vocational Rehabilitation—A well designed program designed to help disabled adults obtain and hold a job.

PSYCHOLOGICAL

Affective Reactions—Psychotic reactions marked by extreme mood swings.

Anxiety—A general uneasiness of the mind characterized by irrational fears, panic, tension, and physical symptoms including palpitations, excessive sweating, and increased pulse rate.

Assessment—The process of gathering information about children in order to make educational decisions.

Baseline Data—An objective measure used to compare and evaluate the results obtained during some implementation of an instructional procedure.

Compulsion—A persistent, repetitive act which the individual cannot consciously control.

Confabulation—The act of replacing memory loss by fantasy or by some reality that is not true for the occasion.

Defense Mechanisms—The unconscious means by which an individual protects himself or herself against impulses or emotions that are too uncomfortable or threatening. Examples of these mechanisms include the following:

> **Denial**—A defense mechanism in which the individual refuses to admit the reality of some unpleasant event, situation, or emotion.
>
> **Displacement**—The disguising of the goal or intention of a motive by substituting another in its place.
>
> **Intellectualization**—A defense mechanism in which the individual exhibits anxious or moody deliberation, usually about abstract matters.
>
> **Projection**—The disguising of a source of conflict by displacing one's own motives to someone else.
>
> **Rationalization**—The interpretation of one's own behavior so as to conceal the motive it expresses by assigning the behavior to another motive.
>
> **Reaction Formation**—A complete disguise of a motive that it is expressed in a form that is directly opposite to its original intent.
>
> **Repression**—Refers to the psychological process involved in not permitting memories and motives to enter consciousness but are operating at an unconscious level.
>
> **Suppression**—The act of consciously inhibiting an impulse, affect, or idea, as in the deliberate act of forgetting something so as not to have to think about it.

Delusion—A groundless, irrational belief or thought, usually of grandeur or of persecution. It is usually a characteristic of paranoia.

Depersonalization—A non-specific syndrome in which the individual senses that he has lost his personal identity, that he is different, strange, or not real.

Echolalia—Refers to the repetition of what other people say as if echoing them.

Etiology—Refers to the cause/s of something.

Hallucination—An imaginary visual image that is regarded as a real sensory experience by the person.

Magical Thinking—Refers to primitive and pre-logical thinking in which the child creates an outcome to meet his fantasy rather than the reality.

Neologisms—Made-up words that only have meaning to the child or adult.

Obsessions—A repetitive and persistent idea that intrudes into a person's thoughts.

Panic Attacks—A serious episode of anxiety in which the individual experiences a variety of symptoms, including palpitations, dizziness, nausea, chest pains, trembling, fear of dying, and fear of losing control. These symptoms are not the result of any medical cause.

Paranoia—A personality disorder in which the individual exhibits extreme suspiciousness of the motives of others.

Phobia—An intense irrational fear, usually acquired through conditioning to an unpleasant object or event.

Projective Tests—Methods used by psychologists and psychiatrists to study personality dynamics through a series of structured or ambiguious stimuli.

Psychosis—A serious mental disorder in which the individual has difficulty differentiating between fantasy and reality.

Rorschach Test—An unstructured psychological test in which the individual is asked to project responses to a series of 10 inkblots.

School Phobia—A form of separation anxiety in which the child's concerns and anxieties are centered around school issues and as a result he/she has an extreme fear about coming to school.

Symptom—Refers to any sign, physical or mental, that stands for something else. Symptoms are usually generated from the tension of conflicts. The more serious the problem or conflict, the more frequent and intense the symptom.

Syndrome—A group of symptoms.

Thematic Apperception Test—A structured psychological test in which the individual is asked to project his/her feelings onto a series of drawings or photos.

Wechsler Scales of Intelligence—A series of individual intelligence tests measuring global intelligence through a variety of subtests.

OCCUPATIONAL THERAPY

Abduction—Movement of limb outwards away from body.

Active Movements—Movements a child does without help.

Adaptive Equipment—Devices used to position or to teach special skills.

Asymmetrical—One side of the body different from the other; unequal or dissimilar.

Associated Reactions—Increase of stiffness in spastic arms and legs resulting from effort.

Ataxic—No balance, jerky.

Athetoid—Child with uncontrolled and continuously unwanted movements.

Atrophy—Wasting of the muscles.

Automatic Movements—Necessary movements done without thought or effort.

Balance—Not falling over, ability to keep a steady position.

Bilateral Motor—Refers to skill and performance in purposeful movement that requires interaction between both sides of the body in a smooth manner.

Circumduction—To swing the limb away from the body to clear the foot.

Clonus—Shaky movements of spastic muscle.

Compensatory Movement—A form of movement that is atypical in relation to normal patterns of movement.

Congenital—From birth.

Coordination—Combination of muscles in movement.

Contracture—Permanently tight muscle or joint.

Crossing the Midline—Refers to skill and performance in crossing the vertical midline of the body.

Deformity—Body or limb fixed in abnormal position.

Diplegia—Legs mostly affected.

Distractible—Not able to concentrate.

Equilibrium—Balance.

Equilibrium Reactions—Automatic patterns of body movements that enable restoration and maintenance of balance against gravity.

Equinus—Toe walks.

Extension—Straightening of the trunk and limbs.

Eye-Hand Coordination—Eye is used as a tool for directing the hand to perform efficiently.

Facilitation—Making it possible for the child to move.

Figure-Ground Perception—To be able to see foreground against the background.

Fine Motor—Small muscle movements, use of hands and fingers.

Flexion—Bending of elbows, hips, knees, etc.

Floppy—Floppy

Fluctuating Tone—Changing from one degree of tension to another, e.g., from low to high tone.

Form Constancy—Ability to perceive an object as possessing invariant properties such as shape, size, color, and brightness.

Gait Pattern—Description of walking pattern including:

> **Swing to gait**—Walking with crutches or walker by moving crutches forward and swinging body up to crutches.
>
> **Swing thru**—Walking with crutches by moving crutches forward and swinging body in front of the crutches.

Genu Valgus—Knock-kneed.

Genu Varum—Bowlegged.

Gross Motor—Coordinated movements of all parts of the body for performance.

Guarding Techniques—Techniques used to help students maintain balance, including contact guarding (when a student requires hands-on contact to maintain balance).

Guarded supervision—When an individual is close to the student to provide physical support if balance is lost while sitting, standing, or walking.

Head Control—Ability to control the position of the head.

Hemiplegia—One side of the body affected with paralysis.

Hypertonicity—Increased muscle tone.

Hypotonicity—Decreased muscle tone.

Inhibition—Positions and movements which stop muscle tightness.

Involuntary Movements—Unintended movements.

Kyphosis—Increased rounding of the upper back.

Lordosis—Sway back or increased curve in the back.

Manual Muscle Test—Test of isolated muscle strength

- normal—100%
- good—80%
- fair—50%
- poor—20%
- zero—0

Mobility—Movement of a body muscle or body part, or movement of the whole body from one place to another.

Motivation—Making the student want to move or perform.

Motor Patterns—Ways in which the body and limbs work together to make movement, also known as praxis.

Nystagmus—Series of automatic back-and-forth eye movements.

Organization—A student's abililty to organize himself/herself in approach to and performance of activities.

Orthosis—Brace.

Paraplegic—Paralysis of the lower half of the body with involvement of both legs.

Passive—Anything that is done to the student without his/her help or coooperation.

Pathological—Due to or involving abnormality.

Perception—Is the organization of sensation from useful functioning.

Perseveration—Unnecessary repetition of speech or movement.

Positioning—Ways of placing an individul that will help normalize postural tone and facilitate normal patterns of movement and that may involve the use of adaptive equipment.

Position in Space—Child's ability to understand the relationship of an object to himself.

Postural Balance—Refers to skill and performance in developing and maintaining body posture while sitting, standing, or engaging in an activity.

Praxis—Ability to think through a new task which requires movement, also known as motor planning.

Pronation—Turning of the hand with palm down.

Prone—Lying on the stomach.

Quadriplegic—Whole body affected by paralysis.

Range of Motion—Joint motion.

Reflex—Stereotypic posture and movement that occurs in relation to specific eliciting stimuli and outside of conscious control.

Righting Reactions—Ability to put head and body right when postions are abnormal or uncomfortable.

Right/Left Discrimination—Refers to skill and performance in differentiating right from left and vice versa.

Rigidity—Very stiff movements and postures.

Rotation—Movement of the trunk; the shoulders move opposite to the hips.

Sensation—Feeling.

Sensory-Motor Experience—The feeling of one's own movements.

Sequencing—Concerns the ordering of visual patterns in time and space.

Scoliosis—C or S curvature of the spine.

Spasm—Sudden tightness of muscles.

Spasticity—Increased muscle tone.

Spatial Relations—Develops the ability to perceive the position of two or more objects in relation to himself and to each other.

Stair Climbing—Methods of climbing include:

◆ mark stepping—ascending or descending stairs one step at a time.

◆ alternating steps—step over step.

Stereognosis—The identification of forms and nature of object through the sense of touch.

Subluxation—A partial dislocation where joint surfaces remain in contact with one another.

Supination—Turning of hand with palm up.

Symmetrical—Both sides equal.

Tactile—Pertaining to the sense of touch of the skin.

Tandem Walking—Walks in a forward progression, placing heel to toe.

Tone—Firmness of muscles.

Vestibular System—A sensory system that responds to the position of the head in relation to gravity and accelerated and decelerated movements.

Visual Memory—Ability to recall visual stimuli, in terms of form, detail, position, and other significant features on both short- and long-term basis.

Visual-Motor Integration—The ability to combine visual input with purposeful voluntary movement of the hands and other body parts involved in the activity.

Voluntary Movements—Movements done with attention and with concentration.

APPENDIX F—SPECIAL EDUCATION
ABBREVIATIONS

ACLC—Assessment of Children's Language Comprehension

ADHD—Attention Deficit Hyperactive Disorder

AE—Age Equivalent

AUD.DIS.—Auditory Discrimination

BINET—Stanford Binet Intelligence Test

BVMGT—Bender Visual Motor Gestalt Test

CA—Chronological Age

C.A.T—Children's Apperception Test

CEC—Council for Exceptional Children

C.P.—Cerebral Palsy

CSE—Committee on Special Education

DAP—Draw a Person Test

Db—Decibel (Hearing Measurement)

DDST—Denver Developmental Screening Test

DQ—Developmental Quotient

DTLA-3—Detroit Tests Of Learning Aptitude-3

E.D.—Emotionally Disturbed

EMR—Educable Mentally Retarded

FAPE—Free Appropriate Public Education

fq—Frequency Range (Hearing Measurement)

GE—Grade Equivalent

GFW—Goldman-Fristoe-Woodcock Test Of Auditory Discrimination

H.H.—Hard of Hearing

HTP—House-Tree-Person Test

Hz—Hertz (Hearing Measurement)

IEU—Intermediate Educational Unit

IHE—Institutions of Higher Education

IQ—Intelligence Quotient

ITPA—Illinois Tests Of Psycholinguistic Abilities

LA—Learning Aptitude

L.D.—Learning Disabled

LEA—Local Education Agency

LPR—Local Percentile Rank

MA—Mental Age

M.B.D.—Minimal Brain Dysfunction

M.H.—Multiply Handicapped

MMPI—Minnesota Multiphasic Personality Inventory

MR—Mentally Retarded

MVPT—Motor-Free Visual Perception Test

NPR—National Percentile Rank

PHC—Pupils With Handicapping Conditions

PIAT—Peabody Individual Achievement Test

PINS—Person in Need of Supervision

PLA—Psycholinguistic Age

PQ—Perceptual Quotient

PPVT—Peabody Picture Vocabulary Test

PR—Percentile Rank

P.S.—Partially Sighted

PSEN—Pupils With Special Educational Needs

P.T.A.—Pure Tone Average (Hearing Measurement)

SAI—School Abilities Index

SCSIT—Southern California Sensory Integration Tests

SEA—State Education Agency

SIT—Slosson Intelligence Test

S.R.T.—Speech Reception Threshold (Hearing Measurement)

TACL—Test for Auditory Comprehension of Language

T.A.T.—Thematic Apperception Test

TMR—Trainable Mentally Retarded

TOWL—Test of Written Language

TWS—Larsen-Hammill Test of Written Spelling

VAKT—Visual/Auditory/Kinesthetic/Tactile

VIS.DIS.—Visual Discrimination

VMI—Beery-Buktenica Developmental Test of Visual Motor Integration

WAIS-R—Wechsler Adult Intelligence Scale-Revised

WISC-R—Wechsler Intelligence Scale for Children-Revised

WISC-III—Wechsler Intelligence Scale for Children-III

WPPSI-R—Wechsler Preschool and Primary Scale of Intelligence-Revised

WRAT-R—Wide Range Achievement Test-Revised

REFERENCES AND SUGGESTED READINGS

Alley, G. R., & Deshler, D. (1979). *Teaching the learning disabled adolescent: Strategies and methods.* Denver, CO: London Publishing Company. (This book is no longer available from the publisher, but may be available in your local public library.)

American Association on Mental Retardation. (1992). *Mental Definition, classification, and systems of support (9th ed.).* Washington, DC: American Association on Mental Retardation.

Bagnato, S., Neisworth, J., & Munson, S. (1997). *Linking Assessment and Early Intervention.* Balitmore: Paul Brooks Pub.

Berdine, W.H., & Meyer, S.A. (1987). *Assessment in special education.* Boston: Little, Brown and Company. (available from Harper-Collins)

Bigge, J.L. (1990). *Teaching individuals with physical and multiple disabilities (3rd ed.).* Columbus, OH: Charles E. Merrill.

Blackhurst, A.E., & Berdine, W.H., (1981). *An Introduction to Special Education.* Boston: Little Brown and Co.

Bloom, L., & Lahey, M. (1978). *Language development and language disorders.* New York: Wiley.

Buros, 0. K. (1972–1996). *Buros Mental Measurement Yearbook* (Editions 1–12). Highland Park, NJ: Gryphon Press. 938.

Campione, J.C., & Brown, A.L. (1987). *Linking dynamic assessment with school achievement.* In C.S. Lidz (Ed.), Dynamic assessment: An interactional approach to evaluating learning potential (pp. 82–115). New York: Guilford.

Carlson, J.S., & Wiedl, K.H. (1978). Use of testing-the-limits procedures in the assessment of intellectual capabilities of children with learning difficulties. *American Journal of Mental Deficiency,* 82, 559–564.

Carlson, J.S., & Wiedl, K.H. (1979). Toward a differential testing approach: Testing-the-limits employing the Raven Matrices. *Intelligence,* 3, 323–344.

Code of Federal Regulations (CFR); Title 34; Parts 300 to 399, July 1, 1993. (Available from the U.S. Government Printing Office.)

Conoley, J. C. & Impara, J. C. (1994). *The supplement to the eleventh mental measurements yearbook.* Lincoln, NE.: The University of Nebraska Press.

Conoley, J. C. & Impara, J. C. (1995). *The twelfth mental measurements yearbook.* Lincoln, NE: The University of Nebraska Press.

Conoley, J.C., & Kramer, J.J. (Eds.). (1992). *Eleventh mental measurement yearbook.* Lincoln, NE: University of Nebraska Press.

Covarrubias v. *San Diego Unified School District (Southern),* No. 70–394-T, (S.D., Cal. February, 1971).

Cox, L.S. (1975). Diagnosing and remediating systematic errors in addition and subtraction computations. *The Arithmetic Teacher, 22,* p. 151–57.

Diana v. *California State Board of Education.* No. C-70 37 RFP, District Court of Northern California (February, 1970).

Elliott, R. (1987). *Litigating intelligence: IQ tests, special education, and social science in the courtroom.* Dover, MA: Auburn House.

Franklin, M.E. (1992). Culturally sensitive instructional practices for African-American learners with disabilities. *Exceptional Children,* 59(2), 115–122.

Goodman, Y. & Burke, C. (1972). *Reading Miscue Inventory Manual: Procedure for Diagnosis and Evaluation*. New York: MacMillan.

Grossman, H.J. (Ed.). (1983). *Manual on terminology and classification in mental retardation* (3rd ed.). Washington, DC: American Association on Mental Deficiency. (This book is no longer available from the publisher, but may be available in your local public library.)

Guadalupe Organization Inc. v. *Tempe Elementary School District*. No. CIV 71–435, Phoenix (D. Arizona, January 24, 1972).

Hammill, D.D., & Bartel, N.R. (1978). *Teaching Children with Learning Disabilities*. (3rd Ed.). Boston: Allyn & Bacon.

Hammill, D.D., Brown, L., & Bryant, B.R. (1992). *A consumer's guide to tests in print* (2nd ed.). Austin: Pro-Ed.

Harry, B. (1992). *Cultural diversity, families, and the special education system: Communication and empowerment*. New York: Teachers College Press.

Henderson, E. (1985). *Teaching spelling*. Boston, MA: Houghton Mifflin. (This book is no longer available from the publisher, but may be available in your local public library.)

Heward, W.L., & Orlansky, M.D. (1992). *Exceptional children: An introductory survey of special education (4th ed.)*. Ohio: Charles E. Merrill..

Hodgkinson, L. (1985). *All one system: Demographics of education*. Washington, DC: Institute for Educational Leadership.

Hoy, C., & Gregg, N. (1994). *Assessment: The special educator's role*. Pacific Grove, CA: Brooks/Cole.

Individuals with Disabilities Education Act (P.L. 101–476), 20 U.S.C. Chapter 33, Sections 1400–1485, 1990.

Jitendra, A.K., & Kameenui, E.J. (1993). Dynamic assessment as a compensatory assessment approach: A description and analysis. *Remedial and Special Education*, 14(5), 6–18.

John, J.L. (1985). *Basic Reading Inventory*. (3rd Ed.). Iowa: Kendall-Hunt.

Kamphaus, R. W. (1993). *Clinical assessment of children's intelligence*. Boston: Allyn & Bacon.

Keogh, B., & Margolis, T. (1976). Learn to labor and wait: Attentional problems of children with learning disorders. *Journal of Learning Disabilities*, 9, 276–286.

Kozloff, M. (1994). *Improving educational outcomes for children with disabilities: Principles for assessment, program planning, and evaluation*. Baltimore, MD: Paul H. Brookes.

Kramer, J.J. & Conoley, J. C. (1992). *Buros Eleventh Mental Measurement Yearbook*. Lincoln, NB: University of Nebraska Press. 428.

Larry P. v. *Riles*, C-71-2270 RFP, Opinion, October 10, 1979.

Lerner, J. (1993). Learning disabilities: Theories, diagnosis, and teaching strategies (6th ed.). Boston: Houghton Mifflin.

Liberman, I, & Shankweiler, D. (1994). Phonology and the problems of learning to read and write. In H. L. Swanson (Ed.), *Advances in learning and behavioral disabilities*. Greenwich, CT: Jai Press.

Lidz, C.S. (Ed.). (1987). *Dynamic assessment: An interactional approach to evaluating learning potential*. New York: Guilford.

Mann, P., Suiter, P., & McClung, R. (1979). *Handbook in Diagnosis. Prescriptive Teaching*. Boston: Allyn & Bacon.

McLoughlin, J.A., & Lewis, R.B., (1990). *Assessing Special Students* (3rd Ed.). Ohio: Merrill.

Murphy, L.L., Conoley, J. C., & Impara, J.C. (1994). *Tests in Print IV*. Vol. 1.237. The University of Nebraska Press.

National Center for Education Statistics. (1992). *American education at a glance*. Washington, DC: National Center for Education Statistics.

Ortiz, A. (1986). Characteristics of limited English proficient Hispanic students served in programs for the learning disabled: Implications for policy and practice (Part II). *Bilingual Special Education Newsletter*, University of Texas at Austin, Vol. IV.

Overton, T. (1992). *Assessment in special education: An applied approach*. New York: Macmillan.

Reid, D. K., & Hresko, W.P. (1981). *A cognitive approach to learning disabilities*. New York: McGraw-Hill. (This book is no longer available from the publisher, but may be available in your local public library.)

Roth-Smith, C. (1991). *Learning disabilities: The interaction of learner, task, and setting*. Boston: Allyn & Bacon. (This book is no longer available from the publisher, but may be available in your local public library.)

Salvia, J., & Ysseldyke, J. (1991). *Assessment in special education and remedial education (5th ed.)*. Boston, MA: Houghton Mifflin.

Sewell, T.E. (1987). Dynamic assessment as a nondiscriminatory procedure. In C.S. Lidz (Ed.), *Dynamic assessment: An interactional approach to evaluating learning potential* (pp. 426–443). New York: Guilford.

Shapiro, E. S. (1989). *Academic skills problems: Direct assessment and intervention*. New York: Guilford.

Stanovich, K. (1982). Individual differences in the cognitive processes of reading: Word decoding. *Journal of Learning Disabilities*, 15, 485–493.

Swanson, H. C., & Watson, B. L. (1989). *Educational and psychological assessment of exceptional children (2nd ed.)*. Columbus, OH: Merrill Publishing Company.

Sweetland, R.C., & Keyser, D.J. (Eds.). (1991). *Tests: A comprehensive reference for assessments in psychology, education, and business (3rd ed.)*. Austin, TX: Pro-Ed.

Taylor, R. L. (1993). *Assessment of exceptional children: Educational and psychological procedures (3rd ed.)*. Boston: Allyn & Bacon.

Taylor, R. L. (1997). *Assessment of Exceptional Students (4th ed.)*. Boston: Allyn and Bacon.

Terrell, S.L. (Ed.). (1983). Nonbiased assessment of language differences [Special issue]. *Topics in Language Disorders*, 3(3).

Vacca, J., Vacca, R., & Grove, M. (1986). *Reading and Learning to Read*. Boston: Little Brown and Co.

Vellutino, F. R. (1979). *Dyslexia: Theory and research*. Cambridge, MA: MIT Press.

Wallace, G., Larsen, S.C., & Elksnin, L.K. (1992). *Educational assessment of learning problems: Testing for teaching*. Boston: Allyn and Bacon.

Wechsler, D. (1958). *The measurement and appraisal of adult intelligence (4th ed.)*. Baltimore, MD: Williams & Wilkins.

Wiederhold, J. L., Hammill, D. D., & Brown, V. L. (1978). *The resource teacher*. Boston: Allyn & Bacon.

Wodrich, D.L., & Joy, J.E. (1986). *Multidisciplinary assessment of children with learning disabilities and mental retardation*. Baltimore, MD: Paul H. Brookes. (This book is no longer available from the publisher, but may be available in your local public library.)